SCUBA

SAFE and SIMPLE

by John Reseck, Jr.

Chapter opening art by
Larry Cushman

PRENTICE-HALL, INC.
Englewood Cliffs, New Jersey

*To my daughter, Michelle, and my son, John, who
have set my personal criteria for training students.
And to those young men who sometime in the 1940's
put up with a young boy asking them questions about
diving.*

Scuba Safe and Simple by John Reseck, Jr.
Copyright © 1975 by John Reseck, Jr.

Printed in the United States of America
Prentice-Hall International, Inc., London
Prentice-Hall of Australia, Pty, Ltd., Sydney
Prentice-Hall of Canada, Ltd., Toronto
Prentice-Hall of India Private Ltd., New Delhi
Prentice-Hall of Japan, Inc., Tokyo

10 9 8 7 6 5 4

Library of Congress Cataloging in Publication Data
Reseck, John
    Scuba safe and simple.
    Includes index.
    1. Skin diving. I. Title.
GV840.S78R45   797.2'3   74-31086
ISBN 0-13-796680-6

• ACKNOWLEDGMENTS

I would like to thank all of the students who have acted as guinea pigs so that we instructors could learn how to teach diving.

I would like to say to my fellow instructors who give so much of their time and soul to making diving a safe sport, "Hang in there. It's worth it."

And to the many of you who have encouraged me and read portions of this book and offered criticism for its improvement, I say thank you, and I hope you enjoy reading it as much as I did writing it.

• FOREWORD

Many years ago a writer who went solely by the initials K. M. S. observed that a preface to a book was like a front tooth—never noticed unless it was missing. Elaborating further, he noted that a preface was also similar to a dandelion in grass over which the reader (like the lawn mower) quickly skipped. If this is true of a preface (which at least has the advantage of being in the author's own words) it must be even more valid in regard to the foreword to a book, which is generally written by a person known to the author who is supposed to set the stage in some fashion for the importance of the book and the qualifications of the author. No amount of eloquence on my part could begin to justify my holding you up from reading what John Reseck has to say, for he, and he alone, can tell you what an expert he is and how exceptionally qualified he is to write this volume. As a teacher and diver and diving instructor, John is without a doubt one of the finest authorities in the world. His humor does not distract from his teaching; as you will see, it thoroughly enhances it. I am certain you will find this book to be instructive, interesting, technically sound, and extremely enjoyable.

Arthur J. Bachrach, Ph.D.
Director, Behavioral Sciences Department
Naval Medical Research Institute
National Naval Medical Center
Bethesda, Maryland

• INTRODUCTION

Steinbeck once wrote that "Boredom arises not so often from too little to think about, as from too much, and none of it clear nor clean, nor simple."* I have made an effort in this book to state as simply as possible the information needed to make a diver safe. The diver, if he understands the basic concepts presented here, will have the foundation that I would expect of a diver just completing a basic scuba course.

I did not go into fine detail in any area. I left a great many things out that could have been included because I felt that a more scholarly treatment would be needed to cover them adequately. I wanted to keep the information given to the bare basics and to keep it as "clear, clean, and simple" as possible.

Though I have tried to create the perfect accompaniment to a beginning scuba course, it hopefully is not written in a "normal textbook manner." It is prepared in such a way that, although the information is there, the diver should enjoy extracting it. I believe that diving is fun and that reading about diving should be fun. Preparing for and learning a new skill should be as stimulating as performing it. The material a diver is exposed to in these pages should point the way to a hundred new doors which he can, and should, open and explore.

A perpetual leave-taker is really what the diver is. Every dive is a different venture and, as we all know, half the fun of a trip is preparing for it. There are many books on diving which the diver should work his way through in preparation for his next trip. He can never learn "enough," but with time, experience, and study he can become knowledgeable.

I envy the person starting on this voyage to diving knowledge. He has many diverse waterways and enticing ports ahead of him.

* *Log From the Sea of Cortez* by John Steinbeck. Bantam Books, N.Y., 1971.

• CONTENTS

1

WHAT'S IT ALL ABOUT?

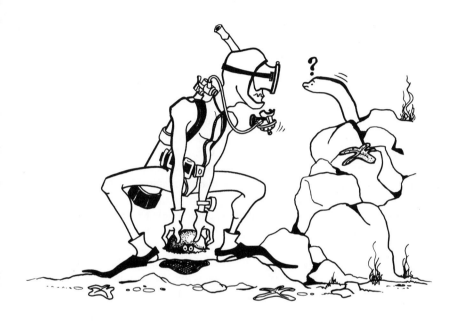

Did you ever wonder what makes a diver tick? Why he puts up with all the garbage he has to just to get wet?

Let's take a look at an average Southern California diver on a normal Saturday morning. He gets up at 5:00 A.M. when the alarm reaches into his head and shakes his brain; drags himself out of bed; stumbles to the bathroom; brushes his teeth in an attempt to get the foreign legion out of his mouth and careens down the hall into the kitchen. He has to be quiet because his wife told him when he got in at 2:00 A.M. last night from a party one of her friends put on that if he woke her up in the morning when he left she would not be there when he got home. He considers it and decides not to make any noise.

He very quietly eats an overdone egg washed down with yesterday's coffee, and then creeps to the garage where he finds all of his dive gear. He takes his wet suit off a special hanger that he's had it hanging on so that it would not get creased and starts to pack all his gear into his dive bag. He knows that when you go diving on a charter boat it is only common courtesy to have all your gear in one bag so nothing gets dropped or mislaid on the deck for someone else to trip on. He has so much junk that each time he goes it's a tossup whether the bag will hold it all. He carries his gear to the front walkway—all 90 pounds of it—and awaits his ride.

He is awake now, and enjoying the sunrise. He takes out a big black cigar (he only smokes them when he is out with "the boys"), lights up, and waits patiently on the curb. He puts on his oldest and most beat-up hat, which is his pride and joy, and looks down the street for the yellow pickup which is ten minutes late. His image is complete. The boys can arrive any time now.

The pickup rounds the corner a little too fast and it appears for a moment bent on running over our diver, but he stands his ground, flexes his muscles, and watches it slide to a stop at his feet. The two men in the truck hop out laughing and they all shake hands. The gear is picked up and tossed into the bed of the truck; our diver climbs in and away they go, cigar smoke pouring out the window.

Mrs. Diver rolls over in her warm bed as the wheels screech around the corner and the roar of the engine fades out. She turns up the electric blanket from "3" to "5", shakes her head muttering something that sounds like "just a bunch of little kids," and goes back to sleep.

The time is now 6:00 A.M. The pickup is parked next to several other vehicles and the three men are carrying their gear down a ramp to a boat. The boat is perhaps 65 feet long and there are 35 to 40 other divers aboard all trying to get out of the way. This, of course, is impossible as all the space on the boat is taken up with bodies and gear. Every time someone wants to go from point A to point B five people have to shift positions. One man throws up over the side and someone comments, "Gee, he usually doesn't do that until we throw off the dock lines!" The engine roars and the boat is underway. Thump, thump-thump, thump-thump. The big diesel will do all the work for the next two and a half hours. The people chat with each other for about 20 or 30 minutes but soon most of them are somewhere asleep. Some find bunks, others are jammed into corners, while still others are standing but appear to be asleep anyway.

Two hours later they are all active and probing for their gear. Soon they will be dressed and in the water pretending they are fish.

Let's take a look at what is meant when we say a recreational diver "gets dressed." We will start with an adult male in swim trunks. As we observe him, we see that his body has what we might call normal human senses and abilities. He now starts to get dressed. First he puts on what he calls a wet suit. This wet suit consists of a pair of pants and jacket, matching of course but not too chic, which are composed of foam neoprene, usually about one-quarter inch in thickness. This suit is designed to insulate the body against the cold water. It does a fair job, too. There is one problem though; in the suit the body no longer bends like it did. There is a great loss of flexibility in all the joints.

2

Our diver now puts on his hood which is made from the same material as the wet suit and is, again, form fitting. The head will now stay relatively warm. There is one thing, however, which he must give up to not have a cool head—his hearing. The wet suit material reduces his hearing to about one-half of normal.

Next he puts on his fins. These are rubber adaptations which make his feet appear to have been run over by a truck. However, they do push him through the water much faster than he can go without them. Of course the fins also present one problem. He can't walk on land with them. His land progress is cut down to a backward shuffle with his neck twisting one way and then the other to try to see where he's going.

Now he puts on a mask. The mask allows for an airspace between the water and his eyes so he can see when underwater. It works, too! The only problem is that it gives the diver tunnel vision (a narrowing of the visual field which we have as ordinary humans). If under normal conditions an individual had the type of tunnel vision the mask gives him, his eye doctor would say he had serious problems.

Our diver now puts on his flotation vest which will strap around his chest and will, if he is not careful, further impede his chest expansion so he cannot breathe normally. It does, however, act as a perfect hydrostatic organ, giving the diver the same buoyancy adjustment capabilities a fish has through use of its swim bladder. The fish or the diver can hang in perfect balance in the water at any chosen depth just by increasing or decreasing the air in the air chamber. It will, as you might suspect, require more energy to swim through the water because of the extra drag on the vest.

He next takes the tank and regulator which he must wear to supply his air underwater. This device gives the diver the air to survive beneath the surface for a rather short stay. The diver cannot do any hard work because the regulator does not supply enough air to the lungs to allow for it. The snorkel, a very important piece of equipment, is now added to the mask. This allows the diver to have about three-fourths the amount of air needed while on the surface swimming to and from the dive spot where his scuba (self-contained underwater breathing apparatus) gear takes over, also giving him three-fourths the amount of air needed. Using the snorkel is much better than having to hold his breath while swimming to the dive spot.

The weight belt is now added—somewhere between 12 and 25 pounds, depending upon the size of our diver, the thickness of his wet suit, and the density of the water. This belt is to compensate for the buoyancy of all the little bubbles that are trapped in the wet suit which afford the needed insulation for warmth. The scuba gear and weight belt, along with everything else, weighs almost 75 pounds.

Our diver is now dressed. He can hear and see only half as well as he used to. He can't talk at all because of the mouthpiece which he must hold in his mouth to breathe. His movement, as well as his breathing, has been drastically impaired, and by now he is overheated from all the exertion of putting on the gear with his wet suit on in the hot sun. He is helped to the rail where as gracefully as possible he loses his balance and crashes into the water.

At this point you nondivers are at a loss. Why would any semi-intelligent organism supposedly with the power of reason do such a thing willingly? Well, it's a long story. Man is a peculiar species. When he goes hunting and gets no game, he says, "I just go for the exercise anyway." When he goes fishing and catches no fish, he says, "I was really lucky. Now I don't have to clean anything. All I wanted was to be out in the fresh air for a while." He will go out and buy a Porsche and say to his friends that he bought it because he gets good mileage. The explanation is ridiculous. He knows it's ridiculous and so does everybody else, yet everyone accepts it. No one really knows why man does the silly things he does, why he insists on fooling himself, so all the reasons we are going to give for our diver going through this trial by physical effort, which he must to become a diver, are pure speculation.

Keeping this fact in mind, we can now be very profound in our reasoning about what makes a diver tick. Any time you get ten million people to agree on anything there must be a multitude of good reasons for it. Let's dissect a few of them and see if we can't find one that might suit you.

One of the best reasons for scuba diving is the thrill of being underwater. Think about it for a minute. There you are, totally weightless, quietly soaring just above the sea floor with only the smallest amount of physical exertion. Small fish come out of their holes to look at you. How about that? You are the curiosity. You are the thing that does not belong. But you don't really feel like an outsider until a seal comes by. You watch him triple your speed and then disappear into the blue haze that signifies the limits of your reality. Now you know you are an outsider in this, the last earthly spot where you really can be. Perhaps this is why you dive. You are taking part in exploring man's last ecological frontier. The very thought would excite anyone whose blood still flows in his veins. The exploration of this liquid universe which man has spent millions of dollars trying to conquer and only made ripples on the surface of, can take many forms. One of these forms we will call the observer. This diver just looks at everything he can. He has the most fun, perhaps, of anyone. He feeds the fish from his hand. He drops a rock onto a moray eel's head. He blows bubbles at a passing turtle. He totally forgets the outside world.

A seventy-year-old man once asked me to teach him to scuba dive. I helped him to a chair and we discussed it. After hearing why he wanted to learn, I agreed to teach him. He was not certified, of course, and he understood his limitations very well. He had a specific use for scuba and was able to perform well enough to do his thing. It seems he was all alone in the world except for a daughter. The daughter was married to a fine man who was doing well and they had asked the father to live with them. He had accepted eagerly, for to be alone and old is not pleasant. However, his five grandchildren, with their normal energy level, their visiting friends, their sibling rivalry, were more than he could stand. He explained that

The lure of the unknown is one of the most compelling reasons for diving.

The quiet excitement of a dive is very difficult to share with those who have not been there.

while sunning himself beside his daughter's six foot deep, heated swimming pool one day he had had an idea. After we had completed his training, he bought a scuba unit and kept it next to the pool. Whenever things got too rambunctious around the house he would go to the pool, roll his scuba gear into the water, and escape the noise and confusion of the day. Perhaps while you are reading this, old Sam is sitting on the bottom of his well-heated pool with a big smile on his face—blowing bubbles. What more could anyone ask?

I recently had the pleasure of diving with a gentleman from Israel off Cozumel Island in Mexico. I asked him why he dived and he gave me a reason I'd never heard before. He said, "It's the only thing I've ever done where I feel light! I've been heavy all my life. But to dive I actually have to put lead on me to get down. It gives me a light feeling and I no longer think of myself as being heavy."

Man being what he is, he must have a reason for diving. Whether that reason be real or fantasy is of no consequence. Most people have not reached the evolutional stage where they can say, "I go diving just because I feel light," or "just because it's pretty," or "just because I like it." There are many interesting activities which can be used as an excuse. Spearfishing is one. Underwater photography is another. Marine biological collecting is still another. We will try to give you a few good reasons in this book that will enable you to justify going off the deep end.

One thing all divers have in common is the desire to share what they have seen with their friends. This usually takes the form, at the beginning, of the diver telling

6

Underwater photography is one of the most rapidly growing reasons to dive.

---

his friends with great emotion and the best of his vocabulary all about it. The blank looks on their faces soon let him know that you just can't tell people what it's like. There are no words to do it.

In 1958 I had the opportunity to go to the Antarctic. I lived in a tent and I saw sights that my mind could record but that I could not verbally recreate. I turned to the camera and captured some great photos which I shared with people, adding words. The audio-visual approach was better but still so inadequate that I soon lost interest in using it. I decided there was no way I could share my Antarctic experience with those who had not been there. And then I had what the psychologists call an "aha" sensation. I realized what the key was. The key in the statement was "others *who had not been there*." When I was with people who had been to the Antarctic, forming the word pictures was simple. I could say, "the Ross Ice Shelf," and they saw and felt what I did, for it drew a picture in their minds of something they had experienced, touched, felt. It was already registered inside. I had not actually created the picture. I had simply brought it to the surface of their attention.

Diving is the same type of thing. The person who has not been underwater has no frame of reference upon which to build an image. Our diver, finding words inadequate, will eventually turn to underwater pictures. After awhile he will find that these too are inadequate to convey his fascination. In diving, however, unlike my Antarctic adventure, there is an ultimate solution to the problem of sharing of experience. While I could not take everyone I talked to back to the Antarctic—a physical impossibility—our diver can, if he chooses, become an instructor and show people his world. I am convinced that men and women become diving instructors, not for the money, not for the prestige, but to end the great frustration in trying to talk to people. If they can get the people to whom they talk underwater, they can then tell them all about their diving and not be faced with those blank looks in the eyes of their listeners. Once the instructor completes their training he can tell them about the sea urchin he saw which was lighter in color than normal, or the garibaldi that bit his finger, and their eyes will sparkle, for they will then know just what he is talking about. He teaches diving as a matter of helping people to be able to communicate. When you think about it, that's an entirely valid reason for teaching diving—to enable others to understand and share with you the thing you feel is the most fascinating in the entire world.

Yes, there are many reasons for getting wet. The marine biologist dives to get closer to his animals and plants so he can see what makes them function. For him diving is a most useful tool. The commercial diver dives for profit which, to me, is the worst reason for diving. It is a shame to take a beautiful, stimulating place like the subsurface marine environment and spoil it for yourself by working in it for a living. The romance is gone—only the dangers and the boredom remain. To the commercial diver diving is only a hard, physical job with a high danger rate due to his long hours of exposure.

The foremost difference between the commercial diver and the good sports diver is not knowledge. There are many sports divers who are extremely knowledgeable. The big difference is that the sports diver can go into the water whenever and wherever he wants to. The commercial diver goes into the water whenever and wherever he is told to. The sports diver does things while in the water which bring him joy and peace of mind. The commercial man does things while in the water which bring him exhaustion and money. The recreational diver has it made. He has the cream of what the sea can offer and very few of the problems. For us, the recreational divers, diving with proper instruction becomes a safe, sane family sport. Mom and Dad and all the kids are able to enjoy it on their own level. Sports diving is one of the dwindling number of activities the whole family will actually look forward to doing together.

The sea is the perfect place for the hunter. Here he can hunt on any skill level without the worry that another hunter may shoot him in error. The game is varied, with something available all year 'round. What he hunts is generally good to eat and not difficult to clean. The conservationist can rest at ease that animals are not normally being killed in order to be hung on someone's wall as a trophy. Admittedly, there is the novice diver who kills the small, friendly reef fish and then lets them rot on the bottom. We all have contempt and pity for this individual. Contempt because he is usually loud-mouthed and ego-blinded. What other type of person would kill a living creature that was not good to eat and no challenge to

This woman and her son enjoy a coral reef together.

The harvest of the sea—accessible to the diver with the simplest of equipment—is a toothsome fringe benefit.

hunt? He does not realize this beautiful environment he finds himself in can be spoiled. We have polluted the air over our cities to the point where people die. We have taken advantage of poor game laws to the point of exterminating many of our fellow organisms. We are, as a society, now becoming aware of our faults and trying to correct them in order to survive. We are to the point where the "dumb-dumb" who kills just to kill is to be pitied, for he is demonstrating to everyone that he has no skill and no knowledge of what he is doing. The person who condemns all spearfishing is on the other end of the pendulum. He is speaking with the same lack of knowledge as our killer. Later in this book, I will explain how to be a sporting underwater hunter and still be a concerned environmentalist.

It would be impossible to try to discuss all the reasons people dive. We have talked about a few. There are still an infinite number of others.* There is the girl who takes diving lessons because her boyfriend is a diver and she feels she must learn to dive just to stay in the competition. There is the boy in college who takes the diving course simply because it fits into his schedule where the handball class does not. There is the person who has always been a little afraid of the water and takes up diving to work out his fear.

Everyone has at least "a little" fear of the ocean. Let's face it, it's the biggest thing in the world and doesn't appear too friendly most of the time. Our fear is normal, and good, because it holds our attention on safety and proper techniques. This *normal,* low-level anxiety is what gives us a feeling of adventure and excitement. Even those of us who have a high level of uncertainty at the beginning of training generally make good divers. As we learn to use the equipment our tenseness is eased. As we discover we can see, breathe, and move about with relative ease and comfort, we become more relaxed. The more relaxed we become, the safer we are and the more we see and enjoy ourselves.

The one reason for becoming a diver which concerns me is the person who believes diving is very dangerous and takes it up to prove to himself that he can conquer it. This person is looking for something dramatic to happen to him, and his attitude is the perfect setting for panic. If the diver uses common sense and basic diving knowledge there is very seldom anything dramatic that can happen so our hero has to invent something. I worked at Catalina Island off California for many years as a diver. One of my jobs was collecting fish for several large aquariums. In one of the tanks we kept 70 to 80 moray eels. This tank was about six feet deep, seven feet long, and five feet wide. Each morning Cliff, one of our crew, would climb into the tank and clean off the glass from the inside. Algae grew on the inside and had to be scraped off daily. The eels were simply pushed out of his way as he wiped the glass with his squeegee. On Cliff's day off I would do the window cleaning. One day I wasn't watching what I was doing and reached out to

---

* A special category in recent years are those who take up diving in the wake of a lifelong crush on Lloyd Bridges.

brace myself, giving a big moray a judo chop in the mouth. Had I been smart and waited a few seconds, he would undoubtedly have opened his mouth and I would have had a few small puncture wounds on my hand. Instead, as I felt him close his mouth and sink his teeth into my hand, my reaction was to yank my hand away. This was, of course, a foolish thing to do. Most small animals, when they bite, will let go if there is no resistance. In pulling my hand away I ripped some fairly large lacerations in my fingers. So now I can say I was bitten by a moray eel. I don't normally mention that I had to put my hand into his mouth and then hit him a good whack to get him to close it, or that I pulled it out of his mouth over his teeth to get the moderately deep wound that I did.

Now, what does my molesting an eel have to do with our hero diver? Well, our hero diver is looking for a disaster so he can be a hero. There is just nothing worse than a hero out of work. You can't be a hero without a happening. He cruises the bottom, muscles tense with expectation. Behind every kelp stock, under every rock, he searches for the big challenge, the "happening" that will again allow him to be a hero. (Being a hero is a difficult thing, for glory lasts but a short time and must be constantly reinforced.) As our diver rounds a rock he sees it—the thing he has been looking for—an open mouth with flashing teeth—two beady staring eyes—a moray eel. He frantically escapes in a mad rush to the surface. As he climbs into the boat, he finds that his ankle is bleeding. He was attacked, but he escaped. His story is courageous. It is breath-taking. It, unfortunately, will be widely spread. He swears, and believes, that he was attacked by an eel. Given a lie detector test he would come out clean. In reality the eel, because of its poor eyesight, probably had its head sticking out of a hole in order to see what all the commotion was that the diver was kicking up in front of his home. His mouth was open because it has to be for him to breathe. He can't help it if he has teeth which hang down. We can't all be good looking. When our hero fled to the top, our eel probably retreated to his lair with the same haste with which our diver was heading for the surface. The rock the eel was under more than likely caught the diver's ankle and made a laceration which bled. And we now have another eel story which will grow bigger and better as time passes. Because of his expectation of danger, our hero is always on a knife's edge with his emotions.

Diving, as we do it for sport, is not dangerous if approached in a sensible manner. By sensible I mean with a "touch of cowardice." The diver who's a bit of a coward and admits it, is my kind of guy. He won't take chances he shouldn't, or try to show off to the boys. I much prefer to teach a scuba class for cowards than I do to teach one for heroes.

There are a few simple rules you must be aware of and follow: the two most important are: (1) dive with someone. What's the use of seeing a shimmering fish or a gigantic lobster if you can't share it? And, (2) be objective as to your own physical ability. Don't get into situations that are not easily handled. Then, when you miscalculate, you have a margin of error in which to work and you know it so

More and more women are sampling the wonders of diving.

you are able to handle the situation calmly. Diving is fun. If it isn't fun, you should forget about it and play tennis or do something which is fun for you. Life is too short not to do the things we enjoy. When we look at the number of people being certified as divers (approximately 120,000 a year by one organization, in the United States alone), we just know it's fun because that many semi-intelligent organisms can't be wrong.

Many women are becoming interested in diving now so they can spend their weekends with their husbands and teenage children who have become divers. One nice thing about being a woman diver is that if you bat your eyes just right you never have to carry any of your own gear.

Whatever reason you wish to use, try diving. It is truly an exhilarating activity. It is not as expensive as skiing or sailing, and it is just as much or perhaps more fun.

2

WHERE DID IT START?

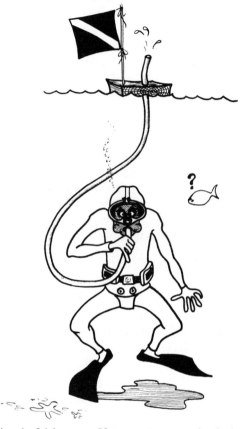

The sport of diving is fairly new. If one were to go back through history and compile a chronological list of sports, he would find sports diving one of the very recent ones to pop its head up. It seems that man has constantly strived to do the impossible and generally accomplished it.

Although sports diving is new on the historical scene, man underwater is not. In the Iliad, Homer writes, "Ye Gods! With what facility he dives!" Later, in the same work, he states, "So then, in Troy it seems are divers too!" These passages indicate that men were diving at least as early as 1000 B.C. Other ancient historians, such as Herodotus, mention divers being used by rulers in their local battles. Xerxes of Persia around 475 B.C. used divers to recover treasure. One such diver, a Greek named Scyllis, used diving to escape from Xerxes' kingdom by cutting the anchor lines of the ships in the harbor during a storm and making his watery getaway while the crews were trying to keep their ships off the rocks. Even

Alexander the Great himself was lowered in a barrel into the briny to steal a look at the diver's world. One of his victories at Tyree, which would have been around 330 B.C., was supposed to have been aided by underwater swimmers.

Throughout history, underwater swimmers and divers have been used by the military of countries which had battles to wage on liquid battlegrounds. Their usefulness was readily recognized by those ancient hawks, and today we have what are known as the SEAL Team and the UDT Team which are very active in underwater warfare in our military.

The diver, then, for one reason or another, has been with us for a long time. It would only stand to reason that once man discovered the beauty of the underwater scene he would attempt to devise a method for staying there awhile. The most obvious method, of course, is to place a tube into your mouth and float the other end of it above the surface, to allow you to breathe. Aristotle, approximately 355 B.C., mentions such apparatus. Knowing what we do today about things like "dead air space" and "carbon dioxide buildup," it is unlikely that anyone actually used these devices. They were undoubtedly conceived and constructed, but they just don't work. The pressure alone on the body increases at the rate of .445 pounds per square inch ("psi") for every foot of water the diver has above him. This means in practical terms that man's muscles are not strong enough to inflate his chest below three feet. Even if the diver could inflate his chest, the CO_2 buildup from the long tube would cause blackout in a matter of a few minutes. Pliny the Elder as late as A.D. 77 wrote of the same type of device. These devices were probably used so the swimmer could stay just under the surface of the water and so be unobserved as he drifted in to do some sort of sneaky thing. They must have been our first snorkels. To remain underwater the diver needs air which is under pressure. The deeper the diver goes, the more pressure is needed to force the air down to him. Some efforts were made to put air into a diving bell (which was generally a barrel or facsimile) to let the diver take the air down with him. The water would compress the air as the diver went down.

There were many attempts at this type of diving between A.D. 1000 and A.D. 1800, but none were very successful. There were two main problems. The first one was sinking the bell. A bell large enough for a man to stick his head and shoulders into was so buoyant that it became too cumbersome to handle when all the weight was added to sink it. The second problem was that if he breathed into the bell even for a short period all the oxygen was used up and the diver blacked out.

In the early 1800s the all-important air compressor came onto the scene. Now air could be pumped down to a diver and circulated so that it did not become stale. Divers started to accomplish what might be called true underwater work. One of the first types of successful diving rigs was the displacement helmet. This is often referred to as the "open dress" because the bottom of the helmet was open to the water. When I was in high school, my friends and I made a displacement helmet out of an old water heater. We cut it in half so it would fit over our heads and sit on our shoulders. We cut a hole in the side and put a glass plate in so we could see outside. We then rigged a harness that would hold it in place. The only problem was that the harness had to come around the body and through the crotch in order to hold the air-filled helmet down. It occurred to me several times while I was diving this unit that it was perhaps better suited for a female diver.

We ran a hose to the pipe that came out the top and pumped air to the diver from a two-cyclinder hand pump on the surface. The extra air would bubble out at the bottom. The lead belt we had to wear was around 60 pounds to compensate for the buoyancy of the helmet. Our only contact as far as communication with the surface was a line which we could jerk, sending pulse signals to the surface. I recall one signal very well. It was a continuous jerking on the line, and was employed when we would bend over too far, allowing the air to bubble out of the helmet. To the man on the surface it meant: pump like mad! In the meantime, the diver sat quietly holding his breath waiting for the air to push the water out of his helmet so he could breathe again. Those were the good old days! Things just aren't the same now—thank goodness!

With the ability to stay underwater longer, new problems began to descend upon the diver. Oddly enough, the diver inherited a mysterious affliction of the construction workers who were engaged in tunnel building. The construction companies built caissons (huge watertight enclosures) under the water to carry out their work and the workers would remain in these caissons all day. In order to keep the water out of the caissons, they were pressurized with air pressure. When the men left the caissons at the end of a 12-hour shift they suffered pains at the joints and often became ill. Some were crippled and others died of "caisson disease." A Frenchman named Bert had insight into what was happening physiologically and suggested slow ascent to reduce the rapid pressure change. In 1907 Haldane found a mathematical equation that explained the problem in terms of nitrogen gas absorption and was able to compile enough data so that the first "stage" decompression system was developed.

Caisson disease is now called "the bends" by almost everyone. The story of how this name came about is an interesting one. The workers would try to ease the pain in their joints by slouching or "bending" a bit at all their joints. Also, it is rumored that at about this same period in time there was a popular dance called "the bends." Because the workers appeared to be doing this dance in their slouched positions they were said to have "the bends."

The first scuba operation occurred in 1825, when a man by the name of James devised and constructed a belt that would carry air. The diver breathed the air from the belt. This concept was good because the water pressure compressed the air in the belt and the diver thus had compressed air to breathe, much the same as scuba

15

divers today have. The problems with the belt were that it could not carry enough air to the bottom to last more than a few minutes and, as the diver used the air, he became heavy due to the loss of buoyancy.

By 1880 Henry Fleuss, an Englishman, had developed a different type of scuba device. This used pure oxygen, which the diver breathed over and over. The rig actually worked but the diver had to be very careful because oxygen under certain pressure conditions becomes a deadly gas to the system. The deepest the diver could go with safety was 30 feet. Fleuss's unit was improved and used by the U.S. Navy in World War II. Its advantages to the military were that it was a closed circuit which would not let off bubbles to give away the presence of a diver, and it lasted a long time.

The real breakthrough in diving apparatus occurred when a steel tank was developed that could hold air under high pressure. This allowed the diver to take a significant amount of air underwater with him so he could stay awhile and not have to worry about the problem that pure oxygen presented. The first use of this tank was in a full-face mask where the air just flowed through and the diver breathed it as it went through the mask. It worked well but was uneconomical as far as the air was concerned. Much air was wasted and the diver's time underwater was short.

In the early 1940s a Frenchman named Jacques-Yves Cousteau made a very important find; he developed an underwater demand-type regulator that conserved air by releasing only the amount of air the diver needed to breathe. This increased the time the diver could stay down on one steel tank of compressed air to approximately one hour if he were in shallow depths. The Costeau rig was simple and inexpensive and marks the beginning of the sport of scuba diving. The sport grew rather slowly through the late '40s and early '50s because, although the diver could now stay underwater for an extended period of time, in most parts of the world he became so chilled he was forced to leave the water after a short stay.

It was in the early 1950s that rubber suits were designed and marketed in quantity. The first ones that came into general use were comprised of a thin sheet of rubber that covered the body like a rubber glove covers the hand. They kept the diver warm but were hard to use due to buoyancy changes, squeezes, and leaks. These old ''dry suits'' were worn over long underwear and sweat suits or sweaters; the clothing acted as an insulator and the rubber suit simply served the purpose of keeping this insulation dry. However, they were so thin they were easily punctured and, as soon as a leak developed, the clothing underneath naturally became wet and all insulation properties were lost.

In an effort to protect the suit from tearing, many of us wore coveralls over our dry suits. Can you imagine the effort we had to expend in order to dive for two or three hours dressed in two sets of long johns, one heavy wool sweater, one rubber dry suit, and one pair of coveralls. We also wore one inflatable life belt, World War II vintage, and either an ammo belt filled with lead or a length of chain wrapped around our waists to sink us with all that ''garbage'' we were wearing.

We were so proud of our gear that we would "dress" at home and walk through town to the beach so that we could be seen and admired by all!

These cumbersome suits always leaked no matter what precautions were taken and we were usually cold, but we always got game. It was not uncommon, in 1953, to dive off the harbor at Avalon, Catalina, in California and take ten 15-pound lobsters in an hour's free diving. It is rare to see even one 15-pound lobster in this area now.

With the advent of the "dry suit" to keep the diver warm, the number enjoying the sport took a jump, but it wasn't until a new strategem called the "wet suit" was introduced that things really began to happen. The wet suit actually trapped a thin layer of water next to the diver's body, which soon heated up to body temperature and acted as additional insulation. Some of the early wet suits were constructed by Terry Cox in a little shop located in Newport Beach, California. Mr. Cox experimented with several materials, one of which was foam polyvinyl chloride. This suit was warm but would not stand up under use. Finally, foam neoprene was selected as being the best material available. When the wet suit hit the market, the average man could go diving in relative comfort in all the temperate waters of the world. I believe the wet suit was as important a step forward as Cousteau's demand regulator.

The first wet suits were mostly custom tailored for the buyer. It was possible to purchase a pattern and construct your own, or use the services of a shop where one would be made to your individual measurements. With growing demand, manufacturers came into the picture with the standard small, medium, and large sizes. As the market continued to increase the neoprene material was improved by making it softer and more flexible, and a backing was put on the neoprene to increase its durability and thus its service.

The market grew still larger and ready-made suits appeared in extra small, small, medium, medium large, large, and extra large sizes. Today, almost anyone can walk into a store and walk out with a good suit that fits.

With all of these recent developments we wonder what the next major breakthrough will be. Modern technology is making it possible to have significant advancements come in rapid succession. The history of sports diving is just beginning and you can be a part of it.

3

THE STUFF YOU NEED

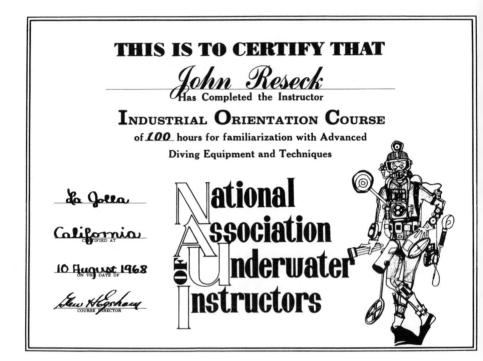

THIS IS TO CERTIFY THAT

John Reseck

Has Completed the Instructor

INDUSTRIAL ORIENTATION COURSE

of *100* hours for familiarization with Advanced
Diving Equipment and Techniques

La Jolla,

California
CERTIFIED AT

10 August 1968
ON THE DATE OF

Glenn H. Gorshow
COURSE DIRECTOR

National
Association
of Underwater
Instructors

The equipment used by the diver is extensive and varied, as we saw when we "dressed out" our diver in Chapter 1. It is not yet perfected. If we were to analyze it in terms of how conveniently he can live and work underwater, we would see that it has a long way to go. When we dressed out our diver we limited him to a large degree in all of his functions; and yet engulfed in this maze of steel, rubber, and glass the diver functions better than without it under the water. Each piece of equipment helps him to perform some chore better than he can without it. Where we have to be careful is to be sure that the same piece of equipment does not hinder some other activity to the point where it becomes a useless trade-off or unsafe.

The equipment we are going to discuss here is that which seems at this time to be usable without creating an undue safety hazard, and extends the diver's capabilities in some specific area. It is interesting to follow the evolution of our equipment through its early stages of development. There are several books on diving published in the 1930s that are worth reading. My very favorite one is called *The Complete Goggler,* by Guy Gilpatric. He tells how they made their own equipment and how disgusted they got at the crowded conditions when they found another diver on the beach where they normally did their diving.

Those days are gone forever. We are flooded with equipment from a dozen major manufacturers and five times that many small ones. Whatever we want seems to be produced for us by someone. We may find ourselves modifying it but we don't have to make it. Dive stores are springing up all over the world. I am often asked to define a "pro dive store," a term used quite a bit now. There is one organization which considers those shops that pay dues to it the only "pro dive stores" regardless of the quality of store or personnel running them. I can't agree. I believe that a "pro dive store" is any store dedicated to diving and divers—one that carries most brands of equipment and is staffed by competent individuals with extensive diving experience, so they can give qualified advice with the interest of the diver at heart and not just the size of his personal bank account. I would suggest to the beginning diver that he trade at a dive store if possible and not at a store that just carries diving equipment along with everything else. It only stands to reason that he will get a better choice of equipment and better advice from behind the counter.

• PRIMARY EQUIPMENT

The basic equipment that is needed to get started in diving includes mask, fins, snorkel, and flotation vest. These are standard anywhere in the world, so we will discuss them first.

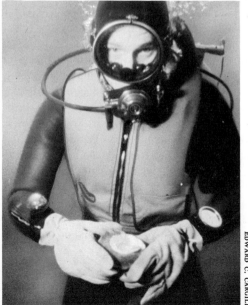

Engulfed in a maze of steel, rubber, and glass, the diver is limited in all his functions, but he functions better with his equipment than without it, under the water.

EDWARD C. CARGILE

19

The Mask

Man has several senses which are important to him, but the ability to see is probably most important. When our sight is impaired our anxiety level rises sharply. It is difficult to imagine what it would be like dropping into the cool ocean and sinking into the liquid world in which we dive if we could not see. The ability to see what is around us releases us from fear. The human eye does a good job of letting us know what we are about to run into on land but underwater, due to a lot of physical facts and laws, it seems that our eye doesn't function too well. Everything looks blurred; the reason is due to the speed at which light travels through materials of different density. The materials of concern to us are water and air. The lens of our eye is adapted to receiving light traveling through air. When we replace the air with water the lens cannot focus the rays where they should be on the back of the eyeball. We end up with a blurred image.

The problem can be solved by trapping air in front of the eyes so the light passes through the air before it enters the eye. This is what the mask does. If we could glue a bubble in front of each eye, we could get the same result. The diver can do the bubble bit if he wants to just by holding his hands on his forehead and looking down as he blows out of his nose. If the hands are held right over the eyes a bubble will be caught over each eye and he can see.

If you have ever tried to hold a bubble and swim, you know why the mask was invented. In days gone by, goggles were replaced by the mask, as the mask helps to keep water from running up your nose and getting into your sinuses, and also allows you to blow air out your nose to compensate for the extra pressure encountered as you descend. The mask turns out to be a good, usable piece of equipment.

Now that I have convinced you of that, which kind of mask should you buy? I do not know how many different masks are on the market, but it must be in excess of 100. Confusion is understandable, but there's a solution so don't get shook. The most important thing to consider when buying a mask is whether it fits your face and makes a comfortable seal to keep out the water. A simple test is to place the mask to your face *gently* without the straps being in place and inhale *slightly* through the nose. This will create a vacuum in the mask and, due to atmospheric pressure, it will stay in place if it fits properly when you let go of it. Don't push the mask on your face and don't suck in hard through your nose, because any mask will stay on if you do that. Do it very gently. Give the masks that don't pass this test back to the salesman and place the ones that fit to the side. Don't be hurried; try them all. It's your face that has to end up wearing whatever you decide to buy.

When you have finished you will have a pile of masks that fit from which to select. If any of them have plastic plates in them, give them back to the salesman, too. Plastic is difficult to see through because water condenses on it and creates a fog you cannot get rid of. Plastic sides are not as comfortable and do not seal as

The almost endless variety of styles and shapes available include masks to accommodate the glasses-wearer.

well as rubber and therefore are not as desirable. Shape is the next consideration. Either a round or an oval mask works fine but an oval mask generally allows the diver a slightly wider view in the water. At best, your vision is limited, but the oval type seems to be less limited than the round. Some masks have side windows; these are okay but do not give the great advantage you might think.

Of the masks you now have left, some will have an extra item called a purge valve. This is a one-way valve located in the bottom portion of the mask, and its function is to allow the diver to remove water from the mask by exhaling through his nose, which pushes the water out with air pressure. The principle is a good one and it works, but what the manufacturers have done with it is something else. There are a great number of masks on the market which were not designed to have a purge valve; the manufacturers have stuck one in at the last minute to make them look a little sexier. When you use one of these, you can tell the engineer who designed it must have been frightened of the water because he certainly never used it himself or he wouldn't have made it. They work very poorly. The only purge mask worth having is one which was originally designed to have a purge. This type is readily distinguished, as the purge is usually quite large—about an inch or so in diameter. It will be located in a projection which sticks out over the nose. This works well. The others give nothing but trouble. Some of the masks have purges built in that you are supposed to open up if you wish to by cutting off the little tabs beneath the nose. Don't open them up. The small purge defeats the purpose and makes it more difficult to clear the mask.

So much then for the purge valve. The rest of the masks you have to choose from will have no purge. You do not need to have a purge to clear the water out of the mask; in fact, I believe you can clear it faster and easier with just a straight mask. At this point, you will have several choices left. You must decide which one you like best. And which one is the most comfortable for your face. Good luck! I generally try a new mask every year. I can't decide either!

MASKS AND THE GLASSES-WEARER • If you wear glasses and can't see well enough to be comfortable without them, then you should wear corrective lenses when you dive also. There are several ways this can be accomplished. If you wear contacts you can still wear them while you dive, though be careful not to lose them when your mask floods. A mask with a purge will help you to avoid losing them if they should be washed out. Another way, and I believe safer and cheaper, is to

21

have your prescription ground into your faceplate glass. It is safer because you don't have to worry about the loss of a contact lens and thus the loss of your sight. It is cheaper because the average custom-ground lens costs about $35.00 while a contact could cost much more if lost. Whatever it takes for you to see well under water, do it. It would be a shame to miss the subtle design and intricate patterning of the various small sea animals and plants which give the sea its unrivaled fascination. It goes without saying that as-full-as-possible vision is an important safety factor, too.

The Fins

Now that you can see underwater, you are going to want to move about so you can see as much as possible. In wearing fins the diver is trying to imitate as closely as he can the underwater mammals. When a diver puts on his fins he has a horizontal tail similar to the seals and porpoises; in fact, man has copied the swimming style of these animals with what he calls a dolphin kick. You will understand why if you have ever had the pleasure of seeing one of these graceful animals swim. They move through the water with no apparent effort, twisting, turning, and somersaulting as they play through their day. Their fins are broad and long, so we make our fins broad and long too. And it works. The swim fins that you can buy at the dive store will push you through the water with amazing ease; you can't swim as fast as a seal because of the greater drag on your body, but if you really turn it on you can make about two and one-half miles per hour for a short time in all of your diving gear. The best thing about the fins is that you can move very slowly (which is the proper speed for diving) across the bottom with almost no effort.

There are two major types of fins and they both work well. One type is similar to a shoe. Your foot slips into a rubber shoe with a fin blade attached to it, generally at a slight angle. The other type has a pocket you put your foot into and a strap that comes behind the heel to hold your foot in the pocket. Again, as with the mask, the fit is of prime importance. The fins must be comfortable; fins that are too tight will cause cramps and cold feet due to loss of circulation. Fins that are too loose will slip back and forth on your feet and rub sores. As a general rule, the shoe type is fairly comfortable just as it comes from the shop. Heel strap fins are generally more comfortable if rubber booties are worn on the feet. The booties serve several functions; they keep the fins from rubbing your feet raw, keep your feet warm, and help you to walk to and from the beach over the rocks. If you decide on heel strap fins, ones that have a replaceable strap would be best because if a strap breaks it can be replaced without having to buy a whole new pair of fins. This could save you money over a period of years.

Now that you know how to pick fins for comfort, what about size? Fins come in all sizes. By sizes, I don't mean foot size. I mean the size of the fin itself. Fin sizes

COURTESY *Skin Diver* MAGAZINE

When buying your gear a proper fit is very important. In a professional dive store the salesmen are all divers and can help you select good equipment that is well suited—and practical—for you.

seem to run something like this: small, medium, large, extra large, and big as hell. The size of the fins should match the size and activity of the diver. A small woman would not want large fins because she would not have the leg muscles to kick with them efficiently. And the 200-pound athlete would not want small fins because he wouldn't go anywhere when he kicked. Keep in mind that the more you swim, the larger the fins you can adapt to. The large shoe-type fins are generally the cheapest good fins and work well for most beginning divers because they give an even thrust and do not tend to cramp the legs as often as the giant size fins. Don't get the gigantic fins until you have the muscle power and the physical conditioning to push them for an hour or so at a time. Too often the big fins are sold on the basis of sex appeal rather than reason. Again, the final decision must be yours.

The Snorkel

Now you can see and move about, but just when you spot a pretty fish you have to bring your head out of the water to get another breath. Well, we can fix that.

There is a strange bent hose that the diver calls a snorkel which is designed to let you lie on your stomach and keep your eye contact with the bottom, and still be able to breathe. The snorkel has many advantages, only one of which is enabling you to see better. By keeping your face down in the water your eyes can adjust to the reduced light and and you can make out details that you could not otherwise see. Because of this, you should learn not to lift your head out of the water more than is absolutely necessary.

Snorkels come in all sizes and shapes, just like masks and fins. There are some simple rules that will help you make a good choice. The snorkel is to allow you to breathe while being face down in the water. Therefore, you want one that will give you all the air you need with as little restriction as possible. The best one would be one foot in diameter and only two inches long with no bends. If one like that worked, you sure would get a lot of air! The idea is to get as close to that as possible. The smaller the tube, the more restriction there is, so you want a fairly large tube. A good rule of thumb is to get a tube large enough so that your thumb (if you don't have an oversize thumb) will fit into the end of it. Every time a snorkel has a bend in it there is an extra drag on the air coming down the tube. So a second good rule is to pick one with as few bends in it as possible.

A third good rule is to reject the type of snorkel called the flex snorkel. In this, the inside of the tube is corrugated and the grooves set up a fantastic drag on the incoming air, cutting down on your air supply. If the inside has a smooth tube, as some flex snorkels do, it helps, but the diameter has to be cut down to put the lining in so the restriction is still far too great. I personally feel that the flex snorkels are a safety hazard and should be taken off the market. In most cases when divers get into trouble, it is because they are tired. A poorly designed snorkel cuts down the amount of air the diver gets on long swims and is a major factor in fatigue.

Your snorkel should have as few bends as possible, be large enough to put your thumb into, and be comfortable in your mouth. To get it comfortable in your mouth, you should move it up and down and back and forth on your mask until it is in the most comfortable position. It should not push or pull on your lips; it should fit very easily in place and you shouldn't have to bite on it to hold it there.

One manufacturer has developed a plastic mouth piece that the diver dips in hot water to soften it, then places in his mouth and bites down on. The mouth piece forms right to the diver's mouth and gives the most comfort of any type yet available.

The Flotation Vest

The flotation vest, or buoyancy compensator as it is more properly called, is similar *in appearance* to the old World War II Mae West. The Mae West was an inflatable life preserver that fit around the neck like a vest so the downed pilot's head would be held out of the water if he were tired or injured. It started out being used for the same reason in diving. It was called a safety vest and was used if the diver got into trouble. There has been quite an evolution of uses for the vest. The more we wore it the more we found it would do for us. Although the basic looks are similar to the old "safety vest," the new "buoyancy compensator" (BC) is changed in most every other way. Buoyancy compensators now have *reliable* automatic filling mechanisms, large oral inflators that really work, better straps to hold them firmly in place when inflated, and do not rot after three months' use.

The BC has become a primary piece of equipment for all *knowledgeable* divers. It has four basic functions: it acts as a hydrostatic organ, similar to the air bladder in most fish; it acts as a surface float, aiding the diver as he swims to and from his diving spot; it acts as a lift bag for light salvage work; and it can act as a safety device in an emergency. Any one of these functions would be reason enough to have one.

This model features a scuba-fed low pressure inflator system which attaches to the diver's regulator, allowing the vest to be inflated with either hand.

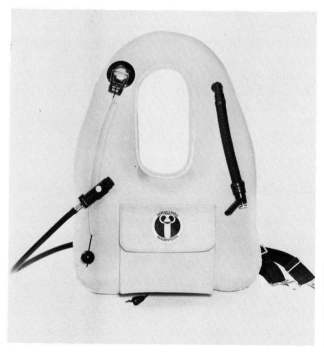

There are two basic types on the market. One works with a small CO_2 cartridge for emergency inflation, and the other works with a small bottle of compressed air. The vest most divers wear is the CO_2 type. It costs about $70 and is satisfactory to a depth of approximately 100 feet if a 26-gram CO_2 cartridge is used and not the small 16-gram one that generally comes with the vest. The air type has both advantages and disadvantages. The advantages are that it can be used in an emergency in depths below 100 feet and will inflate at any depth due to the large amount of air carried in the bottle. The disadvantages are that it is bulky—right on the verge of being too much so—and it is expensive, approximately $150. When you look at the air type closely, the only real advantage is that it will inflate in case of emergency at great depths. But no sensible diver will be diving below 100 feet anyway. I believe that the air vest is more for the commercial diver than the sports diver. I've heard it said that the difference between a man and a boy is just the price of their toys. I would tend to agree. In this case, however, the man can buy a cheaper toy and still play the game safely.

A new kind of flotation vest that may prove to be a compromise between the two standard types is now being offered by some manufacturers. This new type has a hose connecting from the low-pressure port in the regulator to a special filler valve that snaps into the vest. The diver can fill the vest from his tank at any depth without taking the mouthpiece of the regulator out of his mouth. The filler connection alone can be bought separately and fitted to most of the newer vests which have a large filler hose, about an inch in diameter. The price of a vest ready-fitted with the new device lies somewhere between the prices for the other two types and the concept seems to be proving out to be a good one. The diver can inflate and deflate the vest with one hand and play elevator if he wishes. The large oral filler hose is a must. It allows the diver to fill his BC by blowing into it without a great deal of back pressure to tire him. It also lets the diver vent the air out of the BC rapidly so he will not ascend too fast.

. SECONDARY EQUIPMENT

Now that we have discussed how to buy the primary pieces of equipment, we can take into consideration what I am arbitrarily calling secondary equipment. To a great many of you who live in cold water areas, the rubber suit is as primary as the mask.

The Wet Suit

I have thought a long time about what to say about rubber exposure suits. In my local shop they have at least six different makes and brands, all of which work. I am not going to discuss the original type of dry suit at all because it is seldom used nowadays. It is more difficult to use and raises many more problems than the wet suit, although it does keep you very warm when it works. The basic trouble with the dry suit is keeping it functional.

The wet suit became popular in the mid 1950s and proved itself over and over and over again. Basically, it is made of bubble-impregnated neoprene. The gas in the bubbles conducts heat more slowly than water, so the suit acts as an insulator against cold water. The body is able to conserve more heat and the diver consequently stays within his warmth threshold longer. The thicker the wet suit, the longer the diver stays warm. Ideally, the suit would be two inches thick, but remember the trade-off we talked about earlier. A two-inch wet suit would keep the diver warm but he would not be able to move and would have to wear a 100-pound weight belt to sink all those little bubbles. So we compromise. Old Ben Franklin was a smart cookie when he said, "Sometimes we have to cut a little off both ends of a board to make it fit." We must make the suit thin enough that we can still move in it and at the same time keep it thick enough that we can dive as long as we want without becoming too cold.

The thinner the suit, the more comfortable it is and the less tired we become swimming in it. At best it restricts movement and makes you expend more energy. The thickness of the suit a diver will want, then, depends on several variables: the temperature of the water he will be diving in, his general size and physiology, and the length of time he wishes to spend in the water. Fat people can stand much more cold than thin people. Most of us know our own tolerances to cold better than anyone else. Being on the heavy side myself, the figures that I am going to use might be a bit on the cold side for some people and are again arbitrary. (By now you know that I'm fat and I'm arbitrary. Who knows what you will find out if you read on!)

I think I am safe in saying that in water 80° Fahrenheit and above no one needs a rubber suit. This would include places such as the Mediterranean, the Red Sea, the Caribbean, and the South Pacific. Unfortunately, most of us are stuck with something less than that. In temperatures of 72° to 80° Fahrenheit some people can still function well with no wet suit, while others like a thin suit of ⅛" to keep off the chill. In water of 60° to 72° a ³/₁₆" suit will normally do a good job. The ³/₁₆" suit, especially the newer materials which are soft and pliable, does not cut down the diver's mobility too badly. In waters below 60° a ¼" suit will probably be needed and in real cold water, below 45°, some people wear a ⅜" suit, although it is somewhat like a straitjacket.

I have what I think is a great way to attack the problem of what suit to wear. I call it "the wet suit system." I am fortunate enough to dive in many parts of the world and therefore need to adapt my equipment to the conditions in which I find myself at any given time. My system consists of five pieces, worn in various combinations. The first piece is a ³/₁₆" long-sleeved jacket, the second a pair of ³/₁₆" long john pants. For most of my diving in Southern California water this is adequate.

My third piece is really two pieces: my booties. I wear these most of the time anyway to keep my fins from rubbing my feet. When the water gets a little cold I wear my fourth piece, which is a ⅛″ cold water hood. The cold water hood has a large flange around the neck which is tucked in under the jacket and keeps water from leaking down your back, besides keeping your head warm. My fifth piece I wear when I visit Canada and make a dive through the ice with my inland friends. It is a one-piece, ⅛″ short suit which zips up the abdomen. The arms are short, about half the distance to the elbow, and the legs are short, about half the distance to the knees. When I have the short suit on I have $^8/_{16}″$ protection plus an extra film of water between the two suits on all the main parts of my body. On my leg joints and on my arm joints, where little heat is lost anyway, I still have the mobility of a $^3/_{16}″$ suit. If I dive in the warmer waters, I can use just the short suit and be comfortable. I am sure that the "Reseck system" is not new or original, but it does work almost anywhere and can be put together in a module system, one piece at a time. It is a little easier on the pocketbook done this way.

Now that you have some basis on which to choose the type of suit you need, we can talk about how wet suits are made and what to look for. Rubber suit material comes in two main types. One has a lining, generally nylon, impregnated right into the neoprene and the other is not lined, just plain neoprene. I would suggest that a lined suit is best. It is not any warmer than a non-lined suit but it is less apt to tear as you put it on and take it off. The lined suit is also easier to get in and out of as it does not cling to the skin as much as straight neoprene. The seams in the suit should be glued and then sewn to give it the greatest durability. Most suits have zippers. All zippers are bad. They are a constant source of problems and generally break at the most inopportune time. The suit ideally would not have zippers in the arms and legs, but if it does, use them until they break and then glue them shut with wet suit cement. A zipper down the front of a jacket is almost a must, but the real cold water boys have even eliminated that one.

Getting in and out of any wet suit can be likened to getting in and out of an all-over body girdle that is slightly too small. All wet suits tear easily so do it like two sea urchins making love—very carefully. Various companies are working on new materials for suits and perhaps suit selection will be a little easier in a few years. I can hardly wait until the day when the diver just takes three pills: one to keep warm, one to breathe underwater, and one to keep safe.

The Weight Belt

Now that you have decided on your own wet suit system you have to get a weight belt. All of those little bubbles that are nice enough to keep you warm also float. They make the wet suit system anywhere from ten to 30 pounds buoyant. The weight belt is to compensate for this buoyancy. All weight belts have one thing in common: they can be quickly unsstened and allowed to fall off the diver if an emergency arises.

There are several types of release buckles that are standard on the market. The one I like best is the type in which the webbed belt is pulled through the buckle until tight and then the buckle is pressed down to lock it. My reason for liking this particular type is that it is easy to add or subtract weight on it and it can be tightened easily while diving. The wire hookover type also works well but is very time-consuming and difficult to adjust. Some of the newer belts are made of neoprene rubber instead of webbing. I have tried these and like them very much as they cling to the body and do not slip.

That should be enough to guide you on the belt and the buckle. Now for the lead weights. Many dive shops are making their own lead weights. This is good for them and generally good for the diver also. The weights the shops make are usually cheaper than manufactured ones since no middlemen are involved. However, they may raise one small problem of which the diver should be aware. The shops that make their own weights have a tendency to make the type commonly called hip weights. These are large weights of five to ten pounds each, curved so as to sit on the hips more comfortably. If you are diving a wet suit system these are a poor choice. The diver's buoyancy changes with each piece of gear he puts on; some gear is heavier and some more buoyant. His buoyancy also changes with depth; the deeper he goes the less buoyant he becomes due to the compression of the bubbles in the wet suit. If the diver has two nine-pound weights he must use his flotation vest to compensate for any change. This is as it should be except that on every dive a diver is safer if he is properly weighted at the beginning of the dive for what he is going to do on that particular dive.

Because buoyancy is such a changeable factor, especially if the diver moves between fresh and salt water where there is a great difference in density and therefore in the buoyancy, I prefer to use a system on my weights also. I have a belt with ½-pound weights that look like 50 calibre shells strung along it. This enables me to set my weight within a fourth-pound of where it should be. I'm kind of a nut on the proper weighting of divers as I firmly believe that improper weighting is a big step towards creating problems. I test myself for proper weighting by relaxing in the water and taking a normal breath. I should float at eye level. When I exhale, I should sink. This type of weighting enables the diver to keep a perfect equilibrium in the water with just a minimal use of the flotation vest. A diver who is one pound too heavy or too light will use his air much faster than if he is perfectly weighted and therefore neutral in the water.

Half-pound weights are very comfortable on the belt but may be difficult to come by in some areas. A compromise generally has to be made. An example of such a compromise would be to buy two 5-pound hip weights, two 3-pound weights, and one 2-pound weight. With this belt the possible combinations would be sufficient to compensate for nearly all conditions. The diver could wear a belt of 2 pounds, 3 pounds, 5 pounds, 6 pounds, 7 pounds, 8 pounds, 10 pounds, 11 pounds, 12 pounds, 13 pounds, 15 pounds, 16 pounds, and 18 pounds. If he needed more than 18 pounds of weight, he could increase the hip weights from 5 to 6 pounds. The combination system gives the variation needed to make a safe, properly weighted dive.

The Regulator

About the only major equipment left is the scuba gear. I put my discussion of it off as long as I could because I am not sure what I want to say about it. One book I looked at had over 150 pages of text and diagrams on the regulator alone. I don't want to say that much. I firmly believe that the average diver should know very little about how a regulator works. If he knows very much he may try to adjust it himself and wind up at the repair shop with a bag of parts. Regulators are simple but require special tools and gauges for proper setting. If you want to repair regulators, then take a regulator repair class and become competent. Until then, don't mess with it.

All regulators work on what is called the "demand system." This means you must suck on them before the air comes out. The system conserves air, as the only time air is being taken from the tank is when you are sucking it out. If you use the snorkel to swim out to a good diving spot, the air does not escape and is conserved for the actual dive.

Like practically everything else we have talked about, regulators seem to be divided into two major types. I wish someone would just make the best one of everything that would fit everybody so we wouldn't have to be confused!

The two types of regulators are designated as single hose and double hose. This is because one has a single hose and the other has a double hose (I figured that one out for myself!). Ten years ago the double hose regulators were the thing and most people used them. Now the single hose regulators are the thing and most people use them. Both types work well and there are people that swear by both of them and condemn whichever type they don't use. No matter what I say I am going to be in trouble, but here goes!

I have personally dived the two-hose regulator on over 5,000 dives. I like it very much and have never had any trouble with it. About seven years ago I changed to a single hose and now have over 2,000 dives on it and, again, no problems. So the choice is one of personal preference. My choice is the single hose. Though my reasons for selecting it are personal, perhaps they will help you to make a decision. The single hose is more compact than the double; I can store it more easily when I travel. It is much cheaper to maintain than the double hose, mainly due to the fact that hoses have to be replaced periodically. The single hose also eliminates worry about the air escaping if the mouthpiece gets above the regulator, which happens

A single-hose regulator.   Double-hose regulator.

due to a pressure differential in two-hose regulators. In short, I feel the single hose is less complex and simpler to use and maintain than the double hose. However, I still have my two-hose regulator and use it every time I clean the bottom of my boat. To accomplish that particular job, I must work on my back and the same design feature that allows the air to escape if the mouthpiece gets higher than the regulator is now an aid. Working on your back, the air is almost pushed into your lungs and allows you to work rather hard without fatigue from lack of air.

I suggest a single-hose regulator for most everyone. When you are look-ing for a regulator you will find there are a number of different manufacturers and each has several models. I don't think you will go wrong if you purchase one made by any major manufacturer. They all seem to work well enough so that the average diver is not able to tell the difference. This wasn't true a few years ago, but the industry has washed its own hands and seems to be rather clean at the present time. I made some test dives for my own gratification with several different regulators to determine the pragmatic differences. I had talked to the engineers and had been razzle-dazzled about why each company had the best, and they all had wonderful-sounding reasons why they felt they were right. I finally took regulators manufactured by three major companies; samples of their most expensive and their cheapest. Under controlled conditions I dove each one to 200 feet. I found no significant difference at all in any of them. I did not give them a true test because I didn't work hard or run the tank dry. I just wanted to see how they matched up under normal relaxed diving conditions at depths far beyond where they should be used. As far as I am concerned, the normal sports diver will get along as well with the cheapest as with the most expensive. That statement will bring some argu-ments, but actually it is a great compliment to the manufacturers for producing only good-quality regulators!

Underwater Pressure Gauges

In most books and catalogs you will find the underwater pressure gauge is listed as an accessory. Not so, in my book. I consider it a very important tool in accomplishing what we are trying to do. When you get right down to it, we are trying to become as much a functional part of the environment as possible. In order to accomplish this, our minds must be at ease at all times. The underwater pressure gauge is attached to your regulator or to your tank and keeps you posted as to how much air you have left at any given instant. It should be on your regulator and not the tank if at all possible. It will receive less of a beating if stored with the regulator than if stored with the tank, and it will always be handy if you happen to rent or borrow a tank.

The pressure gauge is normally considered one of the diver's several reserve devices, which of course it is because it tells you when you are running low on air, but it is more than just a reserve. You can show it to your buddy so he will know exactly how much air you have and will not start a project which can't be completed. You can turn around and start back to your exit point when you have 700 or 800 pounds left, and finish the dive going home instead of ending up somewhere out to sea, and swimming back. You can figure your personal air consumption at any given depth. The pressure gauge will also tell you how much air you can put into a lift bag (a special device used to lift weight off the bottom) when you are salvaging something without running short of breathing air.

All in all, the underwater pressure gauge is a great piece of equipment with many uses and I highly recommend it. I even use it to tie my depth gauge to. This eliminates the need to wear the depth gauge on my wrist and allows me to check my air supply every time I check my depth, and vice versa.

Tanks

Once you have a regulator it isn't much good to you without a tank. Again, tanks come in several sizes but you don't have to worry much about the quality. The U.S. Department of Transportation does that for you. Every tank must be stamped as to its working pressure right on the tank itself. If you buy a regular scuba tank from a shop, all the controls are in force and all you have to do is pick the size you want.

Some of the standard sizes available are: 80 cubic feet, 71.2 cubic feet, 60 cubic feet, and 50 cubic feet. All of these can be put into a double harness and rigged together so that you end up with double 71.2's or double 60's, and so forth. My personal preference is a single 71.2. It is heavy to handle but not so heavy as to be oppressive to the average man. The girls like the 60 cubic foot tank because it is shorter and lighter. This makes them easier to handle as well as to dive with. The old worry about your partner having a smaller tank than you and therefore running out of air first is true, but not as pertinent as you might think. A girl generally uses far less air than a man due to reasons best known by physiologists. They tell me that her body size is generally less and therefore she uses less air. Her lungs are smaller as a rule and therefore take less air to fill them with each breath. Because of these reasons and other more sophisticated ones, she will be able to stay down with most men on a regular dive just as long as they can with a larger tank. The little 60 cubic foot tank seems to be favorite.

If you decide to buy a used tank, there are several things to look for. First is the hydro stamp. Each tank must have a current hydro date on it. This shows the shop that is filling it that the tank has been tested for safety under pressure. The stamp will indicate the date it was tested and the pressure to which it can be safely filled. This stamp must be less than five years old or the tank will have to be retested. There will also be the letters I.C.C. (Interstate Commerce Commission) or DOT (Department of Transportation) stamped on it. These are the controlling agencies which set up standards. The newer tanks will have DOT. The number "3" followed by the letters "AA" should also be present. If the tank is stamped "A" it was not designed for diving and I wouldn't buy it. It should have an "AA" stamp on it. If the tank is out of date, you will have to take it to a hydrostatic station and have it tested. Testing usually costs approximately $8.00; they will fill the tank to 5/3's the pressure at which it is to be used and check for metal fatigue. They can, if they feel it is a very good tank, put a plus after the pressure stamp on the tank. This means that the tank can be safely filled to a ten percent overload above what it is stamped. Generally the only time a plus is put on the tank is when it is brand new. Most shops will not fill it beyond the stamped pressure anyway, with or without a plus.

A fact of general interest is that you don't get as much air as you think you do in your tank. For instance, the manufacturers' rating of a standard 71.2 cubic foot tank includes the ten percent overfill which you don't get from the shops. When you combine this differential between rating and actual contents with the working temperature of the tank in the water where it is cool, you generally come out with about 65 cubic feet. We have been assuming that your used tank passed hydro—it may not. If it does not pass, the tank is junk. You pay for the test, then cut the tank in half and make a flower pot out of it. One person I know made a fine lamp out of an old tank. Someone else I know uses his old tank to smuggle rum back across the border from Mexico. At any rate, you can't dive with it.

If the used tank you are looking at has a current hydro date on it, don't just accept it. A tank can rust out from the inside in a few short months if it has salt water in it. Take the used tank to a dive shop and ask for a "visual inspection." The shop will take the valve out and run a light down inside for a look-see (most shops charge $1 to $2 for this). It is a good idea to have your tank visually inspected each year in any case, just to make certain it is staying in good shape.

TANK VALVES • There are only two types of tank valves in common use today, the "J" valve and the "K" valve. It is interesting to note how they got their names. In the days when U.S. Divers was the only company that had tanks for sale that were made for scuba diving, they put out a small catalog of their wares. It just so happened that these valves were items "J" and "K" in the catalog. The names stuck.

Anyway, these valves have been improved since 1950 and they are manufactured now by nearly all the major manufacturers of diving equipment. Of course, each one claims that his is a little better than the other guy's. They all seem to work well and I wouldn't worry about it. However, the difference in function of the "J" valve and the "K" valve *is* significant. The "K" valve is the simpler one and nothing more than an on-off valve such as you have in your garden hose. It is straight and uncomplicated; you turn it on for air and off when you are through. Simplicity is an advantage as I have stressed in other parts of this book, but this case may be an exception. You will see why as we discuss the "J" valve.

The "J" valve is also an on-off valve with one additional feature. It has a spring-loaded mechanism which holds approximately 300 to 400 pounds of air pressure in the tank. The advantage of this becomes evident when you are gliding along through a gigantic kelp forest thinking to yourself how fantastic it is to be there and suddenly realize it has become difficult to breathe. All you have to do is pull the lever and release the spring and you have a reserve air supply. This reserve air supply (approximately 300 psi) allows you to come up slowly and safely with no anxiety or rush. If you had a "K" valve and found yourself in this situation, you would have to surface immediately which could mean a hard swim through the kelp. The underwater pressure gauge is a must if a "K" valve is used. It will tell you how much air you have left so you can plan the dive safely. Even better yet is an underwater pressure gauge and a "J" valve. Just in case you forget to look at the gauge.

The tank valves are simple devices. Treat them well and they will last a long time. A few *"don'ts"* that will help them last are:

1. Don't bang them around by dropping them or dropping something on them.
2. Don't lubricate them with oil. Oil will get into your breathing air. Use a silicon compound.
3. Don't turn them on or off very tightly. The metal (generally brass) is soft and will be damaged if you make the valve very tight in the ON or OFF position.

Backpacks

Because it is difficult to dive and hold a tank under your arm, most divers prefer to wear some kind of a backpack or tank harness. I have looked at most of the ones on the market and could use practically any of them without a problem. My personal preference in backpacks is not the same as most other divers'; in fact, the one I liked the best sold so few compared to the others that the manufacturers stopped making it!

I like the simple plastic harnesses that fit right over the tank and have straps coming from them. I do not like the wing-type backpacks. I will repeat, 90 percent of the divers like the wing-type pack better. These are good, but they have three features I don't like. They are more expensive by quite a bit—that's one. They are very easy to break because of their shape; they will break if they are stepped on or dropped—that's two. They generally are attached to the tank by a metal band. During normal wear and tear these bands tend to become loose and let the tank slip out. That's three. Can you imagine coming in through the surf and having a tank slip out of the pack and hang from the diver's neck by the regulator neck straps? Don't laugh—it's happened more than once. Some of these bands have a handle built in which to carry the tank. That's really bad news, because it loosens the bands even faster. The accidents I have personally witnessed have been with this type of pack. Most of the wing-type packs have a quick-release snap on the shoulder strap. That feature I like, but not enough to change over. I'll stick to my old cheap plastic pack that goes clear around the tank.

Accessories

After you have all of your basic gear and take your class to become a certified diver, you will find dozens of accessories available for purchase. Remember: the simpler it is, the longer it will work. I have seen divers enter the water with so much gear they resemble a Christmas tree. All they need are the lights. (Now that I think of it, I have seen a few divers that were pretty well lit!)

There should be good reasons for getting each of the accessories you can buy. Think about each one and make sure you have a reason for buying it. The following are a few of the most common accessories:

THE DIVER'S FLOAT . Most divers take a float with them. The float serves many purposes, and many different type of floats are used depending on the intent and preference of the divers.

Two of the most common floats are the inner tube and the surf mat. These two floats are popular because they are inexpensive, and either one can be used as rescue devices. There are special methods of rescue which must be learned if the diver is going to use his float to the best advantage. These methods cannot be learned by reading about them. You must *do* them. Your instructor can show you how to do a "tube rescue," or a "mat rescue."

The reason most divers take a float with them is to hang stuff on. The first item a diver generally puts on his float is a diver's flag. Then hooks are attached to the float so the diver can hang cameras, lights, goodie bags or anything else he happens to be taking on the dive. In some areas there is a long swim to get to a good diving spot. In these locations many divers use special "boards" or kayak-type boats as their float and transportation.

35

Choose a float that fits your needs and learn all the things you can use it for so you will get maximum use from it.

THE KNIFE • Most divers wear a knife and in general I have to agree that it's a good practice. There is not much to cut down there but then a diving knife is not really to cut with. Divers use their knives as a tool. They pry things like scallops; pound things like rock and coral; scrape things like old ship hulls; and in rare cases actually cut things like fishline and kelp. Most diving knives are sold so dull that they won't cut anything much tougher than a jellyfish anyway. (A *sharp* knife is important in cave and wreck diving.) There always seems to be something to poke at or pry up, so a diving knife is a good thing. You can even use your knife to signal to another diver by banging it against your tank.

In view of its duties, a diver's knife should be of heavy construction. The lighter knives will break the first time they meet a challenge. Some of the smaller girls I know wear knives almost as big as they are. It may look funny, but they come back with a full bag of scallops and not one broken knife blade.

One word about where the knife should be worn. It should be in a location where it can be reached by either hand easily. It must not be in the drop line of the weight belt. The drop line of the weight belt is the path it will take if the diver wishes to drop it for safety reasons. It generally slips over the hips and down the legs. This drop path must always be kept clear. The best place that I have found is the inside of the calf on either leg. There it is readily accessible and out of the drop path. Some divers wear the knife on their weight belt. I don't like it there because if you ever had occasion to drop the weight belt you would also lose your knife. Wearing the knife at the center of the belt, where it must be for accessibility, also makes the release buckle on the belt harder to locate in an emergency. Kelp has a tendency to hang up on a knife if it is worn on the belt, also. The safest and most useful place for it is on the inside of the calf.

THE DEPTH GAUGE • When scuba diving it is a good idea to wear a depth gauge. If you are in a lake or some area where the bottom is constant and shallow, then of course you won't need one. Depth is very important to the diver's safety and he must be constantly aware of it.

Of the great number of different depth gauges on the market, there are two types I like. One is expensive, around $45.00; the other is inexpensive, around $8.00. They work on different principles but both accomplish the same thing. They measure the pressure and are scaled in feet. All the diver has to do is look at them to see how deep he is. The expensive one is oil filled; the water never gets into the works. Because of this it should last a long time and not corrode. It has a movable diaphragm on the back of it which is pushed in by the pressure of the water as you go deeper. It works well but is a little bulky.

The cheap kind is a small tube that is blocked off at one end. When you enter the water the pressure compresses the air in the tube the deeper you go. The deeper you are, the farther up the tube the water is. This is calibrated in feet and works about as well as anything else. One of the frequent complaints heard about tube-type gauges is that most of them only go to 100 feet—who wants to go deeper than 100 feet anyway? You do have to check the tube before each dive to make sure there is no water caught in it. If there is water in it, the tube can be removed and the water blown out.

There are other types of depth gauges, but I have found that they do not give good service so I therefore refuse to talk about them. I am one way about things like that.

THE DIVER'S WATCH • A watch is always a good thing to have. Every diver should keep time on his dive. If he is diving deeper than 30 feet, keeping time is very important in avoiding the possibility of the bends. A watch can be used to coordinate your dive with others in such a way that two buddy pairs finish their dives at the same time in the same area so they can swim back to the boat in a group. It can also be used in navigation; it helps you to return to the boat before it leaves you in the middle of the ocean.

It seems that everyone is making a diving watch now. This type of watch is conspicuous due to the movable dial on the face, which is called a "bezel." The bezel is a timer that the diver can set when he starts his dive and read directly in minutes when he finishes the dive. This timer is really handy. Fliers use it to navigate by; teachers use it in testing; and I'm sure it has many more uses. Because of their usefulness, most diving watches never get wet except perhaps in the shower. The testing standards are not all that great and if you really dive with yours you may find that even the most expensive style will leak from time to time. If you get one that leaks, take it back and get a new one. They are all guaranteed. When you find one that doesn't leak it will last a long time. You may have to return some of the cheaper types four or five times before you get one that works satisfactorily.

You should be able to purchase an acceptable watch for around $80.00. After that you are paying for looks.

THE COMPASS • A compass can be a useful gadget if the diver is in an area where he needs it and if he knows how to use it. Most diving areas don't require a compass because the diver is familiar with the bottom and can navigate visually. If you are in an area that you do not know, then a compass can be used to find a direction from which to start the dive and to which to return when you are low on air, thus helping avoid undue fatigue.

The compass is an important tool when running a search pattern to make certain that you maintain a straight line. Most underwater compasses are not accurate and become hard to read. If you really have a need for a compass, I suggest using a compass board. The U.S. Frogmen put other gauges on the board so they can tell depth and time as well as direction. They call it an "attack board." If the diver holds the board level in front of him with both elbows tight against his sides, he will have a good chance of running a true course. A compass on the wrist is not nearly as accurate as one on the board.

One good time to use a compass is during a night dive or a cave dive where visual navigation aids are hard to come by. If you want to make an "attack board" for your very own, I would suggest that you read "The Compass Board," an article by Bill Hemming in the October 1970 issue of *Skin Diver* Magazine.

THE DECOMPRESSION METER • One of the primary concerns of the diver is not to stay too deep too long. The condition known as the bends, which we will discuss later, is a direct function of time and depth. The Navy produced what are known as the Navy Diving Tables, which tell the diver where he is in relation to the time-depth curve during or after any particular dive. However, it is difficult to remember how these tables work if they are not used often, and accidents occasionally occur even when they are used conscientiously. Another aid is the device known as a Decom Meter which, according to the directions and the advertisement of the manufacturer, supposedly puts an end to all of our worry about decompression. Unfortunately, this is not true. There have been quite a few people treated for bends who were diving on the Decom Meter. Don't misunderstand me. I am not saying the meter is no good. I dive with one myself, with great success. What I am saying is that it does not solve all problems. It must be kept calibrated properly and checked often. The diver still must keep his bottom time accurately and should check his dive against the decompression tables. He must also know how to read the meter.

I have a game I play. When I see a diver wearing a Decom Meter I admire it and ask him how it works. I find that about one in ten users actually knows how it functions. About one in four can read it well enough to at least not get hurt, and about three out of four are sure they know how to read it but in reality do not. The instructions that come with the Decom Meter are very poor and someone should rewrite them. It is a good device, used properly and checked often.

4

SKILLS, TRICKS, AND SNEAKY THINGS

Once you have your equipment it will do you little good unless you develop the watermanship needed to get the most from it. You will find the basic swimming skills required of a beginning diver listed in Appendix A. In addition, you must understand the specific function of each item of equipment and know how to use it in the proper manner. You will be expected to have a minimum proficiency with each piece of gear to successfully pass a scuba course.

This chapter presents exercises you can use to measure your progress in using equipment just as an instructor evaluates the students in his class. The skill levels included here are the same ones I expect of the students in my basic scuba class. I have thrown in a few tricks of the trade now and then and an occasional ''sneaky'' thing or two just for drill. The order I have followed is the same order I use in my teaching but is not necessarily the ''best'' order. It is just one that I like.

We have already discussed what to look for when you buy your equipment. This chapter spells out what you must accomplish with each item and also provides solutions to various problems you may have with particular pieces of equipment.

• MASKMANSHIP

We will assume that your mask fits because it was chosen according to the suggestions in Chapter 3. The first thing to master is putting the mask on.

Place the mask on your face and pull the strap over your head. *Do not* put the strap over the back of your head and pull the mask down over your face. Put the mask on first, then pull the strap over your head. This can be easily done with one hand by sucking in just a little with the nose to create a vacuum that will hold the mask in place while you place the strap over your head. This one-hand maneuver will make the scuba exercises easier when you get to them.

The strap should be positioned carefully around the back of the head. If it is too high or too low the pressure around the mask against the face will not be even and the mask may leak. If the strap is too tight it will give you a headache. If the strap is too loose the mask will leak. Take time and do it right; *proper strap position is very important*. Once you get the strap adjusted "just right" then tape the ends of the strap with electrician's tape to hold them exactly in place. This will simplify your life later.

Your mask is now on properly, fits well, and does not leak. Swim with it for awhile and get used to it. You will notice that things look bigger (about ¼) and closer (about ⅓). The magnification is due to a physical law of light called refraction. It is only important that you know that light travels at a different speed through water than it does through air. You would expect this, of course, because water is so much thicker (more dense) than air. This difference in light travel speed is what makes refractions and therefore is responsible for the magnifying effect. Pick things up and get used to the magnification, so you won't be frightened by a passing minnow.

The art of clearing the water out of the mask, should it become flooded while you are on a dive, without having to come to the surface is next. Mask flooding happens quite often, for instance, when your buddy bumps you and breaks the seal on your mask, or for some other reason, such as laughing underwater.

Depending upon the type of mask you have, purge or non-purge, the technique is slightly different, but the principle is exactly the same. The principle involved is simple air displacement of water. When the mask has water in it the diver can blow air out of his nose and the air will rise to the highest spot. If the top of the mask is held firmly to the face, the air will be trapped and will push the water in the mask out the lowest point. The difference between the purge and the non-purge mask is only which part of the mask must be the lowest point.

If the mask is a purge mask, then the purge valve should be the lowest point. Clearing the mask is accomplished by looking at a 45° angle towards the bottom, holding the entire mask firmly in place, and exhaling through the nose. When using the non-purge mask, the diver wants to make the lowest edge of the mask where it seals against the upper lip the lowest point, so the water will run out and leave the mask clear. Clearing the mask is accomplished by looking at a 45° angle towards the surface of the water, holding the top and sides of the mask (but not the bottom) firmly in place, and exhaling through the nose. When done perfectly, no air should escape except a small bubble which indicates that all the water is gone from the mask. A good diver can clear his mask four or five times on one breath.

Some of the typical trouble spots are worth mentioning. One very common error is blowing air out the mouth instead of the nose. A new diver has difficulty telling just where the air is coming out. He knows he is blowing bubbles but he can't really see where they are coming from. A good way to overcome the tendency to blow out the mouth is to hum while you are clearing the mask. When you are humming the air must come out your nose. I have found through extensive research that it does not matter what tune you hum—they all work.

Another error I see the new diver make with the non-purge mask is trying to hold the mask away from his face to let the water out. This is a "no no." Hold it as described. Soon you will be able to clear your mask with very little air loss and no feeling of stress.

If your mask fogs up on you so you can't see clearly, there are two things you can do. First, wash it (toothpaste is good) to make sure that there is no grease of any kind on it. Then spit into it before each dive. Do this *before* you wet it in the water. Rub the saliva around the inside of the glass as well as the outside. Then rinse the mask off and wear it. It should stay clear.

Now for the first sneaky thing. I learned this stunt from a fellow NAUI instructor. I was sitting on the bottom of the pool grading some divers in skill tests when all of a sudden a voice said, "How are they doing, John?" It is, to say the least, an unusual thing to have someone speak to you when you are underwater. I thought for a minute that the Big Boss was around. I turned around to find my good-looking female colleague rolling on the bottom with laughter at the way I had jumped. It seems that if you have one of the larger masks, you can take a big breath, tilt your head back so the air stays trapped in the mask, and pull it down over your mouth and talk. The air in the mask vibrates the glass and sends your voice into the water.

When all of the women divers learn to do this, Cousteau will lose his "Silent World." With a little practice you can learn to talk into the mask quite well, and nothing is more disconcerting than to sneak up behind your buddy and say "Gotcha."

Trouble-Shooting the Mask

1. It leaks.
   a. It may be a poor fit.
   b. The strap is not adjusted properly.
   c. The mask may have a *leak* in it. Take it back to the store if it's a new one.
   d. You forgot to shave. One or two days' growth of whiskers will make the best mask leak.
2. You can't clear the water out.
   a. You are not holding the mask in the right position when you try to clear it. Look *up* with no purge and *down* with a purge.
   b. You are trying to hold the mask away from your face so the water will go out—this doesn't work. Hold the upper part tightly against your face and the lower part gently *against* your face. The air pressure will push it out.
   c. You are blowing air out your mouth instead of your nose. Two ways to get air out your nose—snort or hum.
   d. You are just "psyched out." Relax. You *can* do it.

. **FINMANSHIP**

Fins are not hard for most people to use because all they have to do is kick their feet. However, there are a few tips that will help a diver get better performance.

The purpose of the fins is to push water away from the diver. Mr. Newton a long time ago decided that for every action there is an opposite and equal reaction. To put this law to work for us we must push the water back to push ourselves ahead. I will never forget the time I was starting a new class and saw one of my would-be students kicking like mad and slowly moving backwards. To get the maximum effectiveness from the fins the toes must be pointed, and the legs only *slightly* bent at the knees. This places the fins in a position to push the water backwards on both the upward stroke and the downward stroke. If the fins are not in this position they will move up and down in the water but will not push.

Another common error is called bicycling. This occurs when the diver brings his knees toward his stomach, the motion of the legs much like riding a bicycle. The fins in this case move a great distance in the water but the motion is back and forth and produces little or no thrust. Bicycling can generally be helped by remembering not to bring the knees forward of the normal position when you are walking. If that doesn't do it, sometimes having a diver swim as hard as he can will. It seems that when we swim as hard as we can, we do not make this particular error.

Once the diver has the feel of doing it right, there is no problem. One of the best kicks for underwater is the dolphin kick. The best way to learn this is to have

Fins help the diver develop the thrust necessary to propel him through the water. Before you take on the larger fins be sure you have the muscle strength necessary to use them without tiring.

someone demonstrate it for you. The diver keeps his feet together and undulates his body. When the kick is done correctly the body appears to be rolling over a series of barrels. It is very efficient and can be done slowly using a minimum of energy.

There are many other kicks which can be used on and off to rest the muscles in the legs. If the same kick is used during the entire dive, there is a tendency to overtire certain muscles. By changing your kick occasionally you can alternate the load and not overtire one set of muscles, thus avoiding cramps. The *Red Cross Swimming Manual* (available at any book store for about $3) describes and illustrates a number of different kicks.

The only way to build your legs up so they can kick the fins without getting tired is to put on the fins and swim. Swim hard, and as often as you can. Your legs will respond rapidly and your kick will become easy and relaxed.

Trouble-Shooting the Fins

1. The fins rub raw spots on your feet.
   a. They could be too loose—try booties.
   b. Your ankle bones stick out at the edge of the straps—try wearing a pair of socks.

2. Your feet cramp up.
   a. The fins could be too tight, jamming the toes.
   b. You are very tense—try to relax.
   c. The fins are too big for you—try a smaller size.
   d. The water is too cold—move to the Caribbean (or get a pair of booties).
3. You don't move as fast as everyone else when you swim.
   a. Make sure your toes are pointed so the blades are in the most efficient position.
   b. You may be bicycling—bringing your knees forward toward the chest. This is a very common and *very bad* error.
   c. You may be in poor shape—work harder.
4. Your fins disappear.
   a. You were dumb enough to let them lay around.
   b. You didn't put your name on them and someone picked them up by mistake. A good way to mark them is to use a wire coat hanger to *brand* your initials in each blade.

. SNORKELMANSHIP

The position of the snorkel on the mask is important. The snorkel should be on the left side. Later, when the diver learns to use scuba gear, the air supply from the scuba will come over the right shoulder. If the snorkel is always on the left and scuba always on the right, even in a stress situation there is no chance of a mix-up. The snorkel should be held on by a snorkel-keeper that comes with every snorkel. Both holes in the keeper go over *the snorkel,* and the mask strap *does not* go through one of them. The strap goes, instead, between the snorkel and the narrow part of the keeper to hold the snorkel *firmly* in place on the outside of the strap, *not between* the mask strap and the head. With the mask in place on the face, the snorkel should be adjusted by sliding it back and forth on the strap and up and down in the keeper until it fits in the mouth naturally without having to be held there with tight jaws. This adjustment is critical for proper use and comfort.

Are you ready for some shocking news? Seventy-five percent of today's qualified divers are clearing their snorkels wrong! What's more, most textbooks are wrong, and many instructors are teaching a less-than-best technique. Granted, there's more than one way to get the water out of that tube . . . but why are we doing it the hard way?

If old man Archimedes were around today, he'd be the first to point out a simple fact of physics: it's a lot easier to *displace* water than it is to *lift* it. Yet every diver is taught to clear the snorkel by the "blast" method—lifting a 15-inch column of water by the sheer force of a muscular breath expulsion. As far as your lungs are concerned, this is one heck of a hard way to dump a cupful of water, particularly upon surfacing from a long, deep dive. And then there's always that gurgle problem—those noisy, nagging few drops of water that survive the blast and

One way to learn proper clearing of the snorkel is to make a large over-size snorkel out of garden hose and practice with it.

remain gurgling in the U-trap of your tube. It's just enough water to make things uncomfortable and restrict proper breathing.

I would like to share with you a much easier way to clear that snorkel—with one-third the effort and twice the comfort. A simple law of physics will work for you so that you can automatically clear your snorkel tube without the huff-and-puff routine. For lack of a better name, let's call this technique the "displacement method" for clearing a snorkel. The name is almost self-explanatory and the technique equally simple:

1. While on the surface, take a deep breath, hold it, and make your surface dive. This part is standard technique for starting a snorkel dive.
2. During ascent, look up toward the surface checking for overhead obstruction. This is also part of the standard operating technique.
3. Keep your head pointed upward, so that the tip of the snorkel is pointing on a downward slant.
4. Gently expel your air into the snorkel while coming up. Because of the downward slant of the snorkel, the bubbles will be trapped in the tube—thus displacing all of the water. Start exhalation approximately two feet from the surface.
5. When you reach the surface, simply roll into your usual swimming position and resume breathing. Since you exhaled underwater, you can start inhaling fresh air upon breaking the surface. Gone are the days of "thar she blows!"

Sounds simple enough. Well, it is. And you can master the "displacement method" in less than 15 minutes. All that's required is timing the exhalation the the last few feet before you surface.

Besides being easy to execute, the "displacement method" is far better than the

45

blast method for your overall diving performance. You'll suffer less fatigue because you no longer need to undergo strenuous diaphragm contraction for that snorkel blast. Over a long period of time, this sort of forceful exhalation can be quite exhausting and sometimes causes total fatigue.

With the new method, you'll also gain more bottom time and faster recovery time on the surface. The elimination of the expulsion and exhalation cycle on the surface really steps up your diving rhythm. This is particularly important to competitive spearfishermen who are trying to attain maximum down-time during a tournament.

Another aspect of snorkel diving which is as important as clearing the tube is proper breathing. Many of the diver's minor annoyances—headaches, shortness of breath, coldness, cramps, etc.—can often be traced back to snorkel respiration. A basic understanding of the snorkel can help remedy such problems.

Breathing through a 12- to 16-inch tube is not a natural form of breathing. In fact, it drastically changes the balance of your entire respiratory system. The snorkel actually doubles the amount of dead airspace which lungs must contend with. If you breathe through a snorkel as you would normally on land, CO_2 (carbon dioxide) begins accumulating in your respiratory dead airspace—the air passages from your lungs to the tip of the snorkel. The lungs just cannot push enough stale air up and out of the snorkel tube in a normal exhalation, so some of that stale CO_2-laden air is rebreathed over and over again. It's this sort of "CO_2 stacking" that causes headaches, short wind, fatigue and, in extreme cases, blackout.

In order to compensate for the extended burden of the snorkel's dead airspace, you must learn to breathe abnormally—what we call modified breathing. By inhaling deeply and exhaling more than usual, you can compensate for this physiological abnormality. At first, this modified breathing cycle will require concentration, much like a singer's breathing exercises for better diaphragm control. Modified breathing should be practiced until it becomes second nature. You'll find that it will make a remarkable improvement in your snorkel diving performance. You'll be able to dive deeper and stay down longer since your respiratory system contains less CO_2. And, you won't get as chilled or suffer cramps as easily because the CO_2 (muscle depressant) has been reduced.

The snorkel is a deceivingly simple apparatus—just a bent tube—but its effect on the human body can be both wondrous and frustrating. Used properly, it is one of the greatest breathing aids invented by man.

More sophisticated snorkel skills will be covered in Chapter 5 under "Breath-Hold Diving." A very important scuba skill that should be learned at this time is to hold the snorkel in place without the mask and swim face down for approximately ten minutes without holding your nose. You must learn to have "selective breathing" to use scuba, and be able to breathe through the snorkel without let-

Mastery of snorkeling skills is an important prerequisite to scuba diving.

ting water come up the nose. This is one of the harder things to learn. Now would be the time to learn it.

The snorkel is very important. Don't develop bad habits with it. Remember, "Only *perfect* practice makes perfect."

A trick with a snorkel is to use it as a horn. If you blow into it as you would a shell horn it will produce a fine tone.

Trouble-Shooting the Snorkel

1. The snorkel hurts your mouth.
   a. The mouthpiece is not the right size to fit your mouth.
   b. The snorkel is not on the mask properly. If it is too far forward on the strap it will hurt your lower gum and upper lip. If it is too far back on the strap it will hurt your upper gum and lower lip. If the strap is too close to the mouthpiece it will pull on the left side of your mouth. If the strap is too far from the mouthpiece it will push on the right side of your gum.
2. There is water left in it after you clear.
   a. You are not using the displacement method.
   b. You are not exhaling just before you break the surface.
   c. You are exhaling too soon and water gets back in before you break the surface.

47

. THE FLOTATION VEST

The flotation vest first came out as a safety device for the diver. There were many problems with it, the most important of which was that it just didn't work all the time. The diver would get himself in a tight place and pull the panic string to inflate his vest, and nothing would happen. Because he was psychologically dependent on the vest he would go to pieces when it didn't work. It acted, in this case, as an anti-safety device.

Eventually the diving manufacturers put their heads together and made some improvements. The newer vests, for the most part, work pretty well, though still not perfectly. They require constant care, and the diver should check out his vest before each dive. The vest should first be inflated and checked for leaks, then the inflation device should be removed and tested to make sure it works.

As the vest was used by more and more divers, they discovered more and more things to do with it, until finally it has come to be considered a tool first and a safety device second. Very few divers ever inflate the vest with the CO_2 mechanism. Everyone seems to use the oral inflation tube. If they want air in the vest, they simply blow into the tube. This can be done underwater with scuba as easily as on the surface of the water, and every basic scuba class should teach this technique. A scuba diver uses the vest to add to or subtract from his buoyancy during a dive. As mentioned before, it is very important to have your weights exact to lessen the fatigue factor and the air consumption ratio. The vest does this magnificently.

Another use for the vest is to compensate for any extra weight a diver may pick up during a dive. This could be a limit of abalone or pismo clams, which are quite heavy, or an old anchor that some unfortunate soul lost overboard. One of the most common uses of the vest is to aid the diver on the swim out to where he plans to dive, and also on the swim back to the beach. The diver can be totally relaxed and rest on his way out and back from the dive. The technique here is to put some air in the vest, turn over on your back, and enjoy a slow, easy trip out and back.

I personally do quite a bit of free diving. I enjoy spearfishing whenever I get into water where the fish present a challenge. I use my vest as a flotation tool while spearfishing. I generally use a 100-foot line on my spear and believe in hanging onto it during the entire fight. I don't use floats that follow the fish around until he dies, and then go back and pick him up. This type of fishing falls into the same category as fishing with the power heads used by some divers which explode and kill the fish on contact. Both of these methods seem a little like fishing with dynamite to me, effective but requiring zero skill.

I like to hang onto the fish for the ride; if I get a big one that looks like he might be able to pull me under, I pop the vest. This gives me a little more buoyancy and thus an additional advantage. I have taken several dozen fish over 200 pounds, five or six over 400 pounds, and one over 600 pounds. They were all taken while free diving with the only aid being the vest which I was wearing. I might add that I have never lost my equipment by having a fish take it away from me. (One shark, an 8-foot hammerhead, took my gun out of my hand, but I retrieved it later.)

One last story illustrates the need for a vest in an emergency situation. Many divers look at the flotation vest as a mark against their manhood. The standard comment is, ''I don't need that thing; I'm not going to get into trouble.'' Those who say this are generally the noncertified divers who have been diving for a long time and who, due to their lack of formal training, do not realize how useful a tool the vest is. In any event, I was diving with such an individual in the Sea of Cortez (Gulf of California) a few years ago when an interesting thing happened. This particular diver was then and probably still is one of the best divers I have ever been in the water with. You know the type I mean—free dives below 100 feet repeatedly all day long. (I hate them all!) Anyway, he was one who wouldn't be caught dead in a flotation vest, and I often joked with him about the fact that if he wore one he probably wouldn't be caught dead at all. But try as I might, he wouldn't wear one. His ''thing'' was spearfishing and he was extremely good at it.

This incident occurred in mid-morning. We happened to be on the surface within 20 feet of each other, which was a lucky break, and only about 15 feet from a rocky cliff. The water was clear and warm and we were having good luck. Big yellowtail were all around us, and it was a great day. I looked up to check where my friend was and saw him slowly roll over on his back with his mask off. He seemed to be floundering. I swam over to him as quickly as I could and shouted at him, ''Are you all right?'' He didn't answer. I gave him a push and he was able to reach the rocks. He recovered in a few seconds, and you'll never guess what had happened.

He carried a large, very powerful homemade rubber-powered speargun. He had just had a shot at a fish and missed it and was in the process of reloading his gun. He had pulled the rubbers back and placed them in the notches on the shaft by placing the butt of the gun against his chest and pulling with both arms, which is the standard method of loading such a gun. He put the last rubber in the notch and started to push the gun away from his chest when it misfired. We never knew just why it misfired. It had never done this before and never did it again, but it did it then. He did not have a tight hold on the gun and, due to Mr. Newton's law, for every action there is an opposite and equal reaction, as the 6-foot long ⅜-inch stainless shaft got underway forward, the gun itself got underway backwards. It was at a distance of about six inches from his chest when it misfired, slamming into him just below the heart and knocking all the breath out of him. He couldn't yell, talk, or breathe. If it were not for the fact that he was in magnificent condition, he could have been killed.

He realized that had he not been right next to the rocks, or had I not been there to help him, he would have had a hard time of it. We talked about the vest on the boat ride home and he admitted that if he had been wearing one he would have been okay. It is surprising how fast we humans forget. To the best of my knowledge, he

49

never did get a vest. The last time I talked to him, he told me that he had cut down his driving time to Guaymas, Mexico, where he did a lot of diving, to 11 hours . . . 850 miles of narrow Mexican roads with cows wandering back and forth across them. I figured if he kept driving like that he probably wouldn't be needing a vest anyway, so I didn't mention it again.

. THE WET SUIT AND WEIGHT BELT

As much as I enjoy diving in warm water where a wet suit is not a necessity, there is one practical point about wearing one. It is probably the best safety device the diver ever has available to him.

If you will recall, the suit is composed of small bubbles which make it very buoyant. There is just no way a diver can sink if he has on a wet suit and no weight belt. This is why weight belts have the quick release buckles on them. The idea is to drop the weight belt if you get into a tight spot. Once this is done, the diver would have to work very hard to be able to get into trouble. Why is it then that in practically all diving accidents the divers do not drop their weight belts? I believe the failure to do this is due to two main causes. The first one is money. The belt represents anywhere from $12.00 to $25.00, depending on what kind it is and where the diver bought it. The diver strangely enough thinks about this when he considers dropping the belt. So, he rationalizes that he is really all right and doesn't need to drop it.

The second cause of failure to drop weight belts is that the diver waits too long. He does not become aware, or admit to himself, that he does have a problem until he takes in a little water. Then, he panics! Very few of us will ever see anyone in a panic situation but, when it happens, the individual has a complete narrowing of perception and focuses all of his attention on a single objective. In the diver's case, he tries to walk on water. He forgets all the safety rules he has ever been taught. He does not drop the belt. I have seen this happen and wondered how to prevent it. I don't have the solution but I have a helpful hint or trick if you will.

When the diver feels the situation is starting to get a little hairy for any reason at all, he should take off his weight belt and hold it in his hand. He would not lose the belt unnecessarily and if he should panic, it would be the first thing to go without thinking about it. I have had several divers use this method and they say that the psychological difference when the belt is in their hand instead of strapped on their back allows them to stay calm and work out the problem. I believe in this method and heartily prescribe it for all divers.

5

THE BIG PLUNGE

Now that you are feeling at home with your essential equipment, it is time to put it all together and start to dive.

In the early days of diving everyone was a "skin diver." Then the tanks and regulators became available and we had to come up with a new term, or a new use for an old term, "free diver." The term "free diver" meant without tank, and "scuba" meant with tank.

Times have changed once more and most of the commercial men no longer use the "hard hat" or "heavy gear" that we see in old movies. Instead they use wet suits and light "hard hats" made of plastics and are supplied with air from the surface through a set of hoses called an "umbilical." When the commercial men talk about free diving they mean without an umbilical.

To keep our terms straight I might suggest the following chart:

Breath-hold diving
Scuba diving } Free Diving

Light gear umbilical
Heavy gear umbilical } Tethered Diving

Breath-hold diving was first historically and still must be mastered in order to master scuba. All scuba does is extend the breath-hold diver's time underwater.

• BREATH-HOLD DIVING SKILLS

Breathing

There is no one thing that will make you a good breath-hold diver, but *not understanding* proper breathing will sure cut you from the ranks in a hurry. For the diver, breathing is not something that just happens naturally, but a skill which must be learned. There are some basic physiological facts you must know and you must also understand *why* they are important:

1. In "normal" breathing the lungs are *not* used anywhere near their full capacity.
2. The thing that makes you want to breathe is *not* lack of oxygen (O_2) but rather the buildup of carbon dioxide (CO_2) in the system.
3. The consumption of O_2 and buildup of CO_2 is directly proportional to the level of metabolic activity. In other words, the more relaxed you are and the fewer muscles you use the longer you can hold your breath.
4. The body is a chemical machine which can adapt, within limits, to the stresses put upon it. This adaptation however, is not instant, and under any given conditions there is a certain speed or rhythm, or "rpm" if you wish, at which it will function most smoothly and give optimum performance.

What is normal breathing? Normal breathing, as I am using it here, means the air exchange in your lungs as you do your "normal" day's activities of eating, sleeping, working, and so on. This is represented as "Tidal Volume" in Figure 5–1.

We have in our lungs reserve areas which we can use when we are under stress. We can breathe deeper than normal until we reach the point where the lungs are

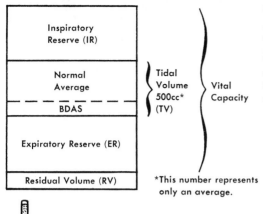

FIGURE 5-1

A diagram of the air capacity of the lungs, showing the breakdown and physiological names of the parts that make up the whole. Tidal Volume represents the "normal" at-rest air exchange. Vital Capacity represents the largest air exchange you can have, taking advantage of the entire usable lung.

Inspiratory Reserve (IR)

Normal Average

BDAS

Tidal Volume 500cc* (TV)

Vital Capacity

Expiratory Reserve (ER)

Residual Volume (RV)

*This number represents only an average.

MDAS 150cc

BDAS 150cc

L L

FIGURE 5-2

A simplified diagram of the air passage to the lungs, including the nasal and mouth spaces, the windpipe (trachea), as well as the first division of the major bronchial tubes. The shaded area represents the "dead air space" we all have. The volume of "biological dead air space" (BDAS) is approximately equal to the volume of a snorkel. The average is 150cc's. The space in the snorkel is called a "mechanical dead air space" (MDAS).

totally full. This is the upper limit of the "Inspiratory Reserve" as well as the top limit of our "Vital Capacity." By taking in air to this limit we get the maximum air input for our bodies. To reach this limit takes energy; muscles have to pull the diaphragm down and lift the ribs. We do not want to breathe this deeply often because doing so will tire us. We can also exhale deeper than normal. When we reach the point where we no longer can push out any more air, we have reached the bottom of our "Expiratory Reserve" as well as the bottom limit of our "Vital Capacity." We will find that a good deep exhalation is more important than a deep inhalation for diving.

Let's move on to item 2 and discuss why we want to breathe at all. Most people believe that when we get low on oxygen we want to breathe. This is why they take a deep breath before a dive. Unfortunately this is not the case. If it were, the diver would be safer, and would not have to worry about "shallow water blackout." The fact is that as we use the oxygen in our bodies to produce the energy we need to function, we produce waste products. One of these products is CO_2. The CO_2 is picked up by the blood and taken to the lungs where it passes into the lungs and is exhaled when we breathe out. When the CO_2 level in the blood reaches a high enough level there are sensors (the main ones are in the carotid bodies located in the neck) which tell our brain that it is time to exchange the gas in our lungs so we can get rid of some CO_2. There is no mechanism in the body that works rapidly enough to tell us that we need oxygen. Fortunately we get a high enough level of

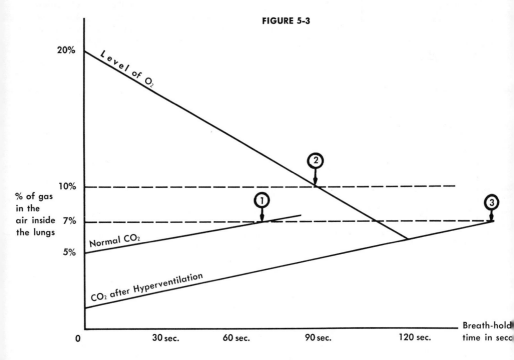

FIGURE 5-3

Figure 5-3 shows what happens to the oxygen and CO_2 in the body as you hold your breath, both normally and after excessive maximum breathing.

When the carbon dioxide in the lungs rises to about 7% the diver will feel that he has to breathe (Points 1 and 3).

When the oxygen in the lungs falls to about 10% the diver will become unconscious (Point 2).

When the diver hyperventilates he **washes out** the carbon dioxide which normally stays in the lungs, so that he will reach the point of unconsciousness before he feels he has to breathe. "Shallow-water blackouts" of this type can be avoided by not taking more than three maximum breaths before a dive.

(1) The normal point at which the diver feels he must breathe.

(2) The point at which the diver will black out.

(3) The point at which the diver will feel he must breathe **after hyperventilation** (TOO LATE.)

54

CO_2 to tell us to breathe before we reach a low enough level of oxygen to pass out (see Figure 5–3). If we were in an airtight room and had chemicals that would absorb the CO_2 out of the air, we would breathe in and out until the oxygen was used up and would just go to sleep. We would feel no stress at all; in fact, we would not even remember going to sleep. This is why in breath-hold diving we must be careful not to purge so much CO_2 out of our system by maximum breathing (as in Figure 5–4C) that we do not have enough to tell us to come up and breathe before we use up all of our oxygen. That is why there is a rule that says: *Never take more than three maximum air exchange breaths (hyperventilation) before a dive.*

It is possible by breathing as in Figure 5–4C to purge all of the CO_2 from the system and hold your breath until the oxygen is used up, and then pass out. This is called "shallow water blackout." The process is more complicated than we have indicated here, having also to do with the increased pressure on your body while you are diving, but the general mechanism is as we have discussed. The best and safest breath pattern when breath-hold diving is as follows:

1. Use maximum breathing, as in Figure 5–4C, for three or four breaths when you surface from a dive to purge the system quickly of CO_2.
2. Then switch to modified breathing, as in Figure 5–4B, until you are fully recovered and relaxed.
3. Switch back to maximum breathing for three breaths before the next dive.

This pattern will give you the best recovery time and still retain enough CO_2 to dive safely.

Relaxation

If there is a single thing that is important to good diving, it is the "art of relaxing." The more relaxed the body, the less oxygen is used and the less CO_2 is produced.

The secret to complete relaxation in the water is to spend enough time in it so you are very much at home there. Any anxiety will make complete relaxation impossible.

Relaxing must be a conscious endeavor when you first get into the water; it doesn't just happen. There are several tricks that will help the body to relax:

1. Lie face down breathing through the snorkel. If you are weighted properly you may have to kick ever-so-gently to keep you from sinking.
2. Take three big, deep breaths (maximum breathing), then on the third *exhalation*, just totally relax. Inhale when your body says to. Repeat until the whole body is completely relaxed.

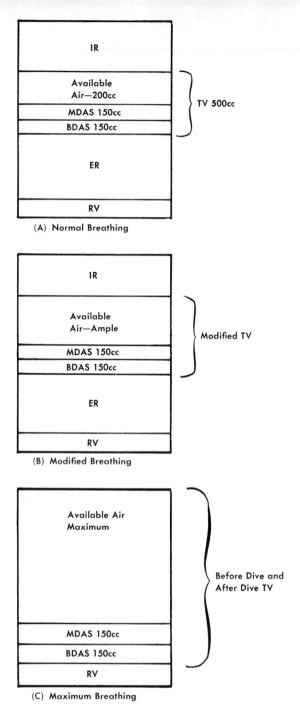

FIGURE 5-4

Note: The numbers used on these charts were taken from several standard physiology texts. They represent only an average. The actual numbers would vary with the individual.

(A) shows available air from "normal" breathing through a snorkel;

(B) shows the improvement of available air if a modified breathing pattern is used, with a larger inhalation and a greater exhalation than normal;

(C) shows the proper use of the lung capacity on the last three breaths before a dive, and the first three breaths after a dive.

3. While relaxing, keep your eyes closed. Light activates the brain and makes it more difficult for you to turn off enough of the neurons in the brain to relax the body. Each time you come up from a dive into a recovery period, it is best to close the eyes momentarily also. This is an aid to quicker recovery.
4. As you proceed with your diving, "tell" yourself to relax often. Repeat in your mind as you descend, "relax, relax, relax . . ." over and over. This is called "auto-suggestion," and it will work. Soon your body will listen and relax.
5. While you are on the surface during a recovery period or during the initial relaxation period when you first get into the water, shake your legs and even your whole body to loosen them up. This technique gets rid of any tightness in the muscles.
6. Since it takes several dives for the body to become fully relaxed, don't push yourself for the first eight or ten dives. You must have a "warm-up" period to give your body a chance to adapt to its new job.

I cannot overemphasize the importance of complete relaxation. Until you master it, you can only be a mediocre diver. Master it and you will be on your way to excellence.

Rhythm Diving

Once you have learned to breathe properly and have mastered the relaxation process, you will want to put them together in the best possible sequence, or rhythm, for maximum performance. Rhythm diving makes use of all you've got. The proper rhythm *for you* is a must.

The human body is a machine, complex to say the least, but still a machine. All machines have an optimal speed at which they function. Two identical car engines will operate slightly differently under the same load. In a like manner each of our bodies will operate differently under a similar load. Every person has a different physiology and psychology. We therefore must define the "load," and experiment until we find our own "optimal speed." The load in this case is breath-holding while we swim under water and do light work. We must determine;

1. How long we can remain under water without undue stress.
2. How long it will take us to recover on the surface from the load.
3. How long it will take us to prepare for the load again.

We have three parts to our dive profile. The load, the recovery, and the preparation for the load again. These three steps should be executed in a definite rhythm. The body, like a machine, works better if it can do the same thing over and over. Each step should take up about the same amount of time on every dive; the diver then develops a dive pattern that is repeated over and over, so we call it rhythm diving.

57

The best way to find your rhythm is to start with a standard and modify it. A good place to start is with a 20-second dive, a 20-second recovery, and a 10-second preparation. On a continuous basis, using a watch to time yourself, this means 20 seconds under, 30 seconds on top, 20 seconds under, 30 seconds on top, and so on. Keep this rhythm for at least 15 minutes so you can establish the stress points in the pattern, and then modify the pattern to eliminate them. The idea is to have as much bottom time as possible with as little surface time as you can and stay comfortable.

My personal rhythm for maximum bottom time is 60 seconds up, and 60 seconds down. This gives me one hour of bottom time for every two hours I'm in the water, and I can keep it up all day. If I change the rhythm, I can stay under for longer periods of time but I start to tire. Keeping a rhythm that allows you to stay relaxed and not tire will enable you to extend yourself when that "big fish" happens to swim by. It will take some time and effort to establish your rhythm, and once you have it you will be changing it slightly as you become better. It is a dynamic process, not a rigid one.

. BASIC SCUBA SKILLS

After the diver has learned how to use the mask, fins, and snorkel, and has been introduced to breath-hold diving, he is ready to learn scuba. This is always a happy time for the instructor because he receives a strong positive reinforcement of what he is doing. In short, the students tell him that they "dig" it.

The first time a person goes underwater with scuba is always a far-out experience. Some of the comments I have heard are: "fantastic," "weird," and "outta' sight." All of these fall short of how the divers actually feel, but there is no way to accurately describe it.

All of these incredible sensations that the new diver experiences when he first takes the tank and regulator under the surface are based on one thing: The fact that suddenly he can relax on the bottom and breathe. Being able to stay underwater and not have to hold your breath is a sensation that the instructor cannot prepare the student for with words. Not until the water closes over your head and all sound disappears except for the roar of your own breathing can you know what it is like. It is fascinating, exciting, and a bit scary. You say to yourself, "I'm actually breathing under water." It takes several breaths before you are willing to trust this amazing phenomenon. Just when you start to realize that you really can, the instructor tells you not to swim off and play yet. There are things you must learn about how to use this marvelous device we call a regulator and the tank that feeds it air, before you can wander away.

The regulator is both simple and complex. It is complex in its engineering but simple in its use. The uncomplicated use of the regulator is a blessing for the diver and is a function of its complex design.* There is much to learn about the regulator. How to clear water out of it is important, and there are other things that are necessary to know for its safe use. The scuba tank must be understood also. This is simply a tank full of air. Nothing mysterious. We use a compressor to push a roomful of air into a small space so we can carry it with us underwater. The regulator allows us to take the air we need from the tank. When we use up all of the air in the tank we come to the surface and pump more in so we can go back down.

In order to learn the proper use of tank and regulator without acquiring bad habits along the way, I give my students the following list of scuba skill activities which they must accomplish in the order they are listed. I do not let them jump ahead even if they are experienced. I demonstrate to the group, but each student progresses as an individual and each skill is checked off after completion by that student.

If you are already a diver, run through this list in order and see what a logical progression of learning it is. If you are not yet a diver, then it may seem difficult. But it is not hard, for you will soon see that each step leads you to the next one. Your instructor is an expert in this step process to accomplishment. He will lead you through his steps and you will be amazed at how simple it is to master the basic skills. Once you find out how easy it really is, don't tell anyone. Let them be amazed at how "good" you are.

Scuba Skills to be Performed for Certification *Without Undue Stress***

(A) From a scuba unit placed on the bottom in four feet of water, be able to:

1. Swim down, pick up the regulator, and breathe from it.
2. Clear the mask while breathing from the unit.
3. Fill a flotation vest with the oral inflator, while breathing from the unit underwater.

* Because of the regulator's complex makeup the diver should never attempt any repairs himself. Only a qualified regulator repair man should dismantle the regulator. The diver who does his own repair work (and, in effect, meddles with his own air supply) without the proper tools and an air flow meter is both foolish and brave. Repairs are not that expensive and should always be done by a skilled technician.
** Throughout this book you will read the term "without stress" or "without undue stress." This is the best way I have of getting across the idea that you must be able to perform the technique of scuba with complete confidence. This includes understanding the function and use of each piece of equipment as well as how to judge the diving area and your personal capabilities. If you feel uneasy about the task you are doing then you are under stress. A small amount of "uneasiness" or "stress" is not bad, but an excessive amount will cause you to perform badly because you will be too "tight" and not thinking clearly.

The good diver dives with his head, not his courage. You should master all the things necessary for you to do on a dive so that you can think out any problems that arise and not "gut" them out. If you still feel stress after you have taken instruction then take more instruction. If you still feel "undue stress" then take up archery.

A student demonstrates skill A-1: picking up a regulator from the bottom in three feet of water and breathing from it.

4. Swim from one scuba unit to another scuba unit without surfacing.
5. Swim down and breathe from a single regulator with anot person, alternating every two breaths, for 2 or 3 minutes

NOTE: By the time students complete these first five activities, they have in reality learned most of what they have to do in the course. There is no anxiety because they are in water in which they can stand up and are not confined by wearing the suit. They, in effect, have learned the most important skills. The list goes on as follows.

(B) With a tank on your back, be able to:

1. Clear the mask.
2. Breathe two people from one tank in several positions:
   a. Face to face.
   b. Side by side.

   NOTE: We stress position *a*. Position *b* is an academic drill and is of little use in an emergency. The students are made aware of this.

3. Clear the regulator of water:
   a. With air in the lungs.
   b. After a full exhalation.
      1. By pumping very short breaths in and out of the regulator.
      2. By using the purge on the regulator.

   NOTE: There is one trouble that the diver sometimes has that can be easily avoided. It is customary to snorkel to the dive site, then switch to scuba and descend. The trouble is in clearing the regulator of water so the diver can breathe. The regulator has a purge valve in the bottom section and will clear easily if in an upright position as it is when the diver is swimming. When the

A student practices skill B-5: taking the tank off and putting it on under water. She is not wearing a mask so she learns to do it by feel.

diver descends head first, however, the regulator is *upside down*. It will not clear. This is averted simply by clearing the regulator on the surface before the descent or by descending feet first. A very simple thing, but many divers have much trouble before they discover it.

4. Take off the tank and put it back on while treading water on the surface.

   NOTE: The overhead method is demonstrated, but any method the student can use smoothly and without stress is acceptable.

5. Take off the tank and put it back on while sitting on the bottom.
6. Take off the tank while on the bottom, leave it there, and return to the surface. Dive back down and put the tank back on while sitting on the bottom.
7. Take all gear off while on the bottom and leave it there, returning to the surface. Dive back down and put all gear back on while remaining on the bottom.
8. Hold all gear in the hand and jump from the side of the pool into the water with the air in the tank turned on, and put all gear on after reaching the bottom.
9. Hold all gear in the hand and jump from the side of the pool into the water with the air in the tank turned off, and put all gear on after reaching the bottom.
10. Exchange all gear with your partner using one tank to breathe from for both of you while on the bottom.
11. Swim the length of the pool from the shallow end to the deep end underwater with one partner in full gear and the other one in swim suit only, buddy-breathing while you go. Upon reaching the deep end of the pool, transfer all gear to the partner who had swim suit only and return to the shallow end without surfacing.

Number 11 is my final pool test, upon completion of which students receive their final watermanship grade. They seem to be fairly competent after completion of these exercises. Since the exercises are sequential in nature, I rarely have anyone who cannot complete them. I follow up these exercises with four ocean dives because I feel it is important for a student to gain confidence in open water where he will be doing most of his diving.

Ocean Dive 1

We learn to enter and exit the surf without using tanks. Students are given the opportunity to try several methods, such as walking in with fins on, walking in frontwards, walking in backwards, walking in up to their waist and then putting

This young woman demonstrates the proper method of ascending to the surface. Hand up, head back—and, of course, she exhales all the way up.

It is important for the student to gain confidence in open water, where he will be doing most of his diving.

their fins on, and crawling on their hands and knees or "polliwoging in" as it is normally called. They enter over sand and over rocks and exit over sand and over rocks, accomplishing approximately 12 entries and exits in a one-hour period in the water. They finish this exercise with a one-half mile ocean swim. By then they are tired and it is time to quit. They are no longer frightened of surf and are somewhat used to the wet suit.

Ocean Dive 2

Again no tanks are used. Students dive in buddy-pairs along a reef that we have locally and must stay in water for a minimum of one hour. They cannot take camera gear or spear guns with them. They may only look and touch. This is strictly a dive to allow them to rid themselves of some of the normal anxiety that comes with being in open water, and to become more accumstomed to the wet suit. If you are a certified diver, try leaving your tank at home sometime and float along in shallow water and practice the art of "look and touch." Even with a tank a "look and touch" dive is a lot of fun. You will see more than you ever dreamed was there.

Ocean Dive 3

The third dive is my students' scuba check-out. This is generally done from the beach, in 25 to 30 feet of water. The diver must perform personally for the instructor (that's me because I'm the head honcho) *without stress* the following skills:

1. The ability to descend and clear the ears properly.
2. The ability to take the mask off and replace it, clearing it of water.
3. Buddy-breathe with the instructor. (The main importance of this exercise is that I can then tell how nervous the student is by how tight he holds me as we buddy-breathe together.)
4. Control his buoyancy by the use of the oral inflator on his flotation vest.
5. Perform a controlled emergency swimming ascent.
6. Complete at least a 30-minute scuba dive with his partner in 30 feet or less of water.

Ocean Dive 4

The second scuba dive is a fun dive, generally off a boat. It is just to give the student that little extra experience he needs so badly at this time in his training. This second scuba dive is also required by law in some areas.

He then becomes a certified NAUI diver. Before I will certify a diver I must be able to say to myself honestly that I would let him dive as a buddy with my young son or daughter.

There are any number of other scuba skills that could be outlined here, but the ones I have mentioned I feel are adequate for a first class in scuba diving. I might add that these are *the minimum skills a diver should have to be a safe diver.* They still do not make him a diver; what they do is give him the skill level he needs to be safe while he goes out and gains the years of experience it will take to make him a diver.

When a student has mastered the basics, and becomes certified, he should make as many open-water dives as possible the first year. NAUI has a sports diving program intended as the next step.

• DECOMPRESSION AND REPETITIVE DIVING

Repetitive diving and its relationship to decompression is a subject that is taught in depth to a deep-diving class, but a fundamental understanding is necessary for the beginning student so he will appreciate the problem areas and know enough to avoid them until he receives training in them.

The decompression and repetitive dive tables are often confusing to the student because they look complicated. In fact, they are not complicated, and can easily be mastered.

The theory which the tables are based on is Haldane's theory that the partial pressure of nitrogen (if you are breathing air as scuba divers do) can reach a level of twice the pressure of that gas without harm. (This is explained more fully in Appendix K, "High Altitude Procedures for Repetitive, Decompression, and Flying After Diving.")

The more pressure a diver is under, the higher the partial pressure of gases he is subjected to. As would only make sense, the more pressure that is pressing on him, the faster he will absorb gas. Therefore, a diver at 20 feet is not absorbing gas as fast as a diver at 25 feet. The deeper a diver goes, the faster gas is absorbed. The tables are based on the time it takes the diver to absorb twice the amount of gas he would have in his system at normal sea level pressure of 14.7 pounds per square inch. This is a predictable time at any given depth. Through research and much testing the rate of gas absorption has been determined for the *average* person. The tables, therefore, are based on the average person. Because the tables were developed by the Navy for their divers and not for sports diving, *there is no safety factor figured in*. This means you should never "push" the tables. You can figure in your own safety factor by figuring to the next greater depth than you actually used on your dive.

The first table you should become familiar with is the "No-Decompression Limits Table." This is listed as "Table 1–11" in the U.S. Navy Air Decompression Tables, and is reproduced here in full. The No-Decompression Limits Table tells you how long you can stay at any given depth before you reach your limit of saturation that requires decompression.

Note that you look in the left-hand column to find the depth you will dive. The next column over tells you how many minutes you can stay at that depth without absorbing enough nitrogen (N_2) to have to decompress. It is interesting to note that at 30 feet and above you will not absorb enough to have to decompress. Stay above 30 feet and you will never have to consider the decompression tables. If you go to 40 feet then you are limited to 200 minutes without having to decompress, and at 60 feet you only have 60 minutes. The deeper you go the more pressure is on you, so the faster you absorb gas and the less time you have. By looking at this table you say, "Well, I just won't stay down longer than the limit and I won't have to worry." This is true *if you only make one dive in any 12-hour period*. It is not true, however, if you make several dives. Each dive after the first one within a 12-hour period is called a repetitive dive. The problem lies in the fact that the nitrogen you absorb during your first dives takes time to slowly work its way out of your body after you reach the surface. If you go back into the water anytime up to 12 hours after your first dive, there is still nitrogen left in your system that has not had a chance to work its way out yet.

Instead of starting the second dive with normal ambient pressure of nitrogen, you are starting it somewhere above that level. This must be figured into the table some way. In order to do this the Navy prepared two more tables that helps you figure out what your present level is or, to say it another way, to calculate the "residual" nitrogen left in your system and turn it into a number that can be plugged into the No-Decompression table. The first step in this calculation is to

TABLE 1-11.—*No-decompression limits and repetitive group designation table for no-decompression air dives*

Depth (feet)	No-decompression limits (min)	Repetitive groups (air dives)													
		A	B	C	D	E	F	G	H	I	J	K	L	M	N	O
10	----------	60	120	210	300											
15	----------	35	70	110	160	225	350									
20	----------	25	50	75	100	135	180	240	325							
25	----------	20	35	55	75	100	125	160	195	245	315					
30	----------	15	30	45	60	75	95	120	145	170	205	250	310			
35	310	5	15	25	40	50	60	80	100	120	140	160	190	220	270	310
40	200	5	15	25	30	40	50	70	80	100	110	130	150	170	200	----
50	100	----	10	15	25	30	40	50	60	70	80	90	100			
60	60	----	10	15	20	25	30	40	50	55	60					
70	50	----	5	10	15	20	30	35	40	45	50					
80	40	----	5	10	15	20	25	30	35	40						
90	30	----	5	10	12	15	20	25	30							
100	25	----	5	7	10	15	20	22	25							
110	20	----	----	5	10	13	15	20								
120	15	----	----	5	10	12	15									
130	10	----	----	5	8	10										
140	10	----	----	5	7	10										
150	5	----	----	5												
160	5	----	----	----	5											
170	5	----	----	----	5											
180	5	----	----	----	5											
190	5	----	----	----	5											

Instructions for Use

I. No-decompression limits:
This column shows at various depths greater than 30 feet the allowable diving times (in minutes) which permit surfacing directly at 60 feet a minute with no decompression stops. Longer exposure times require the use of the Standard Air Decompression Table (table 1-10).

II. Repetitive group designation table:
The tabulated exposure times (or bottom times) are in minutes. The times at the various depths in each vertical column are the maximum exposures during which a diver will remain within the group listed at the head of the column.

To find the repetitive group designation at surfacing for dives involving exposures up to and including the no-decompression limits: Enter the table on the *exact or next greater depth* than that to which exposed and select the listed exposure time *exact or next greater* than the actual exposure time. The repetitive group designation is indicated by the letter at the head of the vertical column where the selected exposure time is listed.

For example: A dive was to 32 feet for 45 minutes. Enter the table along the 35-foot-depth line since it is next greater than 32 feet. The table shows that since group D is left after 40 minutes' exposure and group E after 50 minutes, group E (at the head of the column where the 50-minute exposure is listed) is the proper selection.

Exposure times for depths less than 40 feet are listed only up to approximately 5 hours since this is considered to be beyond field requirements for this table.

find out how much nitrogen was in your system when you got out of the water from the first dive. To do this you use the other numbers on the No-Decompression table. Here again, the Navy has made it easy. Instead of saying you are 37 percent saturated or using some other confusing number, they divided the amounts of saturation from 0 to 100% and gave each portion a letter name. They call these "groups." So when you use the table you will find that you are in a certain group, such as *C* or *F*.

Let's find out what our group would be if we were diving to 50 feet and had stayed there for 20 minutes. We look at "Table 1–11" and go down the left-hand column until we find 50. We see that we could have stayed for 100 minutes without decompressing, though we only stayed 20 minutes. We continue to the right in the 50-feet column and we find the numbers 10, 15, 25, 30, and so on. These numbers represent the time of our dive in minutes. This is called "bottom time." At this point we must define bottom time. Unfortunately it *is not* the time you *spend* on the bottom. It is, instead, the time from when you *leave the surface* and start down until the time you *leave the bottom* and start up. If we were to draw our dive it would look like this:

"D" would represent depth and "BT" would represent Bottom Time. In our dive D = 50', and BT = 20 minutes.

Our *BT* of 20 minutes we would then use in the table. But alas there is no 20 minutes in the table. When this happens you always go to the next greater time. In this case that would be 25. Once we have found this point we follow the column straight up and get our group. It is, in this instance, group *D*. We would then add this to the drawing of our dive showing the group we were in when we came out of the water.

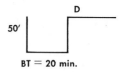

As we eat lunch or rest before the next dive, some of the nitrogen is leaving our system. This is called "out gassing." The longer we are out of the water, the more nitrogen will leave; in 12 hours it is all gone and we are back to our normal amount. The length of time we spend out of the water thus is important to us in figuring what amount of nitrogen we have left at the beginning of the second dive. This interval we spend on the surface between dives is called the "surface interval"

Table 1-12.—*Surface Interval Credit Table for air decompression dives*

[Repetitive group at the end of the surface interval (air dive)]

Z	O	N	M	L	K	J	I	H	G	F	E	D	C	B	A
0:10 / 0:22	0:23 / 0:34	0:35 / 0:48	0:49 / 1:02	1:03 / 1:18	1:19 / 1:36	1:37 / 1:55	1:56 / 2:17	2:18 / 2:42	2:43 / 3:10	3:11 / 3:45	3:46 / 4:29	4:30 / 5:27	5:28 / 6:56	6:57 / 10:05	10:00 / 12:00*
O	0:10 / 0:23	0:24 / 0:36	0:37 / 0:51	0:52 / 1:07	1:08 / 1:24	1:25 / 1:43	1:44 / 2:04	2:05 / 2:29	2:30 / 2:59	3:00 / 3:33	3:34 / 4:17	4:18 / 5:16	5:17 / 6:44	6:45 / 9:54	9:55 / 12:00*
	N	0:10 / 0:24	0:25 / 0:39	0:40 / 0:54	0:55 / 1:11	1:12 / 1:30	1:31 / 1:53	1:54 / 2:18	2:19 / 2:47	2:48 / 3:22	3:23 / 4:04	4:05 / 5:03	5:04 / 6:32	6:33 / 9:43	9:44 / 12:00*
		M	0:10 / 0:25	0:26 / 0:42	0:43 / 0:59	1:00 / 1:18	1:19 / 1:39	1:40 / 2:05	2:06 / 2:34	2:35 / 3:08	3:09 / 3:52	3:53 / 4:49	4:50 / 6:18	6:19 / 9:28	9:29 / 12:00*
			L	0:10 / 0:26	0:27 / 0:45	0:46 / 1:04	1:05 / 1:25	1:26 / 1:49	1:50 / 2:19	2:20 / 2:53	2:54 / 3:36	3:37 / 4:35	4:36 / 6:02	6:03 / 9:12	9:13 / 12:00*
				K	0:10 / 0:28	0:29 / 0:49	0:50 / 1:11	1:12 / 1:35	1:36 / 2:03	2:04 / 2:38	2:39 / 3:21	3:22 / 4:19	4:20 / 5:48	5:49 / 8:58	8:59 / 12:00*
					J	0:10 / 0:31	0:32 / 0:54	0:55 / 1:19	1:20 / 1:47	1:48 / 2:20	2:21 / 3:04	3:05 / 4:02	4:03 / 5:40	5:41 / 8:40	8:41 / 12:00*
						I	0:10 / 0:33	0:34 / 0:59	1:00 / 1:29	1:30 / 2:02	2:03 / 2:44	2:45 / 3:43	3:44 / 5:12	5:13 / 8:21	8:22 / 12:00*
							H	0:10 / 0:36	0:37 / 1:06	1:07 / 1:41	1:42 / 2:23	2:24 / 3:20	3:21 / 4:49	4:50 / 7:59	8:00 / 12:00*
								G	0:10 / 0:40	0:41 / 1:15	1:16 / 1:59	2:00 / 2:58	2:59 / 4:25	4:26 / 7:35	7:36 / 12:00*
									F	0:10 / 0:45	0:46 / 1:29	1:30 / 2:28	2:29 / 3:57	3:58 / 7:05	7:06 / 12:00*
										E	0:10 / 0:54	0:55 / 1:57	1:58 / 3:22	3:23 / 6:32	6:33 / 12:00*
											D	0:10 / 1:09	1:10 / 2:38	2:39 / 5:48	5:49 / 12:00*
												C	0:10 / 1:39	1:40 / 2:49	2:50 / 12:00*
													B	0:10 / 2:10	2:11 / 12:00*
														A	0:10 / 12:00*

Repetitive group at the beginning of the surface interval from previous dive

Instructions for Use

Surface interval time in the table is in *hours* and *minutes* (7:59 means 7 hours and 59 minutes). The surface interval must be at least 10 minutes.

Find the *repetitive group designation letter* (from the previous dive schedule) on the diagonal slope. Enter the table horizontally to select the surface interval time that is exactly between the actual surface interval times shown. The repetitive group designation for the *end* of the surface interval is at the head of the vertical column where the selected surface interval time is listed. For example, a previous dive was to 110 feet for 30 minutes. The diver remains on the surface 1 hour and 30 minutes and wishes to find the new repetitive group designation: The repetitive group from the last column of the 110/30 schedule in the Standard Air Decompression Tables is "J." Enter the surface interval credit table along the horizontal line labeled "J." The 1-hour-and-30-minute surface interval lies between the times 1:20 and 1:47. Therefore, the diver has lost sufficient inert gas to place him in group "G" (at the head of the vertical column selected).

NOTE.—Dives following surface intervals of more than 12 hours are not considered repetitive dives. Actual bottom times in the Standard Air Decompression Tables may be used in computing decompression for such dives.

(*SI*). Let's say, in our example, we rest for 2 hours and 40 minutes before our next dive. Our surface interval (*SI*) is then 2:40. To calculate the amount of nitrogen that has left our system during that time, we use "Table 1–12," the "Surface Interval Credit Table." Our drawing now looks like this:

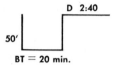

We are interested in knowing how much nitrogen is left in our system when we *start* the next dive, which is another way of saying "at the end of our SI." We look at the Surface Interval Credit Table, 1–12, in the slanted left-hand column to find our repetitive group at the *beginning* of the surface interval. We find *D*. By going to the right we locate the period which contains our *SI*. Our 2:40 falls between 2:39 and 5:48. We now go straight *up* this column and find our new repetitive group to be *B*. We enter this in our drawing. It now looks like this:

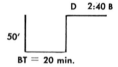

We plan our next dive. The important part is the depth. We must know how deep we are going to dive. We will go back to the same place we were before so our depth will be 50' and we add this to our drawing:

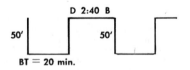

Now we have to find out how many minutes group *B* is equal to at 50' so we can subtract that much from the no decompression time we have at 50'. "Table 1–13," the "Repetitive Dive Timetable," does this job for us. We go down the left-hand column until we find our group, which is *B*. We then go to the right until we are in the column that represents the depth we are going to dive. We decided on 50 feet. We would then go over to the second column, which has 50' at the top. By coming down the 50' column and across to the right in the *B* column we find they intersect on the number 13. This number 13 represents the number of minutes at

TABLE 1–13.—*Repetitive dive timetable for air dives*

Repetitive groups	Repetitive dive depth (ft) (air dives)														
	40	50	60	70	80	90	100	110	120	130	140	150	160	170	180	190
A	7	6	5	4	4	3	3	3	3	3	2	2	2	2	2	2
B	17	13	11	9	8	7	7	6	6	6	5	5	4	4	4	4
C	25	21	17	15	13	11	10	10	9	8	7	7	6	6	6	6
D	37	29	24	20	18	16	14	13	12	11	10	9	9	8	8	8
E	49	38	30	26	23	20	18	16	15	13	12	12	11	10	10	10
F	61	47	36	31	28	24	22	20	18	16	15	14	13	13	12	11
G	73	56	44	37	32	29	26	24	21	19	18	17	16	15	14	13
H	87	66	52	43	38	33	30	27	25	22	20	19	18	17	16	15
I	101	76	61	50	43	38	34	31	28	25	23	22	20	19	18	17
J	116	87	70	57	48	43	38	34	32	28	26	24	23	22	20	19
K	138	99	79	64	54	47	43	38	35	31	29	27	26	24	22	21
L	161	111	88	72	61	53	48	42	39	35	32	30	28	26	25	24
M	187	124	97	80	68	58	52	47	43	38	35	32	31	29	27	26
N	213	142	107	87	73	64	57	51	46	40	38	35	33	31	29	28
O	241	160	117	96	80	70	62	55	50	44	40	38	36	34	31	30
Z	257	169	122	100	84	73	64	57	52	46	42	40	37	35	32	31

Instructions for Use

The bottom times listed in this table are called "residual nitrogen times" and are the times a diver is to consider he has *already* spent on bottom when he *starts* a repetitive dive to a specific depth. They are in minutes.

Enter the table horizontally with the repetitive group designation from the Surface Interval Credit Table. The time in each vertical column is the number of minutes that would be required (at the depth listed at the head of the column) to saturate to the particular group.

For example: The final group designation from the Surface Interval Credit Table, on the basis of a previous dive and surface interval, is "H." To plan a dive to 110 feet, determine the residual nitrogen time for this depth required by the repetitive group designation: Enter this table along the horizontal line labeled "H." The table shows that one must *start* a dive to 110 feet as though he had already been on the bottom for 27 minutes. This information can then be applied to the Standard Air Decompression Table or No-Decompression Table in a number of ways:

(1) Assuming a diver is going to finish a job and take whatever decompression is required, he must add 27 minutes to his actual bottom time and be prepared to take decompression

according to the 110-foot schedules for the sum or equivalent single dive time.

(2) Assuming one wishes to make a quick inspection dive for the minimum decompression, he will decompress according to the 110/30 schedule for a dive of 3 minutes or less (27+3=30). For a dive of over 3 minutes but less than 13, he will decompress according to the 110/40 schedule (27+13=40).

(3) Assuming that one does not want to exceed the 110/50 schedule and the amount of decompression it requires, he will have to start ascent before 23 minutes of actual bottom time (50−27=23).

(4) Assuming that a diver has air for approximately 45 minutes bottom time and decompression stops, the possible dives can be computed: A dive of 13 minutes will require 23 minutes of decompression (110/40 schedule), for a total submerged time of 36 minutes. A dive of 13 to 23 minutes will require 34 minutes of decompression (110/50 schedule), for a total submerged time of 47 to 57 minutes. Therefore, to be safe, the diver will have to start ascent before 13 minutes or a standby air source will have to be provided.

50′ that the nitrogen left in our system represents. We call this "residual N_2 time" (RT). We add this to our drawing:

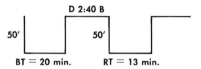

We now go back to the No-Decompression table. We find 50 feet and see we have 100 minutes without decompression available for us to use. We *plan* our dive for a bottom time (don't forget how to calculate bottom time) of 40 minutes. We add this to our drawing.

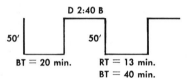

Now we total our *RT* and our *BT* to make sure the total does not exceed the 100 minutes that Table 1–11 gave us.

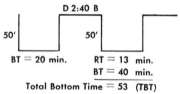

We do not have to decompress on the second dive because we did not exceed 100 minutes of total bottom time.

Each successive dive would be calculated in the same manner. To figure our group when we come out of the water from dive 2 we would go across the 50′ foot column on Table 1–11 to 60. Remember, you go to the next highest and 60 is next from our 53. Our group would be *H*. We would enter it in our drawing and proceed with the steps just as we did with dive 2.

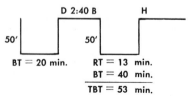

A series of practice problems is provided in Appendix F. Work them and practice until you do well and *understand* the procedure.

The "Standard Air Decompression Table" (Table 1–10) is for use when the times in the No-Decompression table are exceeded. This should not be attempted without specific training. The table is easy to read and understand and is included in Appendix D but should be used only by trained divers on well-planned dives.

• THE DIVER'S FLAG

The diver's flag is a feeble attempt to keep the diver safe from boats passing overhead. The idea is that a diver takes the flag out with him on a float. He then dives within 100 feet of the float and all boat skippers can see the flag and will not come closer than 100 feet.

Several problems arise when we put this flag-safety theory into practice. One is that we cannot decide on a standard worldwide flag. There are at least four that are fairly widely used. You would think that at least within a single country there would be agreement. This may be in some countries but not here in the U.S.A. We have several that are used. The Navy uses an all red flag. The sports diver uses a red flag with a white stripe running from the top of the mast diagonally to the lower corner on the opposite side. Some say it must be rectangular in shape, others that it must be square. At the moment the square shape is the most "acceptable."

A second major problem is that boaters don't know what the flag means. Recently, I sat through a U.S. Power Squadron course on basic boat handling during which the instructors talked about flags for a half hour but never mentioned the diver's flag. Many boaters just don't know what the flag is supposed to mean. If they did know that they were not supposed to get within a couple of hundred feet of the flag, it wouldn't do any good anyway. The diver can easily be a quarter to a half mile away from the flag before he realizes it. Some areas require use of a flag to dive there; unfortunately they are fooling themselves and no one else.

Before the flag idea will work we must train the diver to never dive out of the immediate area of his flag, and then get the boating public to recognize and honor the protected area indicated by the flag. If people can ever be taught to respect the flag, it will be good for diving. As it stands now the flag is probably a bigger hazard than safety factor because the Sunday boater, who took a Power Squadron course several years ago in which the flag was not mentioned, will run over to see what it is.

• LENDING A HELPING HAND

Divers nearly always use the buddy system of diving. What is the buddy system? For some divers it means calling up your buddy and going diving, but in different directions. This is *not* what it means to use the buddy system. When the buddy system is used as it is meant to be, your buddy checks your gear and you check his gear just before you enter the water. Then the

The buddy system insures that someone will be there, should you need help of any kind. It is also more fun to share your diving experiences with a buddy.

two buddies stay close enough together that if one needs to be helped in any way, the buddy is right there to help.

Being *able* to render aid to a fellow diver is of the utmost importance. The entire buddy system is invalid if the buddies do not have the know-how to render aid to each other. Courses like the Red Cross lifesaving program for lifeguards are of extreme value and a diver should take such a course as part of his continuing education plan in diving. The lifesaving courses, however, do not specifically teach diving lifesaving. Many of the basic techniques used to aid a swimmer in trouble will not work well in dive gear. We will try here to point out some of the techniques for rendering aid to a diver that are not in the Red Cross or YMCA books on lifesaving.

As a buddy, part of your responsibility is to recognize when your partner needs help. To do this you must be actively aware of your buddy and what he or she is doing. This awareness should start on the beach or in the boat, *before* you enter the water. A general discussion of what the two of you plan to do is important. This "pre-dive plan" may take the form of a five-minute chat while you are getting suited up, but is necessary so the two of you are somewhat tuned in to the activity of the dive. Any special signals can be worked out and old signals reviewed to insure they mean the same thing to both of you. Particularly important are the signals for "I'm out of air," "I'm going up," "I need to buddy-breathe," and "I need help." These signals vary from area to area and should be clear in both divers' minds *before* the dive.

The next important aid the buddies should render each other is an inspection of each other's gear after they are suited up. Make sure the weight belt is clear in case it needs to be dropped, the flap on the wet suit jacket or snap on the wet suit crotch is done up, and generally check to be certain everything looks in order for the dive. We always seem to forget some little thing, and a buddy check is really a great help.

Now we enter the water. At this point our main concern with our buddy is that he is comfortable and not under stress. There are signs that will aid you in knowing how relaxed your buddy is. Watch his breathing. If it is short and rapid then he is *not* relaxed. Slow down the pace and come up for a chat. Tell him you noticed that he is breathing hard and ask him if everything is okay. Generally calling this rapid breathing to the attention of someone is in itself enough to stop it. If he continues to hyperventilate (breathe rapidly) then you should call the dive off. Hyperventilation is dangerous due to a CO_2 buildup and although a person may feel fine, problems can develop all of a sudden and he can be in bad trouble. The symptoms are generally explained by, "I can't catch my breath." If you can't get him relaxed in a few minutes, *get out of the water*. Calm him down and try again. Hyperventilation is a bad danger sign. Fortunately, by being aware of it we have plenty of lead time to act safely.

Another sign that a diver is in trouble is when he keeps lifting his head out of the water. This is not a natural position in dive gear. Be particularly careful when the diver lifts his head up and takes the snorkel or mouthpiece out of his mouth. This is a sign that he thinks he needs more air, and quite often is the prelude to panic. This is a good time to take a weight belt off and hold it in the hand so it can be dumped quickly if need be. One of the best ways to determine how your buddy really feels

The skill of buddy breathing can be an important one in an emergency.

75

is to watch his feet. If he is kicking in a relaxed slow kick he is okay, but if the feet are really working, trouble is at hand. Take some weights off him, inflate the vest, or do whatever else seems to ease his mind so he can relax.

What if you miss the signs and your buddy panics? Try talking to him. Chances are he won't hear you, but try. If that does not work you must drop his weight belt. If you are in scuba gear put your regulator in your mouth and come up behind him underwater. Watch out for his feet and his tank. Reach around and undo his belt and make sure it drops off. A panic victim will generally be arching his back to keep his head up and this will pinch the belt under the tank. You may have to pull it free. If he is in a wet suit and the belt is dropped, that is generally all that is needed. Don't let him take hold of *your* tank. Once he gets on your back you won't be able to get to him. If you can inflate his vest do so. *Do not* take off his mask. It will keep water out of his eyes and nose, which will help calm him down. At this point generally you both can swim back to the beach or boat. *Do not* pull a diver by the collar of his flotation vest. This will tend to choke him. You can tow him by the tank, pulling him on his back if he needs help.

What do you do if your buddy gets a bad leg cramp? Leg cramps can be very painful, especially if the cramp is in the thigh area. Most cramps fortunately are in the calf and although they hurt and hinder swimming a great deal, they do not panic the diver. The best thing to do is to stretch the muscle out as soon as possible. This means stretching the leg out and bringing the toe back as far as possible towards the head. Rubbing or kneading the cramped area helps too.

If the cramp will not go away there is a good swimming assist you can do to help your buddy back to dry ground where he can work out the cramp. This swimming assist is good also if your buddy just gets tired and needs a "push."

First, have the tired or cramped person lie on his back with his legs straight out and stiff. The knees must be locked rigid (this is good for the cramped person as it relieves the muscle by stretching it). Next, come up to him and place his feet on your shoulders. Then hold his feet on your shoulders by holding each calf with your hands and kick. (You are swimming on your stomach and the victim is being pushed on his back.) This will push him through the water and you can rub his cramp as you push him. You can also talk back and forth, which is a great comfort to the hindered person. Talk only positively, saying things like "It's not very far to shore," or "These doggone cramps, I get them myself sometimes." If you can get him to talk about something he will be more at ease. Ask him simple questions: "Where did you start diving?" "Do you take underwater pictures?" Simple light conversation will help the person keep his mind off the fact that he is having trouble. Have him keep his body as rigid as possible. If he bends at the waist his rear end will create drag. Try this method of assist a few times—it really works well and a few practice sessions will make it easy to effect if you ever have to do it for real.

Next we have to consider what to do if you look over at your buddy and find him unconscious. When you are watching carefully as you should be, this probably will never happen for if a person is in trouble you can tell it long before he reaches this state if you are tuned in. We have to consider the possibility, however, of something like a heart attack. The first course of action is to get the victim to the surface. In bringing an unconscious diver to the surface, the airway should be kept open. In other words, the head should be back, not against the chest. This will allow air in the lung area to escape and reduce the chances of embolism from expanding gas as we ascend. This can be accomplished in several ways. You can bring up the victim by grabbing him under the chin so the head is back, you can grab his hair (one advantage of long hair), or you can grab his feet and bring him up feet first, in which case the water pressure on the chin will hold the head back. *Do not* grab the tank and bring him up that way. This will push his head against his chest and close the airway, thus trapping the gas in the lungs. If the unconscious diver is over 20 feet deep, drop the weight belt first to add lift. If this is inconvenient, drop yours. If you can drop both his and yours, *do not* inflate *your* vest. You might lose your grip on the way up and not be able to get back down to grab him again. When you reach the surface, call for help if any is available. Leave the mask on and the mouthpiece in as you tow him in. This will keep water out of his eyes, nose, and mouth. Time is the important thing here. If you can get to shore or a boat in *under four minutes,* do it. The best tow is probably by the top of the tank. Try to keep his head out of water. As soon as you reach a practical point, start mouth-to-mouth resuscitation. If you are so far from anything that you can't get there in under four minutes, start mouth-to-mouth in the water. Keep towing towards shore but concentrate on the mouth-to-mouth, not the tow. Inflate the diver's vest, *not yours.* You will be able then to turn his head and administer mouth-to-mouth. Mouth-to-mouth in the water is tricky. Practice it sometime with a friend to get the technique down. If you have to give mouth-to-mouth in the water, naturally you will have to take the mask off. It becomes very important then to maintain the face clear of the water.

Special symposiums on scuba lifesaving are run by NAUI. These symposiums include both lectures and water work and generally are held over a weekend. If you can't get to one yourself make sure the people you dive with get to one. At least they could save you!

6

MOTHER NATURE'S PART

Close your eyes and try to imagine a world that had no physical environment. There would be no light, sound, heat, cold, wet, dry, smell, touch, or anything else. What an awful place in which to live. We are lucky to have a very real and active physical environment surrounding us at all times. It protects us as well as threatens us on every edge of our territory as we move through life. If we understand this environment we can use it to our advantage, or at least avoid that which is to our disadvantage.

In diving, there is one law of nature that seems to dominate. That law is pressure. The part of the physical environment that changes most for the diver is the pressure of his environment on his body. A long time ago, Robert Boyle, an English chemist and physicist, noted a few things about pressure as it relates to the volume of gases. He recorded his observations and became famous. All he said was that the harder you push on a gas the smaller it gets. He didn't say it in quite

FIGURE 6-1

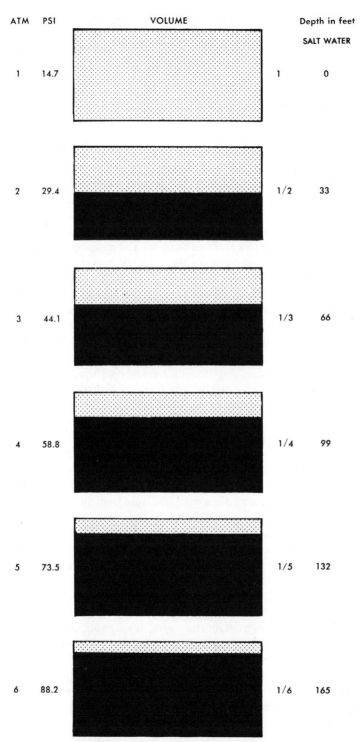

ATM	PSI	VOLUME	Depth in feet SALT WATER
1	14.7		1 0
2	29.4		1/2 33
3	44.1		1/3 66
4	58.8		1/4 99
5	73.5		1/5 132
6	88.2		1/6 165

The deeper you dive the greater the pressure due to the weight of the water. The more pressure, the more the air is compressed, until it is pushed into just a fraction of what it was at the surface.

those words but what he said meant the same thing. He used scientific terms: the volume of a gas is inversely proportional to the pressure exerted upon it, that is, of course, if the temperature remains constant. Within these few words is where most divers' problems lie. Let's take a closer look at air, the gas we live in. After all, it's all around us and we really should know at least what it's made of and how much it weighs.

Air is composed of three gases that are of concern to the diver. These are nitrogen, which makes up almost 80 percent, oxygen, approximately 20 percent, and carbon dioxide, approximately .03 percent. Minute amounts of other gases and things such as smog, dirt, dust, and so on are also in the air, but I choose at this time not to discuss them. (Incidentally, another good reason to scuba dive is that you get to breathe good, clean, filtered air. The air you breathe from your tank is more purified than any other air you can get.) The gases in the air mix together to make the atmosphere surrounding the earth. We even know how much the atmosphere weighs. The weight of the entire atmosphere is a number so large that it could not be written on this sheet of paper. If you are like most people, you prefer to deal with small numbers, so we will weigh just one square inch of the earth's atmosphere. A column of air from the surface of the earth at sea level, one square inch in area and running out into space ten miles or so, would weigh 14.7 pounds. Physicists tell us that this weight pushing down on a unit area of something gives us "atmospheric pressure" equal to 14.7 pounds per square inch. To make that number even smaller, let's call it *one atmosphere*. Actually the physicists thought of that before I did or I could have been famous too. Hold your hand out, palm up. The average hand is approximately 15 square inches in area so you are holding up approximately 220 pounds of air in your palm right now. Sounds great, but you are cheating. Because pressure is exerted in all directions, you are using the air on the bottom of your hand to push up and balance the 220 pounds on top of your hand. It's lucky for you that a gas or liquid exerts a pressure in all directions equally. If this were not true, then our bodies would collapse from the air pressure around us. Instead, the air works its way into our bodies and pushes out to keep us from being squashed. It goes into holes in our head called sinuses and into various other cavities in our body like the lungs, the stomach, occasionally by mistake, the ears, and even dissolves in our blood and body tissues. This is a good thing. Nobody wants to be squashed.

We all know that water is heavier than air. The physicists, being curious devils, wanted to know how much heavier. So they weighed it. They found that if they used the same square-inch column they used to weigh air, that it took only 33 feet of ocean water to weigh the same as one atmosphere (14.7 pounds per square inch) of air. That made it simple for us divers. Every 33 feet we dive beneath the surface of salt water (34 feet in fresh water), we increase the pressure on us by one atmosphere. At 33 feet we would have two atmospheres of pressure on us, the real one and the watery one. At 66 feet, we would have three atmospheres and so on, all

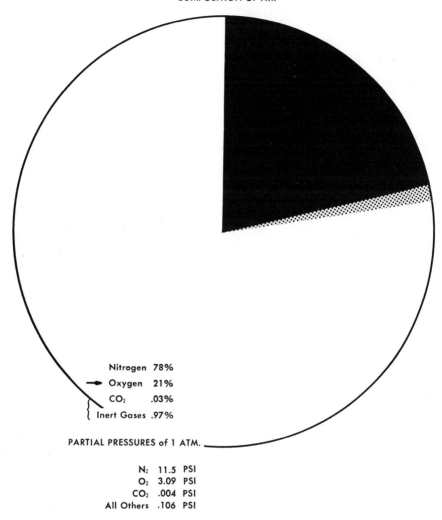

FIGURE 6-2

COMPOSITION OF AIR

Nitrogen 78%
Oxygen 21%
CO_2 .03%
Inert Gases .97%

PARTIAL PRESSURES of 1 ATM.

N_2	11.5	PSI
O_2	3.09	PSI
CO_2	.004	PSI
All Others	.106	PSI

This pie in the sky is one the diver should be aware of.

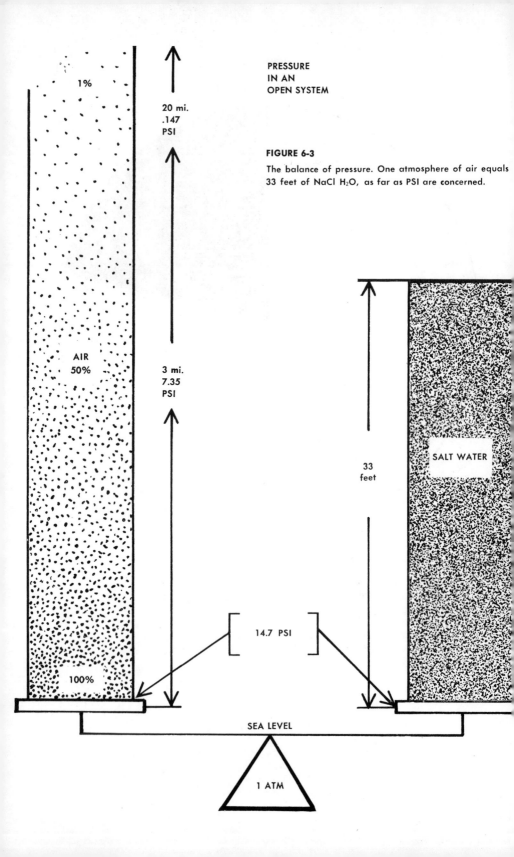

PRESSURE
IN AN
OPEN SYSTEM

FIGURE 6-3

The balance of pressure. One atmosphere of air equals 33 feet of NaCl H_2O, as far as PSI are concerned.

1%

20 mi.
.147
PSI

AIR
50%

3 mi.
7.35
PSI

SALT WATER

33
feet

14.7 PSI

100%

SEA LEVEL

1 ATM

BOYLE'S BUSTED BALLOON

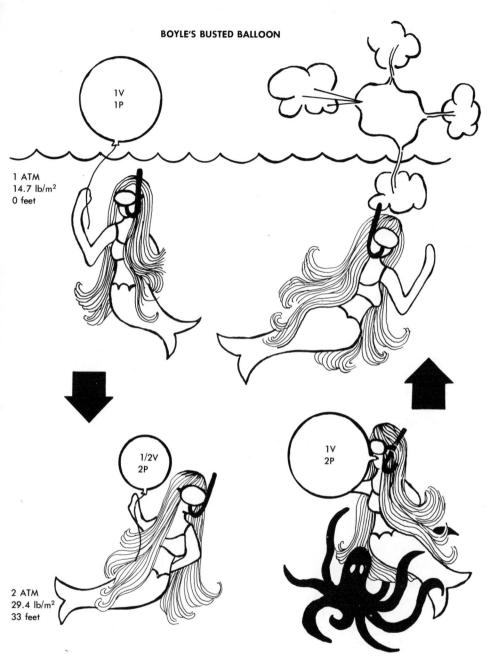

1 ATM
14.7 lb/m²
0 feet

2 ATM
29.4 lb/m²
33 feet

FIGURE 6-4

With one volume (V) and 1 pressure (1 atmosphere) on the surface we have a full balloon. If we take the balloon down to 33 feet we find we have 1/2 V because we have twice the pressure (2P). If we then refill the balloon at 33 feet with pressure air from our scuba tank to its original volume we have 1V at 2P. If we take the balloon back to the surface it will expand as the ambient pressure decreases until it reaches twice the volume at the surface but generally the balloon will burst before it reaches the surface. A balloon reacts much the same as the lungs under these circumstances.

the way down. Now that we know how the pressure increases underwater, we can go back to old man Boyle and his law. Remember that he said the more pressure you put on a gas, the smaller a volume or space it will take up. One thing for sure, as we dive deeper the pressure is going to increase on us one additional atmosphere for every 33 feet. We also can recall the reason we didn't squash is that the air got inside us and pushed out. By doing a little quick figuring and remembering that Boyle said it was an inverse proportion we are concerned about, we can see that at a depth of 33 feet we have twice the pressure on us that we had on the surface. Therefore, the air that is pushing out from the inside would be squashed or compressed to half its original volume. We therefore need more air inside to keep us in a happy state, about twice as much as at the surface. If we were at 66 feet, we would need three times as much to keep our system at a pressure equilibrium with the water. The pressure around us is called *ambient pressure;* the object is to keep our inside pressure the same as or in equilibrium with the ambient pressure no matter where we are. That goes for the bottom of the ocean, or the top of a mountain where the pressure is less than one atmosphere. The scuba regulator is designed to measure the ambient pressure and give us air to breathe that is exactly the same pressure as the ambient pressure at whatever depth we choose to dive. This is why we can dive to 100 feet and not squash.

The only problem is that when all that air is in our body and we start to come up, the ambient pressure decreases and of course the air expands as Boyle would have predicted. If we hold our breath and don't let it out, it will expand to the point that we will explode, figuratively, of course. The air will rupture blood vessels generally in the lungs and let blood into the lungs and air bubbles into the blood. This condition is called air embolism and is about the worst thing that can happen to a diver. The bubbles work their way through the blood vessels to the brain and stop up the small capillaries. This stops the blood flow and thus prevents oxygen from reaching the brain cells and the cells die. Death may result. The solution is simple: don't hold your breath while you are using scuba. Just continue to breathe and expanding air will come out the same way it got in, through the lungs. A good diver will breathe slower and deeper than normal. This modified type of breathing helps to compensate for the mechanical dead airspace in the regulator or snorkel. Steady breathing is the way to avoid most pressure problems.

There are other scientists who got into the act of diving physics also. Back in 1801 one of the Dalton boys did some experiments. He found that in a mixture of gases each gas keeps its own identity. Thus the total pressure of a gas is equal to the sum of the separate pressures of the gases that comprise it. He called these pressures, which added together make the total pressure, partial pressures. In air, for example, if the total pressure is 14.7 pounds per square inch and is 80 percent nitrogen, it is easy to see that 80 percent of the 14.7 pounds per square inch is nitrogen pressure and 20 percent is oxygen pressure. It only makes sense. If you have 25 marbles all the same size and weight, 20 red ones and 5 blue ones, 20

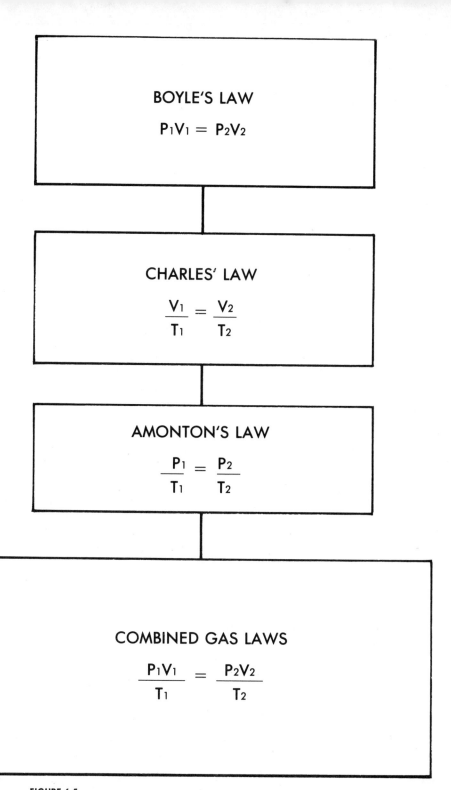

BOYLE'S LAW

$$P_1V_1 = P_2V_2$$

CHARLES' LAW

$$\frac{V_1}{T_1} = \frac{V_2}{T_2}$$

AMONTON'S LAW

$$\frac{P_1}{T_1} = \frac{P_2}{T_2}$$

COMBINED GAS LAWS

$$\frac{P_1V_1}{T_1} = \frac{P_2V_2}{T_2}$$

FIGURE 6-5

The beginning diver need not *memorize* these formulas. But if inclined to such things you can have a lot of fun with them.

percent of the total weight of the marbles would be from the blue marbles. This partial pressure of gases becomes important to the diver mainly when he is diving deeper than 100 feet. The most obvious way to show a partial pressure problem is to take a look at the gas oxygen. We know that oxygen (O_2) is needed for us to live. It comprises about one-fifth, or 20 percent, of the air we normally breathe. The pressure of this air we have said is 14.7 pounds per square inch at sea level, which is our normal breathing pressure. For convenience, let's call one atmosphere equal to 15 pounds per square inch. If oxygen is one-fifth of this, then its partial pressure is equal to three pounds per square inch. It has been found by the physiologists that if the oxygen pressure reaches approximately 30 pounds per square inch (or two atmospheres), it may become a deadly gas for us to breathe. Another way to say the same thing is that if air reaches the pressure of ten atmospheres it may become a deadly mixture of gases for us to breathe due to the partial pressure of oxygen reaching 30 pounds per square inch at that point ($^1/_5$ of 150 p.s.i. = 30 p.s.i.). This is one reason why commercial divers use different gas mixtures when they do deep diving. Ten atmospheres of pressure would equal a dive of approximately 300 feet.

Another physical law that diving books like to talk about is Charles' law. It is a simple law and does not really have too much practical use to the diver. Charles said that gases expand when heated and contract when cooled. The significance of this law to the diver is that because the air in the tank is confined, it cannot expand in the tank. Therefore, instead of expanding, the pressure goes up. If the tank is left in the sun and gets hot, the pressure in the tank will increase approximately five pounds for every degree Fahrenheit rise in temperature. This increase is not important because the pressure changes under normal conditions are not great enough to affect the tank; an increase or decrease of 50° F equals an increase or decrease of approximately 250 p.s.i. in the average tank of 2,200 p.s.i. However, it does cut down the amount of pressure in the tank and therefore the volume of air available to the diver when the diver is in very cold water. When the tank is cooled to 40 or so degrees, the pressure is decreased a hundred pounds or so from normal. This lessens the diver's time on the bottom with the tank. No big deal! Just interesting!

You can use old Archimedes' law to find out what the volume of your body is if you want to. The next time someone asks you how big you are you can tell him you are 2.87 cubic feet. The way you figure your volume is simple; our physics friends have found that sea water weighs 64 pounds per cubic foot. Archimedes discovered that when an object floats in water it pushes aside or displaces its own weight in water. All you have to do is check your buoyancy as described in Chapter 3 until you reach a point where you are in equilibrium. Then weigh yourself, and divide your weight by 64. The answer will be the number of cubic feet your body displaces. In fresh water such as a lake or a pool you can't use 64 because fresh water isn't as heavy as salt water. In fresh water you must use 62.4. A cubic foot of fresh water weighs that many pounds. A totally useless fact, but fun. I personally am proud to say that I take up 3.1 cubic feet of the ocean every time I go diving.

There are a few more interesting facts that a diver should be aware of. One such fact is that water carries heat away from the body much faster than air does. If you were to stand nude in 32° air you would be cold, but could hop around a bit and last a long time. In 32° water you would be unconscious in just a few minutes, and would die shortly thereafter. This is why we consider 70° a good air temperature, but not a good water temperature. My ice-diving friends are shouting great profanities at me about now. They think that 45° water is warm. As Einstein said, "All things are relative."

In the performance physiology lab at UCLA, Dr. Glen Egstrom and Dr. Weltman have performed some experiments in cold water that show there is a memory loss when the diver is exposed to cold water. It seems that the mind forgets even simple instructions, which makes any job, no matter how simple, a rather difficult chore. This particular loss of memory brings on in the diver a type of inner frustration so that he doesn't really care just what he is doing. It has been termed by some as the "what-the-hell syndrome."

7

HYPERBARIC MEDICINE—WOW!

Medical problems for the diver are like accident problems for the motorist. There are so many possibilities that it would be impossible to name them all in several volumes. Luckily, as for the motorist, most of the more common possible accidents can be grouped into basic cause groupings. For the motorist they would be, for example, following too closely, excessive speed, changing lanes, driver error, and equipment failure. For the diver we could generalize diver error, marine life, equipment failure, and pressure-related conditions.

There is a word which you should know at the outset so you will sound knowledgeable in the field of Hyperbaric (more than normal atmospheric pressure) Medicine. The word is "barotrauma." Barotrauma is any injury caused to the tissue by a pressure change. It is a good word to drop now and then, as in: "It sounds like barotrauma to me!!" Or, instead of saying your ears hurt and you had to equalize, you could say, "I sensed an approaching barotrauma as I descended. I pressed my digits to my nose and relaxed my diaphragm. Gas rushed through my cranial labyrinth to cause a homeostatic condition behind my tympanic membrane. Thus, the pending barotrauma was averted." Your diver friends won't know what you said because most divers have only a 600-word vocabulary anyway, but your nondiver friends sure will be impressed. Be careful about the backgrounds of the people to whom you are talking, however, as they will interpret things differently depending on their personal experience. For example, if you were to say "bull shit" to a sailing enthusiast and did not pronounce your words carefully, he would think you were talking about a line with which you lead a bull around. Pick your audience. It's ridiculous to use big words on someone who doesn't know enough to be impressed!

You have now been exposed to three terms which you must know in order to be a diver. To review them, not necessarily in order of importance, they are: hyperbaric medicine, barotrauma, and bull shit! All very important to the diver! I will try to give you enough information on hyperbaric medicine and barotrauma so that you can tell your diving friends "bull shit" when they come up with some of their wild stories.

In this chapter I will touch briefly on diver error and equipment failure as causes of diving accidents, describe in some detail a number of pressure-related hazards, then discuss several female problems and their effect on the diver. The more common sea life hazards are dealt with in Chapter 9 and so will not be considered here except to remind you always to check with local divers for their particular local "no-no's." A comprehensive outline of diving diseases and accidents and general first-aid procedures are presented in Appendices H and I.

• DIVER ERROR AND EQUIPMENT FAILURE

Diver error, the first major cause of diving medical problems, is best avoided by being truly objective about your ability. Make sure you understand your physical condition and the difference between the end of last summer and the beginning of this one. Go back to Chapter 4 and review the basic diving skills so you know your memory hasn't slipped. Sometimes our mind remembers—it's just that our body seems to forget!

Equipment failure does not seem to be much of a problem. If you are diving less than 60 feet and keep cool you can get out of practically any trouble you can get into due to equipment failure. The exception here is the situation in which you have restricted your ascent path, as for instance in places such as caves, wrecks, and ice. A diver can make it up from 60 feet and shallower depths quite easily, so dive where you belong and you won't have to worry much about equipment failure.

• PRESSURE-RELATED HAZARDS

You will recall that barotrauma injuries are pressure differential related hazards. Depending on where the injury occurs, we have different names for the condition. These names, although they sometimes seem long and complicated, generally give the precise location of the problem in Latin.

One type of barotrauma is referred to as a "squeeze." Squeezes can occur on the face (mask squeeze), in the middle ear (aerotitis media), the lungs (thoracic squeeze), the sinuses (such as maxillary sinus squeeze), and any other place where air is trapped, such as under a dry suit. The mechanism causing damage is the same in all cases—unequal pressure.

Let's take a look at the two most common squeezes; from these, you should be able to understand something about the others.

Mask Squeeze

Mask squeeze is common with the new diver. The general symptom is the feeling that your face is being pushed out into your mask, and that's exactly what is happening. As the pressure builds up on the diver during his descents, the airspace in the mask becomes a low pressure area. The skin on the face, being rather plastic or flexible, is pushed out to help fill the low pressure area. All the diver has to do to stop the condition is increase the pressure under the mask so that it equals the pressure on the outside.

Blowing air out of the nose is the simplest way to achieve this equal pressure. Humming will do it nicely. If for some reason the diver gets a severe mask squeeze, the small capillaries of the eye will rupture and the eyes will turn bright red. This condition has been called "cherry eye syndrome." It will go away in a few months and is guaranteed to make you a hit at every party! One look at your bright red eyeballs and everyone will throw up and go home.

Cold compresses seem to be the best treatment for mask squeezes. Apply the compress to the injured area and relax—that's all you can do for it.

Aerotitis Media

Aerotitis media is just a fancy name for middle ear squeeze. This is one that we all encounter every time we go diving. Water pressure builds up pressure on the outside of the eardrum and we must "equalize" to stop the uneven pressure from hurting the eardrum.

On the inside of the eardrum there is an airspace called the middle ear. Having air on both sides of the rather delicate eardrum allows it to vibrate. The middle ear airspace is good for hearing but poor for diving. The air pocket acts like the air in the mask. It becomes a relative vacuum as the pressure increases around it if more air is not added to bring up the pressure until it is "equalized" with the tissue around it. In the mask we use the nose to inject air into the chamber; in the ear we use a small (sometimes too small) tube that runs from the middle ear to the throat, called the "Eustachian tube." There is one on either side of the throat so each ear has its own personal duct for air passage. The Eustachian tubes are important to avert barotrauma of the middle ear.

In the case of ear squeeze there is great pain right from the onset of pressure change. This pain is good because it warns the diver he must equalize or he will do damage to his eardrum. What would happen if the diver ignored this pain and continued to descend without clearing? Very simply, the eardum will stretch to its capacity and then tear. We call this a ruptured eardrum. When this happens, water goes through the hole and equalizes the pressure. This would be okay except for a few other considerations.

Obviously, if the eardrum is torn, you can't hear well until it is repaired. A visit to your mechanic (doctor) will generally, along with six to ten weeks of time, take care of the repair job.

What happens if your intelligence level is high enough so that you stop your descent when you first feel the pain? In this case the eardrum would not have holes in it but, if you allowed the pain to get rather intense, you will have a swelling of the eardrum from the distention which was forced upon it. Your hearing will be impaired for a few days; generally things will sound as if you're in a barrel, but this effect goes away in a few days and you are fine. Swelling of the eardrum is a common occurrence.

After the diver puts his eardrum through this a few hundred times, it will begin to lose some of its elasticity. The result will be a hearing loss of 5 to 20 percent, or even more in severe cases. That is why old-time divers say "huh?" a lot.

Up to this point we have taken pains to motivate the diver into doing the right thing, but now we are going to enter into an area of judgment.

Good judgment is needed to avoid what is known as a "reverse block." Everyone says that you shouldn't dive if you have a cold or are congested for any other reason. The reason for this is not obvious until you put some of our basic information from several different areas together. Congestion causes excessive mucus and phlegm on the mucus membrane of the respiratory tract. This excess mucus could easily cause a plug in the small Eustachian tubes which would cause nonpassage of air, preventing equalization of the middle ear.

We mentioned earlier that the scuba regulator gives us air under ambient pressure. This means that the air we breathe while we are diving is at the same pressure as the water pressure around us. Groovy! Now, the judgment. You have a cold. You want to dive. Your friends are all there getting ready for the dive and you decide to go. At that moment you blew it.

The next couple of events seem okay. You clear your ears at your descent, a little more difficult than normal, but no big deal, and have a great dive with your friends. The dive is so great that you stretch it out until your underwater pressure gauge says only 200 psi of air left. Time to come up and have a beer.

You start for the surface and, ouch, pain in the ear. You are running out of air, you have to come up, but the pain gets more severe as you do. If you are lucky, there will be a squeaking sound and a rush of air in your head, and all will be okay. If you are not lucky, your eardrum will rupture from the inside out on the way up. (A good reason for a J valve, so you won't run your air too low on your way up.)

What happened is simple. Your ears cleared on the way down then, due to the congestion, the physical change due to your dive, and any number of other possibilities such as a bounce-back reaction from some drug like antihistamine that you were dumb enough to take, the Eustachian tube plugged up while you were down. When you started up, the pressure on the inside couldn't get out and ruptured the eardrum outward. Don't get caught in this trap. It's a painful one, and "common horse sense," as my mother used to say, "is the best solution to the problem." Another good rule is not to take any medication while diving, unless prescribed by a doctor *who understands diving.*

There are other squeezes that react in a similar manner, such as sinus squeezes. What we said about the ear is mostly true for the sinuses also. If you are congested, try just snorkling for the day; you will still enjoy yourself. A word of caution about your ears. Don't try a bunch of home remedies on them. Many divers rinse the ears with alcohol when they finish a dive. This is good for the ear. A disinfectant rinse is not a bad idea, but alcohol dries out the tissue, which is what we want. Check with your doctor about what, if anything, to use. I personally use an 80 percent hydrogen peroxide-20 percent glycerine solution. I don't know if it is harmful or not. The doctors I have talked to don't seem to think it is, and I have had no trouble using it; but, on the other hand, I do say "huh?" a lot! Perhaps some doctor with greater insight and experience with the problem is bouncing off the walls about now. I would much appreciate the formula for a better ear wash (free, of course) from anyone with the wisdom to have worked one out. Anyway—check with your doctor. He's your best bet.

Respiratory Barotrauma

The chest, which contains the lungs, is also an airspace, so barotrauma can take place here also. The problems which occur here are generally more serious than the ones we have been discussing.

There are two main considerations which make respiratory barotraumas very bad. First, they concern a vital organ for life, the lungs. Secondly, there are few pain sensors in this area to warn you that you may have a pending problem. It is possible to do irrevocable damage to the vital organs and feel no pain at all.

Consequently, we are now discussing a problem area which can cause death without warning. Pay attention! The danger arises when the air in the lungs reaches a higher pressure than the outside pressure (lung tissue, in the area where the actual gas transfer of oxygen and CO_2 takes place, is very thin). The two ways in which a diver can incur damage to his lung area are by holding his breath as he ascends, allowing the air inside to expand and over-inflate the delicate tissue as the pressure outside drops, and, secondly, having a bronchial tube clog from congestion. The latter situation, although uncommon, can have the same effect as the former, though in a smaller area. These maladies only exist when using pressured air, such as scuba or surface-supplied air. There are other ways to take in pressured air; for example, breathing out of an air pocket in a wreck or cave, but these are rare enough not to consider here.

Both of these usual causes of lung damage are easily avoided. Always breathe normally on ascent and never hold your breath under pressured air breathing conditions. Never dive when congested, and always come up slowly to give the air a chance to escape.

Now that we know the causes and preventions of respiratory barotrauma, let's take a look at its symptoms and treatment. If the injury actually occurs and the lungs rupture, air will escape. It has two places to go: first, into the thoracic cavity and, second, into the blood. Where it goes depends on where and how the puncture happens. If the air escapes into the thoracic cavity, the symptoms will vary depending on what area the air escapes into. It is possible that the air could escape and be trapped in the cardiac area. If this happens, the bubble could put pressure on the heart and possibly cause heart failure. The problem is compounded because, as the diver comes up, the air bubble will expand due to the lowering of the pressure and become much larger than it was when it first escaped. This air in the central chest is called a mediastinum pneumothorax, and also puts pressure on the heart. If the air escapes to the general pleural cavity (the cavity in which the lungs are located) the expanding bubble could very easily collapse a lung.

Sometimes the bubble gets loose in the thoracic cavity and causes a lump in the throat area. This condition is generally called a pneumothorax and can be treated only by a doctor. He will generally puncture the body and simply let the trapped air out. This has been known to cause a slight bit of discomfort for the diver. It has been said by the wise men that an intelligent organism can stand pain, but that he avoids it whenever possible. Next time you have pain in your ears or any other part of your body, think of the wise men!

If the air escapes into the blood, the problem is even more serious. This will cause a condition known as air embolism. Embolism means a blockage. In this case the air bubbles travel via the arteries to the small capillaries, where they tend to stop the passage of blood and thus oxygen transport. The insidious aspect of this blockage is that the nerve tissue in the brain is very susceptible to lack of oxygen, and in about four to seven minutes the cells will die. If you have a *very* minor embolism, you will just get a little dumber, but normally this condition is not minor and the patient dies.

We used to think that air embolism was the major cause of diving deaths, but upon recent analysis we find that plain old-fashioned drowning seems to be the leader. Nevertheless, the fact that the breath must never be held while diving with scuba gear cannot be overemphasized. The treatment for air embolism is a recompression chamber. By increasing the pressure we can squeeze the bubbles down to a small enough size that they will pass through the capillaries. All you have to do is get the victim into a chamber in less than four minutes and down to pressure. Not too practical. Just avoid it (*don't hold your breath!*); it's much simpler!

The Bends

The next item to consider is what is commonly called "the bends." We discussed the bends in Chapter 2 and how they were discovered in construction workers many years ago, so we can limit the discussion here to what happens to the body.

The bends is a malady which is related to a time-depth curve. If the diver stays beyond a certain time at any given depth, he will more than likely have a problem. The decompression tables the Navy developed have been used for years. They are not designed for much of the diving the sports diver does, but they are the best we have at present.

The Navy tables were developed by and for Navy divers. Navy divers are, in general, leaner and in better shape than most civilian divers. The Navy also says that men over forty-five don't dive. We know that there is no safety factor built into the diving tables even for the Navy diver. It would only stand to reason that for fatter (fat tissue takes up and holds nitrogen five times more efficiently than most other tissue) and more out-of-condition individuals (being out-of-condition slows the circulation, helping to bring on the bends), the tables are even less safe. For activities such as ice diving in which the cold water causes a major physiological change in metabolism, and altitude diving such as in Lake Tahoe in California where the difference in atmospheric pressure changes all of the partial pressures, the Navy standard tables are not even in the ballpark.

Unfortunately, there are no tables that are accurate. Many people, some in rather high positions, claim to have worked out special tables to handle these situations. They don't understand the problem. You can't just take the standard table and throw in a factor and come out heads up. The metabolic curves don't react that way. What these people have done is to create a safety factor on the standard table that fits their circumstances, and then tried it. They weren't bent, so they figure they have a winner. For them, in that particular circumstance, it may be. For you, it may not be. The person who thinks he has a perfect high altitude diving table is ignorant of the problems; however, there have been some sharp troops who have made their own table for altitude which seems to be fairly safe for them to dive in lieu of nothing else. Hopefully, someday someone will have the time and expertise to do it right.

What are the variables that give us the problem? There are so many that we will mention only a few here in an effort to get across the idea of the complexities involved. The major variables, ás I see them, are temperature (particularly extremes of cold or heat), anxiety, fluid content of the body, physical condition, and workload.

To see how these things affect the diver, we must have a basic understanding of how the bends come about.

We all know that gases dissolve in liquids. If this were not so, there would be no life in the sea because there would be no oxygen dissolved in the water for marine life to respire. The bends is a direct result of the solubility of gases—the solubility of nitrogen in particular if we are diving with straight air for a breathing gas. If we are on mixed gas, then the inert gas used in the mixture is of concern.

The readers of this book should all be air breathers, so we will concern ourselves with the dissolved nitrogen. Decompression sickness, which is really what the bends are, is caused by having so much nitrogen dissolved in the blood that it cannot be disposed of by the body in a normal manner. The amount of nitrogen which dissolves in the blood is directly proportional to a time-depth curve. In other words, the deeper you go, the more pressure your body is under. Therefore, at any given depth the rate of nitrogen flow from the air in the lungs through the lung tissue into the blood and the tissues of the body is proportional to this increase in pressure. The rate of flow is not as great under the pressure of 50 feet as it is under the pressure of 75 feet, and so on. It therefore takes longer for the diver to absorb a dangerous amount of nitrogen at 50 feet than it does at 75 feet.

Because of this differential in the amount of nitrogen dissolved in the blood in any given time period at each depth, the important thing to consider is the time spent at the depth of the dive.

In Chapter 5 we discussed the Navy No Decompression Table, which tells the diver how long he can stay at any given depth without taking up a dangerous amount of nitrogen. This is the table for the sports diver to live by. It is simple to read and simple to follow. The only hang-up is that, using this table alone, a diver can only dive one tank of air in any 12-hour period. If he stays too long on any air dive and exceeds the time allowed on the No Decompression Table *or* makes several dives, the accumulated nitrogen in his blood will be more than can come out via the lungs, like it went in. When this happens, the excess nitrogen forms small bubbles as the pressure is released on ascent and the bubbles are the causative factor in the symptoms which designate the bends.

These symptoms can be very slight or very severe. The main symptoms of the

95

bends are: a prickly or itching sensation on the skin, a mottled skin rash, excessive fatigue after the dive, muscle weakness, paralysis, pain in the limbs, numbness, convulsions, vomiting and, in extreme cases, death. The rash, itching, and fatigue will generally go away in a few hours. The other symptoms need treatment by a chamber and a physician (*as soon as possible*) who understands the problems. The average M.D. is of little use in a bends case because he has had no experience with them. Seek out a diving doctor. Normally 85 percent of the symptoms will show during the first hour. Ninety-five percent will show within three hours. In very rare cases a lag of 24 hours goes by before the onset of symptoms.

We have said that these symptoms are caused by the formation of bubbles in the blood and tissues. It is interesting to note that the nitrogen is absorbed more slowly in areas of poor circulation, such as fat. Conversely, nitrogen comes out of the body more slowly from areas of poor circulation. Any condition which slows the circulation or thickens the blood will make an individual more susceptible to the bends. It is a good bet to drink a lot of water before a dive and immediately after to keep the blood as fluid as possible. Beer and coffee are not particularly good to drink because they act as diuretics and thus are not efficient.

The actual formation of bubbles depends on many things. One we can mention here is the total pressure of the gases in the body. If the diver has been working hard, the CO_2 in his body will be higher. If the CO_2 is high, it will form very small bubbles which seem to act as seeds to start formation of the larger nitrogen bubbles. Because of this, a diver should totally relax for a few breaths before he starts up. This will expel excess CO_2 and stop the seed formation of nitrogen.

We said earlier that there were many variables. The most important seem to be those which impair circulation. An injury such as a sprain, or any swelling in the body, is an example. Cold water which causes a shunting of blood away from certain areas of the body is another. Older people have poorer circulation in general and should not push it.

Heavy drinking before a dive (for example, the night before) causes diuresis, which thickens the blood and is very bad. All I can say is let common sense and not peer pressure or ego plan your dive, and you will not have bends problems.

There are other problems which could arise, such as oxygen poisoning. This is rare and is discussed in Appendix H so we will not discuss it here.

Carbon monoxide (CO) poisoning is not rare, though the majority of divers think it is. Most books say that CO poisoning is the result of bad air. This is correct. The example of the air intake on the compressor being located where it will pick up exhaust fumes from a gas engine is generally given. However, the average diver gets his CO poisoning from a different source.

Let's take a look at the mechanism of the condition. The blood contains a pigment called hemoglobin which carries oxygen and CO_2 back and forth between the lungs to the tissue. Some oxygen is carried in the plasma (liquid protein of the blood), but not enough to sustain life, except in one family of fishes that live in the

Antarctic. Our stamina, therefore, depends a great deal on the efficiency of our oxygen transport system to the tissues of the body. If we are exposed to CO, a chemical change takes place in our blood. The physiologists call the condition "carboxy hemoglobin," a long word meaning "bad news." Here is what happens.

When CO is inhaled into the lungs, it moves across the lung wall into the blood like any other gas, except that it has a stronger tie with hemoglobin than oxygen has. The CO will take the place of the oxygen on the hemoglobin and render that particular red blood corpuscle useless to our oxygen transport system. When this happens even to a handful of red corpuscles, our efficiency is cut down. A concentration of only .4 percent in the air we breathe will cause serious symptoms if breathed for a period of one hour. The reason for the time element is that the effect is cumulative.

Now, why are most of the books mistaken when they say CO poisoning is very rare? Simple. They are only considering the severe cases which need treatment. They are not considering the impaired efficiency of the person who is a "little" poisoned.

How do you get a "little" poisoned? Very easily. All you have to do is live in the smog belt of any large city, or travel a while on a congested freeway, or smoke cigarettes. The person who smokes cigarettes lives in a perpetual state of semi-efficiency and mild CO poisoning. The air inhaled through a cigarette is the direct product of combustion and is very high in CO. As fast as the body can make new, fresh hemoglobin, the smoker renders it useless. What it amounts to is that if you don't mind working at less than your innate ability, then smoke. If I were an employer, I would want to hire someone who could work at his peak ability. A smoker can't do that. Think about it.

Inert Gas Narcosis

The inert gas in the air we divers breathe is nitrogen, under most circumstances. The air is about 79 percent nitrogen. It has been noted that when the body is subjected to high pressure, the increase in partial pressure of nitrogen or any other inert gas will cause what has been termed "rapture of the deep." The heavier the gas the faster the effect seems to take hold. Helium is used instead of nitrogen for deep dives because it is much lighter and rapture of the deep comes on at a much deeper depth than with nitrogen. We will concern ourselves with normal air, and thus nitrogen.

The exact mechanism of what happens to the body physiology is not completely understood. There are several theories which do not warrant time here. The symptoms, however, are very important to recognize. They normally occur in the area of 100 feet; some feel it shallower, some deeper. The normal signs of narcosis are a numb tongue and lips, musical bubbles (your bubbles sound like they are being played by an orchestra), general euphoria and, in more severe cases, loss of manual dexterity. The reasoning ability of the diver is hampered, and he will start to make rather poor decisions.

At 200 feet everyone is affected and some *very* poor decisions could be made—decisions such as not to come up when you know you are low on air. The sensation is similar to that of being on a very happy drunk or a good trip. The effects of the narcosis, however, can be much more dramatic because a slight error in judgment at depth could be fatal.

Any dive below 150 feet *will* affect the diver. Any dive below 100 feet *may* very well affect him, one more reason why deep diving is very foolish.

When the diver feels the effects of narcosis, he should ascend. As soon as the pressure on the body drops, the effects go away.

What it all comes down to is: stay relaxed, breathe at a normal rate, don't dive below 100 feet, keep watch on your bottom time—and you "can't hardly go wrong"!

• MS. DIVER

There is another area of diving medicine generally overlooked in the books which is of great interest and importance to at least one group of divers in our midst. We might call it the area of female problems and their effect on the woman diver. The one that causes the most concern seems to be how the menstrual flow will affect the shark population of the area. Every woman who considers diving has also considered the attraction that blood has for sharks. As Dr. Woodruff put it at the Third International Conference on Underwater Education held in Dallas, Texas, in 1971, the woman in her period doing a giant stride entry off the back of a boat is sure there is a great white shark waiting right there to gobble her up. In reality, the blood flow impeded by the usual absorptive measures is so small that it wouldn't make any difference anyway.

There is, however, the problem of the mess involved with water-soaked sanitary napkins or tampons of any kind. The girl diver can avoid this, if it is too much for her, by using one of the rubber cups she can obtain from her local drugstore which traps the flow and holds it until a more convenient time without any mess at all. If our girl has cramps or is "sick," then she should not dive anyway. A normal menstrual period is no reason not to dive.

Should a pregnant woman dive? Pregnancy is, again, not a sickness. It is a normal condition. If there are no complications, the girl should be able to dive just as she did before she became pregnant. She will have to avoid stress situations such as heavy surf, but little else will change. If she was not a diver before she got pregnant, then she should wait until she is not pregnant to take lessons and learn. A pregnancy is not a particularly good time to take on a new sport, but she should be

The Ama divers of Japan have been harvesting the sea for over 100 years. These women are among the greatest breath-hold divers in the world.

This lady says diving keeps her young. She claims to be the oldest active woman diver on the West Coast.

able to continue doing the things she is used to doing. The pregnant woman should consult her doctor. Realize, however, that most doctors are completely ignorant of diving and the types of stress it puts on the body. They live in great unwarranted fear of an unknown, like your next-door neighbor who is not a diver, and because of this some of them will say "no diving" just to cover their ignorance. If your doctor simply says "no diving," then consult a doctor who dives. He will at least be realistic. Further information for lady divers may be found in Appendix J, "What Every Girl Should Know About Diving."

8

NEPTUNE'S WORLD

Because of its great expanse of scenery and animal life, the ocean is where better than 90 percent of all diving occurs. There are some basic understandings of the ocean as it relates to the diver that can help us enjoy our dives, reduce the effort they require, and insure our safety in the ocean.

Talking about the ocean is difficult because it is so variable depending on where you happen to be. Off British Columbia the ocean is cold, and calm normally, with some hellish currents that take knowledge and skill to navigate. Off Southern California the ocean is moderate in temperature but the surf gives special and real problems. In the ocean off Florida the extreme clarity of the water can present safety problems to divers not used to it. Realizing that the ocean is different everywhere, let's talk about some general things that a diver should be aware of, and some of the specific factors involved in them. There are so many topics we could discuss that we will have to limit ourselves to the more important ones: the land-water interphase, currents, clarity, and basic location awareness.

With over 80 percent of everything alive on earth now living in the sea, there are thousands of breathtaking sights to see and enjoy. This school of silvery fish is in perfect unison, all eyes studying the diver as the diver is studying them.

• THE EDGE OF THE SEA

When a diver decides to visit Mother Ocean (if we exclude boats from our discussion), he walks, crawls, or stumbles across land and into the water. (All three are acceptable under certain conditions.) The important thing is to be tuned into the particular situation you are dealing with in every case.

Entries and exits are worthy of attention for several reasons. First, if you have trouble getting in or out, you get excessively fatigued. Secondly, your ability at entries and exits seems to be a fair indication of your competence as a diver.

When discussing entries into the water it is easy to fall into the trap of stereotyping the kinds of entries and surface dives. For years now we have learned just how to hold each part of our body as we make a particular "entry" into the pool. When we go into the ocean or any other body of open water, the situation is generally quite different from that presented by the pool. Our pool entry does not seem quite right so we change it a little, or a lot. Why stereotype at all?

There are two entries into the water from the side of a pool or "anything similar," the front entry and the back entry. A few basics remain the same in any entry, and these the diver *must* know and do instinctively.

1. Hold the mask in place with your hand. The best way is to standardize by placing the right hand with the palm directly over the nose, the fingers spread out over the top of the mask and the thumb under the lower edge. The hand then holds the mask in place *and* covers the glass in case the diver slips and falls into the water in a face-flop position, which could break the glass in his face.
2. Check the water carefully before you jump in. Make sure it is deep enough so that you won't hit bottom.
3. Have all of your gear in place and checked out before you make the entry.
4. If you want to stay shallow when you jump in, spread out your arms and legs as you hit. You'll stop right on the surface. If you are going in from an awkward place such as a small boat, just roll over the side in a little ball.

On any entry the important things are to hold everything in place, to make sure the entry area is safe, and to hit the water in such a way that you do not hurt yourself. The ocean entry situations most commonly found are sand and rock entries. On a sand entry, the diver just walks out, puts his fins on, and enters. If it is a no-surf entry, he walks out until he is waist deep, puts his fins on and swims out. If there is surf he puts his fins on, enters the water in a backward shuffle, then swims out. If rocks are present, however, a different approach is required. A rock entry is not more difficult than a regular surf entry, just different.

103

What Is Surf?

Before going further in our discussion of ocean entries, we have to come to terms with surf. An oceanographer will tell you that surf is a wave that gets its bottom hung up and the top of it spilled over. To really understand what happens would take a lengthy explanation. You can get the general idea without going too deeply into the physics just by knowing a few facts. Some of the terms you have to know are wavelength and wave height. The wavelength is the distance *between* two waves. If you measured from the top of one swell to the top of the following swell, you would be determining wavelength. If you measured from the top of a swell to the bottom of the trough, you would be determining wave height.

The wavelength is important because the water will move back and forth at depth as the wave passes overhead. This movement is called the "surge" because the water surges one way then surges back. The deeper a diver goes, the less surge there is. The surge will generally become negligible at a depth of one-half the wavelength. Knowing this, a diver can stand on the beach, look out at the ocean, and tell what the surge conditions will be before he goes in. If the surge is going to be heavy and the bottom is sand, then why go in? The ocean will be dirty.

The wave height is important because a wave will have sufficient drag on the bottom that the top will fall over, making white water surf, when the water is about the same depth as the height of the wave. A six-foot wave will thus break in approximately six feet of water. A diver can tell how deep the water is as he watches the surf. Observing wave height is also a good way to spot reefs and sand bars that lie off shore.

Surf Entries

To a person who has never been in surf, a wall of white, rushing, tumbling, churning water four feet high advancing rapidly toward his body is a horrifying experience. The same breaker to a beach kid means "lots of fun." He can dive under it, ride it to shore, let it tumble him like a rag doll, or stand there and see if he can withstand the impact.

To someone raised in an area where there is surf, it poses no problems. He accepts it, he understands it, and he has no fear of it. He appears to just walk into it, and swims away with such ease you can't believe your eyes. You think to yourself, "There is nothing to it." You pick up your gear, walk into it, get knocked down, rolled around, and finally crawl up on the beach wondering "what happened." Surf entries are easy if you remember a few rules:

1. Never stand up in the surf.
2. Get through the surf line as fast as you can. Don't stop to adjust something halfway through.
3. Never let a breaker catch you broadside. Be either head into it or feet into it so you will not be rolled sideways.

4. Hold your mask on with your hand every time a breaker goes over you. It will come off if you don't.
5. Always go *under* a wave, never over it. Remember, the force of a breaker is *on top*. If you dive under the white water, the force is far less.
6. Once you start out or in, don't stop until you are clear of the surf.

Simple rules, but they *must* be followed.

The answer to the surf problem is to play in it until you are not afraid. A diver should not tackle surf that is heavier than he feels confident in, and he should never go diving through the surf if frightened. Unless he is confident of his ability to handle it, he will panic very quickly if he should lose a fin, mask, or get tumbled. The surf is a special environment and must be treated as one. It falls in the same category as kelp. Perfectly safe as long as you understand it.

Surf entries are variable because surf conditions are so variable. There are three basic ways to enter the surf and as many variations as there are breakers:

1. All gear on and in place. The diver walks backwards into the surf because he has his fins on, and cannot walk frontwards well. He keeps a close watch on the surf by looking behind him as he enters so a wave does not sneak up and knock him down. This is a good entry when the beach is steep and the break zone (area of white water) small.
2. All gear on and in place. The diver gets on his hands and knees and crawls into the water. As soon as the water is a foot or so deep, he starts to swim with his fins and "dog paddle" with his hands. This type of entry is sometimes called a "polliwog." It is a good entry if the bottom is rocky and irregular.
3. All gear in place except the fins which are held in the hand. The diver walks in frontwards until he gets waist or chest deep, then puts on his fins and swims out. This is a good entry if the slope of the beach is slight and there is a long surf line. The diver must remember to use a "shuffle"-type step as he goes out so he will not step on a stingray.
   A variation of this entry which is worth mentioning is used by experienced divers in a steep beach situation with a large crashing single surf break. The diver waits, fins in hand, for the break then *runs* into the surf as the water rushes back from the breaker, dives under the next breaker, puts one fin on (which should take no longer than 4 or 5 seconds), and swims out on his back kicking with one fin while pulling on the other. This is a good entry if the diver is competent and used to the surf. It is the fastest and easiest way to "punch" through the surf.

Diving through surf is not difficult or dangerous if done properly. Put your fins on, leave your mask off, and practice. It's a lot of fun.

Surf exits are the same as entries. Generally you should come out of the water

Small boats that can be launched through the surf are a must in some areas where the diver must travel to reefs that lie too far offshore to swim to safely.

the same way you go in. If in doubt, keep swimming until you "bottom out," stand up, and *walk out backwards* until you are clear of the water. Again, once you have committed yourself, swim hard until you are clear out, and don't forget to hold onto your mask.

Rock Entries

Rocky areas often make for interesting diving. The water is clearer than in other areas, with less sand to obscure the diver's view, and with great variety of life forms that make their homes in and around the shelter of rocks.

Rock entries are fairly individual, depending on the particular spot and water conditions. However, there are a few general rules that should be followed:

1. Do not *walk* into water with a rocky bottom. Swim as soon as the water is 18 inches deep or even less.
2. Never let the water drag you across the rocks. Hang on tightly to the rocks when the surge goes in or out. Don't let your body be rolled over them.
3. Time your entries so you go in when the water is high (at the top of a surge). You can then swim out with the water as it runs back.
4. Time your exits so the surge brings you high on the rocks, then *HANG ON* with everything you've got so you are not dragged out when the water runs back. As soon as the water has receded *scramble out fast*, before the next wave comes in.

Barnacles, common in rocky areas, are a hazard the entering or exiting diver should not underestimate. Their sharp, jagged edges can inflict painful wounds that infect easily.

The diver who tries to walk in over rocks which are a foot or two underwater will end up with a cut foot or broken leg. Generally, the best way to enter over a rocky bottom is to crawl on all fours until your body floats and you can kick your way out using your hands to protect your face plate. This can be done quite easily even in moderately heavy surf. If there is deep water next to the rock you are going to enter from, then the entry is as easy as your timing is good. To enter into deep water, the diver waits for the water to rise (assuming there is a surge action with the water rushing in and out) then jumps in on the high water and is sucked right out away from the rock with the water as it rushes back. Coming in takes the same type of timing. The diver waits just far enough from the rock that he won't get bashed on it when the water rushes in but close enough so that when the rush comes he can swim hard and come up with it to the highest part of the rock he can grab. *Now the most important part:* He must hold onto the rock like glue. If he allows himself to be pulled away by the water as it recedes, he will get cut up by barnacles. He must *hang on.* As soon as the water is gone he then scrambles to the high ground before the next wave comes in. It sounds like more work than it is. If you dive in this type of environment your instructor will show you how it is done. If you visit this type of area to dive, then have someone who is experienced show you the proper timing.

Mud Entries

Mud is not a normal entry in most ocean areas but does occur in freshwater

107

lakes. I once had the experience of diving in a lake in Texas and did not realize that the bottom was soft mud. My Texas "friends" led me to the water's edge and suggested that I "walk out and take a look." I took two steps off the bank and was in mud up to my knees. I looked around to find my "friends" rolling on the bank with laughter. They finally helped me out and brought to my attention several times that day "how dumb California divers were to walk out in the mud." Some day I'll get even.

When entering a muddy area the idea is to stay off the bottom so you won't muck up the water. The best method is to swim as soon as possible and try not to touch the bottom or kick hard so the fins won't stir up the mud.

Surface Dives

The ocean is ever-changing so our ways of entering it must be ever-changing. We are not going to be concerned here with the "names" of each kind of surface dive, or, for that matter, all the different kinds. Let's break down surface dives into their basics and then let *you*, the diver, put the basics together in a personalized group of dives that work well for you, rather than trying to mold you into the methods used in the Red Cross book that wasn't written for diving.

All surface dives have some common denominators. These must be kept in mind so you can "build" your own set of dives.

1. A dive should be as quiet as possible. All dives should avoid splash and commotion if you want the fish to stay near.
2. The body should be trim. In other words, the body and whatever equipment is being used should be held in such a position as to cause as little drag as possible. Little things make a big difference, such as pointing a spear gun at the bottom as you dive instead of holding it in the middle, and making sure your toes are pointed so your fins will cut the water cleanly instead of acting as brakes.
3. The diver must be weighted properly to dive *well*. A diver who is two pounds light will have trouble diving. Your buoyancy must be *exact* for optimum performance, and if you accept less than optimum performance from yourself, then there is not much anyone can do for you.
4. As little effort as possible should be expended. The dive should be a slow, relaxed, controlled sinking. Not the fast, thrashing that you normally see. Every molecule of oxygen that you don't use getting down will let you stay down longer. Complete relaxation is the key.

There are basically two kinds of dives, head first and feet first. The headfirst dive should be used 99.99 percent of the time when breath-hold diving, and the feet-first dive should be used 99.99 percent of the time when you are scuba diving.

The diver must be careful with all head-first entries. The diver above is going to hit the water at a bad angle and will probably knock his mask off. This type of entry is normally done only by actors making movies, or hot shots impressing their girl friends.

A back roll entry from a boat. The diver sits on the edge of a low-draft boat, holds his mask with his left hand and his regulator with his right, and falls back over the edge of the boat. Care must be taken with this and all entries that the water is clear of other divers or obstacles, and that the diver's fins do not get caught on something in the boat.

The headfirst dive is used by breath-hold divers because it allows for a faster descent and constant eye contact with where you want to go. If you were to use a feet-first dive you would have to stop your descent, turn around, and then proceed. Your stay underwater would be cut considerably.

The feet-first dive should be used by scuba divers because it acts as a good check on their weighting, keeps the head in an upright position for easy ear clearing, takes less energy, and keeps the exhaust valve in the regulator in the right position for clearing water out of it.

It is indeed unfortunate that someone a long time ago named the feet-first dive "the kelp dive." I've seen a lot of seals come up into kelp, but I've never seen one do a "feet-first" dive. They just nose over and go down. A breath-hold diver should be just as trim. The idea of having a whole arsenal of equipment (camera, spear gun, goody bag, bulky depth gauge, knife on the belt or on the outside of the leg instead of on the inside of the leg where it belongs) is ridiculous and unsafe. The diver should wear only what he needs to do *the job* he sets out to do. It's fun to spearfish, take pictures, collect shells, and catch lobsters, but do them one at a time and you will do a better job and do it more safely. With scuba you are not trim because of the tank, so you would do a feet-first dive, but then you should anyway no matter where you are.

Remember, when you dive, don't splash, don't use any energy, and be trim.

Kelp

In some areas of the world the seaweed, or kelp, grows into thick underwater forests. These forests have the grandeur of the great redwoods, the strange shapes of the bristlecone pine, the mystic quality as you swim through them of a

Kelp is a good hunting-ground for the underwater photographer.

snow-covered grove of evergreens. Kelp grows from a "holdfast" system that holds it to the rocks on the bottom. Along its stalk as it grows are little gas-filled bladders that lift the stalk towards the surface. The stalk is composed of small strands the size of your finger, each strand being lifted from a common holdfast to the surface by its system of bladders. Some stalks have a hundred or more strands and are three feet in diameter. When they reach the surface they fan out or lie with the current and float on the surface where they can pick up sunlight for photosynthesis like any other plant.

A kelp bed is, to me, the most stimulating and aesthetic environment in the underwater world. I have dived in many locations, from the ice-filled waters of the Antarctic to the coral reefs of the Caribbean, and none of them holds a candle to a kelp forest on a clear day for sheer artistic setting.

These same finger-size strands that compose the kelp's stalk and fan out on the surface to interlace with other strands from other stalks give some divers concern for their safety. This is understandable. The diver, with his tank on his back, and the various straps and other equipment he might carry, is a series of hooks swimming through the kelp. It is easy for the strands to snag him as he swims by. To the new diver this is frightening. The experienced kelp diver never even thinks about it. He keeps on swimming and just shrugs off the kelp as he goes through. He reaches back and pulls it free as he swims on. The experienced kelp diver will hold his head back so the strands will not catch on the tank valve. If he holds his head down the tank on his back makes a big hook and he will have to keep reaching back to pull the kelp strands off all the time.

I have mentioned that kelp strands grow up from a holdfast and fan out on the surface. It is as easy to swim under this surface mat among the stocks as it is to walk through a forest. It is more difficult to swim on the surface through the mat, as it

111

would be to work your way through the tops of the trees in a forest. Swimming through the surface mat can be done, but the diver must go slowly and push the kelp out from in front of him; or, if he does not have too much stuff hanging from him like goody bags or cameras, he can swim right over the top of it. Kelp is not dangerous if the diver does not get excited and move rapidly, which could entangle him. If you leave enough air in your tank to swim back to the boat or shore under the canopy, you will never have any problems with kelp.

. CURRENTS

Currents are very important to the diver. They take him where he wants to go, if he understands them. If he does not understand them, they take him where he does not want to go. Going where you do not want to go can be very embarrassing at times as well as scary.

Currents are caused by water running from one place to another. The diver with knowledge of his area can predict them and have a great deal of fun with them. There are many different types of currents. Here, we will discuss three of them: rip currents, tidal currents, and standing currents.

Rip Currents

Quite often rip currents are improperly called "rip tides." They have nothing to do with the tides and therefore are simply "currents." Rips are small local currents that normally come and go depending on conditions. They are often found in surf areas. The water sucks in and flows back out as it runs off the beach. A rip will occur if there is some change in the bottom that will channel the water as it runs back out. Changes in the bottom that can cause rips are channels in the sand which have been dug by heavy surf, and channels dug in the sand by water rushing around rock reefs or pilings of a pier. Or perhaps a rock formation that reflects water when it comes in at a particular angle.

The water in these rips will move out to sea until the water is deep enough or open enough for it to dissipate. They rarely have influence more than 100 yards off the beach. Due to their nature, they are seldom very wide and the diver can swim out of them just by swimming sideways or parallel to the shore for 50 yards or so. Because of their small area they normally create no problem for the diver who understands them.

Rips are quite common in the *center* of coves, because the water is deflected by the sides of the cove towards the center. Divers, being lazy, like to exit from their dive at the center of a cove to avoid rocks or a long walk back to their gear. Check over your area carefully *before* you go into the water. Rips can normally be spotted from the beach because the water in a rip is dirtier than the water around it. The water in the rip will be moving faster than the water around it and will carry sand and what have you seaward. A rip can also change the breaker line, and can be detected as a breach in the evenness of the surf line. It can save you a lot of energy. When you find one, use it for a free ride out, dive, and avoid it when you come in.

Tidal Currents

Currents which occur because of tidal changes are completely predictable. There are tide tables the diver *should* have which are free or very cheap depending on the area you are in. The tides occur as a result of the moon and the sun's positions relative to the position of earth at any given time. Some areas have four tides a day, others have two, and still others have almost none. In areas where the tidal change is great—6 to 25 feet—the water can run very rapidly in and out. The strongest currents occur where the water is diverted into a narrow channel, such as at the mouths of bays, between two islands, or between an island and the mainland. The most dangerous aspect of these currents is a diver's lack of knowledge of their occurrence. Between tides or at "slack water," the water will be calm with no current at all. The diver who enters the water at this time may find that a four-knot current exists 30 minutes later. Places that are famous for this type of current are the Pacific Northwest, the Sea of Cortez (Gulf of California), and the Gulf of Mexico. A diver who is not careful in these areas or others like them may find himself on a long sea voyage he wasn't planning on.

Standing Currents

Standing currents are those which flow the same way practically all the time. In the Gulf of Mexico, for example, there are many standing currents which do not follow the tide. They are very unpredictable in some areas, and the diver must be extremely careful of them. In other areas they seem to flow steadily like a river. The Gulf Stream off the coast of Florida is one of these steadily flowing currents.

If the diver knows the currents in his area he can use them to help him make some fantastic dives. These are known as drift dives. The diver enters the water and drifts with the current. A boat follows him (by his bubbles) so that when he comes up the boat is right there. The diver uses very little air because he is not working. He covers a great area because he is moving at two to five knots (he can only swim at about 1.5 knots). Drift dives of this type have been some of my most memorable experiences underwater. The same type of experience can be had in a clear water river or stream, though the diver must keep alert to avoid getting entangled in an old tree stump or some other type of obstruction.

113

Drift diving along the edge of Palancar Reef, Mexico.

• CLARITY

When you think about hazards to the diver you probably never think of *clear water* as being a hazard. Given the right set of circumstances, however, clear water is indeed hazardous.

First we have to define the term *normal environment*. The diver's normal environment is where he normally dives. It is not necessarily near his home. He may be in the habit of traveling several times a year to Hawaii to dive. Hawaii would then be part of his normal environment. The conditions in his normal environment are what he will respond to automatically.

Once on a dive boat to Catalina we pulled up to our favorite spot and anchored. The water did not look as clear as we thought it should so we asked for someone to go down and have a look before all the rest of us suited up. An eager young man leaped over the side and went hand-over-hand down the anchor line. He came up all excited a minute later and said it was "fantastic." We all suited up, put on our tanks, and jumped in. Ten minutes later we were all back on the boat. The visibility was about eight feet. We asked the "brave scout" what he was talking about, what was this "fantastic" junk. It just happened that he was from an area that had two feet of normal visibility and to him eight feet *was* fantastic. We moved the boat a few miles and dropped him in a 60-foot visibility and told him this was fair for Catalina. He couldn't believe it. All things are relative.

Let's take this diver who is used to two-foot visibility and drop him off Palancar Reef in Mexico, where the visibility is 200+ feet. The bottom starts about 30 feet and drops off rapidly to well over 500 feet. Our diver can't believe his eyes. He zooms off to the bottom, does somersaults, shouts, waves, and is in seventh heaven. He investigates the caves, feels the sponges, and tries to point out all the neat things to his buddy, who is in the same state of euphoria. Suddenly it gets hard to breathe; he pulls his reserve. Then he spots something new—"Look at the size of that sponge!"—and has to have a closer look. It's hard to breathe again. Get to the surface quickly. He starts up, looks at his depth gauge. It can't be right. 150 feet! On the long swim to the surface he realizes it was right. He makes the surface because he is a well-trained diver. He doesn't panic because he had experience in emergency ascents in his certification class. What would have happened had he not experienced and practiced emergency ascent in class? What would have happened if he did not have experience enough not to panic? No doubt about it—bad things would have happened. How did he get into this circumstance to start with? Simple. In clear water a diver has no perception of depth. He can move downward 40 or 50 feet if he is interested in something and not even realize it. Our diver came out all right. He didn't get the bends, because he was excited and breathing hard and used up his air rapidly. He is very unhappy, however, because he has to sit on the deck while the other people make several dives that day. He went deep enough that the nitrogen in his system won't let him make another scuba dive down to the reef for several hours. Had he stayed in 60 or 70 feet of water, *where he had intended to*, he could have dived several more times that day.

Clear water is *very* deceptive. Don't let it catch you and mess up your diving day.

. KNOW WHERE YOU ARE

A diver should be aware of his location at all times. This doesn't sound hard and it isn't, but most divers get lost most of the time. By lost I don't mean they can't find their way home. I mean they come up after a dive out of air and a long way from where they have to get out of the water. They then must endure a long snorkel swim back to the boat or beach. If there are currents in the area or kelp covering the surface of the water the swim back can be a difficult and tiring one. You should keep track of where you are so you can start back towards your exit point before you run out of air. Then, when you do run out, it is an easy swim. You are not tired and soon you are back in the water diving again. The underwater pressure gauge tells you when to start back. Use it.

How do you tell where you are? Normally it is not difficult if you are alert. Even the best divers get lost sometimes. A diver can navigate much the same as a backpacker does. The backpacker will generally use watershed areas to tell him where he is. The diver can do the same thing. When you first go into the water note the slant of the bottom. Is it on your left or right? If there is a kelp or weed note whether it is "leaning" one way or another due to a slight current. Note the way the fish are facing. They generally will face into a slight current. Note the direction of the sun's rays as they penetrate the water. On a sand bottom there may be ripples. What is their direction? By being aware of these features and any others that you can think of, a diver generally will know approximately where he is. Watch the time you travel in each direction and see how close you can come to the exact spot of exit just as you run out of air. This is a game of wits and skill and can be played by teams in any environment, freshwater or salt. Have a club navigation championship. Two categories would be in order—with compass and without compass. Games of this type improve skill and confidence, and increase safety in diving.

9

NO-NO'S THAT LIVE IN THE SEA

Fear of the unknown has for centuries been the nemesis of man. He has created gods, lived in fear, started wars, and died—all for the lack of knowledge. If we leaf through the pages of history, man's greatest quest has been to explore the unknown. As we explore, each step brings us more information and our fears go by the wayside only to be replaced by more "unknowns" and new fears. The average person has anxieties he cannot explain about the creatures of the sea. He knows that they exist and sometimes take strange forms. He also knows that some of them are poisonous, others bite, and still others have painful if not deadly stings. It is no wonder that he is reluctant to leave the safety of his swimming pool and venture into the unknown of the sea.

   As with all things, knowledge brings peace of mind. The diver should learn all he can about the marine environment that he will be diving in so his fears can be forgotten, or at least be put into the proper perspective.

The most dangerous animal in the sea.

Each area of the world has its own population of hazardous marine life. No two areas are exactly the same. The diver must learn to make the right inquiries of local people to gain the knowledge he needs to be at ease wherever he ventures to dive. Fortunately, the dangers in most parts of the world are slight, as he will discover for himself as he progresses. If one were to look at the several volumes entitled *Dangerous Marine Animals,** by Dr. Bruce Halstead, each containing about 1,000 pages, he would wonder whether it were safe to be close to the ocean, let alone dive in it. If he studies each animal in turn, however, he will find that very few pose a problem to him as a diver. Most of the creatures of the sea are shy, wild animals like those of the land environment. They have no interest in man other than as a curiosity. Many cannot even see the diver but simply protect themselves instinctively from any danger.

A good rule is: If you don't know what it is, don't mess with it. Look at it and let it look at you if it can, and part friends. If you take the attitude that everything you see is a friend (it's just that some of them are a little touchy), you will enjoy yourself hour after hour visiting with them.

The critters we are going to discuss are the ones that for one reason or another, are fairly well-known. They have earned a reputation as being the grouches of the sea. When we encounter them, our guardian angel looks over our shoulder and whispers, "No, no, don't touch!" The normal reaction when we are told not to

* U.S. Government Printing Office, Washington, D.C., 1955.

touch is to sneak just one little touch. This accounts for a lot of unpleasant errors in judgment.

As you read on you should replace fear and ignorance of the unknown with respect and common sense.

• SHARKS

Sharks have a reputation that extends far beyond their watery homeland. Almost everyone, no matter how far inland, has a fear of sharks. I believe the only animals that are feared as much as the sharks by the general public are snakes. In both cases this fear arises from lack of knowledge.

As with snakes, the majority of species of shark is harmless. The diver who is fortunate enough to have warm or temperate water to dive in, however, could conceivably come face to face with one of the large dangerous varieties of sharks. But chances of him being bitten are so slight that the fear generated in the diver in such a meeting is usually far in excess of what it need be.

Although the larger sharks are very unpredictable, there are a few general traits which seem to hold true for most species. The shark has three main senses with which he finds his food: sight, smell, and low-frequency vibrations in the water (such as the vibrations sent out by a diver's fins as he is kicking). If the shark can see the diver, he will generally have no more than a passing interest. The diver does not look like any of his normal food. He may swim around the diver for a couple of minutes to satisfy his curiosity and then move on.

There are several procedures which a diver can use when this happens. One of these is to swim like a turtle. I have found through experience and have talked to other divers who also seem to find this true, that if you swim with a breast stroke and a frog kick similar to what a turtle might do, the shark loses interest and takes off. Perhaps most sharks have tried to eat a big turtle and have not had much luck. I don't know what the reason is, but they seem not to be too interested in you.

Secondly, if you swim toward the shark, this seems to upset him and makes him nervous because he is not really used to having things swim toward him. A good practice drill for this procedure is to lie on your stomach in bed and do the breast stroke with your arms and the frog kick with your legs while saying over and over to yourself, ''I am a turtle. I am a turtle. I am a turtle.''

If the water in which you encounter a shark is dirty and the visibility low, the shark may decide to attack before he realizes that you are not a fish. A high percentage of shark attacks occur at dusk, which is a natural feeding time for the shark. At these times the sharks are wandering around looking for food and the visibility is low enough that they are using their senses of smell and vibration, rather than sight, to a high degree. Shark-infested waters in times like these are a poor combination of environmental situations for the diver to be in.

The shark has a sense of smell many times more sensitive than a human's. He can detect the smell of blood in the water at very low concentrations. If the diver

The shark can inspire unreasonable fear even in nondivers.

has been spearing fish, the blood in the water will radiate and very likely bring a shark to the scene.

The most important sense that the shark has, I believe, is his lateral line sense. This is a series of special nerve endings that runs down the shark's body on each side from his head to his tail. These nerve endings are the ones that pick up low frequency vibrations so that he can locate them and rush to them. The most common low-frequency vibration that he is alert for are the struggles of a fish which has been injured. Unfortunately, a diver's fins kicking rapidly in the water could very well be mistaken for a struggling fish if the shark cannot see the diver. Vibrations in the water seem to excite a shark very rapidly. One more reason for gliding very slowly and easily along the bottom as you dive.

A fish fighting on the end of a spear will very often bring a shark to the scene. I have had more than one fish taken off my spear by a passing shark. A diver who sees a shark and starts swimming as fast as he can to get away will set up a vibration much like an injured fish, and could cause the shark to get excited and attack. Common sense tells us to get out of the water if we are aware of the presence of a large shark, but the speed with which we get out of the water sometimes is hard to control. There is an old saying that might bear repeating here: "When you are up to your ass in alligators it is sometimes difficult to remember that your primary objective was to drain the swamp."

Remember, in the case of a shark, that your primary objective is *not to cause a commotion in the water which may excite the shark.* Getting out of the water, in reality, is secondary. This becomes at times difficult to remember. If you can, you should always stay eyeball to eyeball with a shark. He is less apt to come at you in this position, and if he does decide that you could be a tasty morsel, you have him in view. You present a smaller target for him by facing directly at him than with your back turned.

I have personally never been bothered by a shark, although I have been in the water with a great many of them. When I see one I swim toward it, as I have stated. This seems to make the shark very uneasy, and he usually doesn't hang around very long. I must admit, though, that I have a secret. As I swim toward a shark, I always cross my fingers!

I have given a great deal of thought to what I would do if I were actually attacked. The only answer that I have been able to come up with would be that I would try to hide in that big brown cloud that would form around me!

. KILLER WHALES

The killer whale has been reported to be a bad hombre for many years. Recently, however, we have found that in reality he is probably not very dangerous. Several divers have come face to face with killer whales, and the whales seemed to have only passing curiosity for the human. We now have them in tanks, and divers work with them regularly without any trouble. One NAUI instructor was checking out a new student off La Jolla kelp beds in California when a killer whale swam between them. The whale swam around them as they came up and went on his way. The people on the boat said they could hear the divers' heartbeats like a jackhammer 50 yards off. But the divers said they weren't scared at all. When questioned about the size of their eyes as they surfaced, they stated that their eyes were always six inches in diameter!

I would not suggest purposely getting into the water with a killer whale. It is only good sense to avoid all possibly dangerous situations. If I found one in the water with me, my fear would stem more from his size than from his temperament.

. BARRACUDA

The barracuda is one of those creatures of the sea that really looks mean. He is sleek with a long, protruding underjaw and a great many teeth. The danger from the barracuda does not seem to be that he would attack a man in the manner a shark might, but rather from the fact that he is a game fish and attracted by any shiny object or fast movement. He is likely to rush in and strike at the glitter of a ring or watch or other piece of equipment that a diver might be wearing, and take a hand by mistake. It is a good idea to avoid wearing jewelry (or any flashy object) in barracuda waters.

JON HUBER

The barracuda, a formidable pred-
ator of warmer waters, is best dealt
with cautiously.

Barracuda grow quite big in warmer waters—about eight feet long. They are
also very curious. This is a bad combination. They seem to have very little fear of
man and think nothing of cruising in at arm's distance from the diver. It is very
disconcerting to discover a five or six foot barracuda just a few feet away looking
over your shoulder when you were totally unaware of his presence. The best action
in a case like this is to put your hands under your armpits so as not to tempt him
with a dangling morsel that might draw his attention and induce a strike. If he
hangs around for very long, it would be best to get out of the water (slowly,
avoiding fast or sudden movements) for a while.

. **EELS**

Eels have a bad reputation that they have
had to live down for a long time. As more divers have encounters with eels, we are
finding that for the most part they are just creatures of the sea trying to get by like
everything else. Their reputation is slowly being exonerated.

It seems that most girls are frightened of snakes, and because most mothers are
usually girls they instill a fear in their children of any long, slim, undulating
animal. The poor eel looks enough like a snake that this fear is transferred to it. I
wouldn't be surprised if at this point eels actually enjoy scaring divers. I can just
hear an eel chuckling to himself as a diver streaks away toward the surface, "Heh,
heh, I really got that one!"

The moray eel is the most common scary animal that divers in temperate waters
encounter. There are several species ranging up to ten feet long. They are not
aggressive creatures for the most part, and generally stay in their holes during the
day, roaming only at night. Unlike most other fish, if they are threatened, they will
stand their ground and fight. They feed mainly by smell and are easily attracted to
food. Like barracuda, they, too, are attracted to any shiny, fast-moving object.
The divers who are bitten by morays are generally those who pry off an abalone, an
oyster, or some such tender morsel, and reach back into a hole to get it. The eel
smells the food he is accustomed to eating and comes out looking for it. He isn't
too bright and could easily mistake the diver's hand for the food.

If you should get bitten by a moray, the bite is not poisonous and should be
treated as what it is—a bad laceration. Stop the bleeding, put on some disinfectant,
and sew it up if necessary. Then, chew yourself out for being stupid.

122

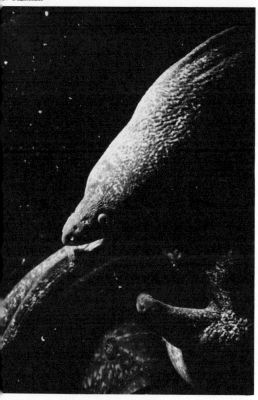

The moray eel looks much worse than he acts.

A green moray displays the gaping mouth characteristic of its genus.

123

The moray does have its good points. It's a fine eating fish. The flesh is white and flaky and has an excellent flavor (in some areas morays can be poisonous, however, so be sure to check locally before eating one). If you should spear a moray, remember that they do fight back and are capable of inflicting a severe wound on the diver. The only place to spear one is in the head. If you can't get a good shot at the head, then don't spear one at all.

Certain other eels may be trickier to tackle than the moray. The conger eel and the wolf eel also have bad reputations. I have no personal experience with either of these two; however, those who have had such experience tell me they think the conger is more aggressive than the moray.

The best way to treat any of the eels is to admire their gracefulness in the water and respect their desire to live a solitary life.

. SEA REPTILES

There are two common sea reptiles: the sea snakes and the turtle. Whereas the eels are not normally dangerous, the snakes can be. There are many species of sea snake, the most common of which is the yellow-bellied sea snake. This animal is rarely aggressive, but at times it can be. Should a diver be bitten, he has a severe problem.

Sea snakes are usually smaller than three feet and normally live a docile life. They have a somewhat flattened body and are good swimmers. An interesting fact about them is that they can swim backwards as well as they can forwards. They are not well adapted to biting, so the diver is relatively safe if he is careful. Their mouths are very small, but they are extremely poisonous should they effect a bite.

Their bad reputation comes not from divers but rather from fishermen. Most sea snake bites have occurred when commercial fishermen were taking them out of their nets. Even I would bite in that particular situation!

About all I can say is to avoid sea snakes. They reside in tropical Pacific waters and should be left entirely alone. If the diver should be bitten, he must keep as still as possible. A restriction band should be applied above the bite and left in place while the diver is taken to a hospital for antivenin treatment.

There are some harmless water snakes, so if the snake can be caught (without getting bitten yourself), it would be a great help to the attending physician. The traditional cut-and-suck method for treating snakebites is not recommended. In fact, it isn't recommended for any snakebite any longer. Packing the area of the bite in ice is the preferred treatment if ice is available, until professional help can be obtained.

The turtles are the other common reptiles in the sea. They are excellent eating and, because of their food value, are one of our endangered species. There are rather large turtle fisheries which have thinned out the turtle population to a dangerously low point.

Sea snakes should be left entirely alone.

In the water these clumsy looking animals coast along with very little effort and are beautiful to behold. If approached and frightened, they can move with more speed than you could possibly imagine. The first turtle I ever saw was in the Gulf of California. He was a small one and was drifting lazily along watching me. I had seen pictures of people riding turtles and thought "here is my chance." I swam over to grab hold and go for a ride. When I got close to him, he took off with such speed he just seemed to disappear. Since then I have seen a great many turtles and I am still astonished by their great speed.

Three species—the green turtle, the hawkbill turtle, and the leatherback turtle—can be poisonous to eat if found in the areas of the Philippines, Ceylon, and Indonesia. Because it is not known just why they are poisonous in these areas, it is recommended that they not be eaten if taken there. However, if you are in any other area and are offered a turtle steak, don't turn it down. It is one of the most delicious pieces of meat you will ever eat, and not too many of your friends will have ever eaten a reptile. If you play the game of "one-upmanship," that could be important.

• SEA LIONS

Just like the sheik of Araby, the male or bull sea lion keeps close watch on his women. During the breeding season (generally during the summer months) sea lions form rookeries. The bulls fight for territories, then they accumulate female sea lions. A big bull could have fifteen or twenty females in his harem. They are male chauvinists and don't want the girls out of their sight. They want the females in their territory, but *nothing* else. If a diver gets too close, a bull will normally make passes at him to scare him off. If he

125

does not scare, he could be attacked. The diver would have no chance against a big bull sea lion. Stay clear of sea lions when they are in a rookery, and if they try to scare you off, don't be a hero—leave.

• STINGRAYS

The stingrays are a group of fish which are flattened in body shape so they can take cover on a sandy bottom. They normally settle on the sand and then flap their wing-like fins to lift the sand up into the water so it will settle over their bodies. The end result of such action is to cover the rays' bodies with sand, leaving only their eyes sticking up and two small holes called "spiracles," with which they breathe, showing. The spiracles allow them to take in water to run across their gills for respiration. The stingers are located on the tail and under certain circumstances can deliver a very painful wound.

The stingrays are not aggressive animals and will never hurt the diver if left alone. In order for them to inflict a wound, the victim must be right on the back of the stingray and in contact with it. This usually happens while a swimmer or diver is walking on a sandy bottom. The rays quite frequently come into shallow water and bury themselves in the sand. If stepped on by a wader, they bring the tail up and jam the stinger into his foot. I once saw a big he-man type lifeguard showing off for a group of girls at the beach. He was going through the whole peacock ritual—strutting, flexing his muscles, and the like, when he walked out into the water. He was about knee deep when he stepped on a small stingray. Surprised by the human, and unable to escape, the ray stuck its one-inch stinger into the side of his foot. He let out a yell and ran back up onto the beach. The wound was a very small puncture and did not look bad at all. He tried to be brave for a while, but finally the pain was so intense he sat down and cried. For him to do this under the circumstances told me that the pain had to be severe. I saw him a week later, and his foot was a mess—black and blue and puffed up. He was on a crutch. Three weeks later he was back on the beach doing his thing again, but I noticed he didn't go wading.

Like most other wild animals, the stingrays are placid, handsome creatures in their own right that, like man himself, are equipped for defense from danger. When frightened or threatened they use every means of escape and defense at their disposal, just like you would.

If stung by a ray, a diver should go to a doctor as soon as possible. Because of the nature of such a wound (generally a ragged puncture wound), antibiotics to stop the infection and soaking the wound are about all that can be done for it. If suction can be applied to the wound quickly, some of the poison might be removed. For this reason, some divers carry a suction pump from a snakebite kit with them.

Stingrays are easily avoided by scuffling your feet as you walk along in the water. This forewarns the ray of your coming and, as he doesn't like being stepped on, gives him a chance to leave.

126

This diver looks at a passing electric ray and decides not to touch.

Even when not covered by sand, a sting ray can be difficult to see on the bottom.

. ELECTRIC RAYS

The electric rays have a strange biological storage battery. This is a physiological phenomenon they share with the electric eels of fresh water. When they are touched they can give off a charge that will shock the toucher. This shock is strong enough that it isn't funny. It won't kill you, but it is something you certainly want to avoid. It has been said that civilized man has two traits. First, he can stand pain if he has to, and second, he avoids it at all costs. We all know that divers are civilized, so avoid the electric ray.

. JELLYFISHES

Another group of animals that share the sea with us are the coelenterates. The ones we are concerned with are generally lumped together by divers under the term "jellyfish." The jellyfish are rather jelly-like in appearance, but in no way resemble a fish. There was a time when practically everything in the sea was referred to as a fish. The jellyfish is a remnant of those days, as are the starfish and the crawfish.

The jellyfish are mainly free-floating characters of the open sea. They drift up to our shores and divers often come in contact with them. They have a stinging cell that can inflict minor to severe pain depending on the species. The stinging cells are small and contain a dart-like mechanism that is ejected and penetrates the skin, injecting a poison. When the diver gets "stung," it is by a great many of these cells, not just one. They are microscopic and exist in great numbers along the tentacles of the animal. As a rule, they produce a local skin irritation that will pass in an hour or so.

There are two forms that a diver should avoid at all costs: the Portuguese man-of-war and the sea wasp. The man-of-war's stinging cells are very strong and cause a most severe skin irritation that could place the diver in the hospital for a while. In reality, it is not a true jellyfish but rather a colony of small animals. It is found in the Atlantic Ocean but has a kissing-cousin which is found in the Indo-Pacific and around Hawaii and Japan that is almost as bad. The sea wasp, one of the most deadly animals in the ocean, has been known to cause death in less than eight minutes. It is a jellyfish-like organism which is difficult to see in the water and is found in the Indian Ocean and off the Philippines and Australia. Sea wasps are good swimmers. They can swim about as fast as the diver, and feed on fish. When the water is very calm they will come to shallow water close to the beach. They are most abundant during the warm summer months. Care must be taken to be alert for and to avoid them.

For the lesser jellyfish stings which cause minor skin irritation there are several first-aid procedures professed to be of help. Rubbing sand over the rash is one.

Jellyfish can sting a diver if he gets too close.

This assists in ridding the skin of the stinging cells lodged therein. Alcohol rubbed on the rash should help, also. One of the best treatments is dilute ammonium hydroxide. If you don't have any ammonia with you, I might bring to your attention the fact that urine has ammonia in it. Here's a chance to see who your real friends are! Cortisone ointments and antihistamine seem to be of the most help in severe sting cases.

Other coelenterates worth mentioning are the corals found in tropical waters. The corals' main danger lies in their sharp edges. Those edges can cause cuts that, although not deep, can become seriously infected. A coral cut generally has in it small pieces of coral that have broken off, as well as sting cells similar to those of the jellyfish. One species, the fire coral, is famous for its stinging abilities. A coral cut should be cleaned promptly and thoroughly and then disinfected. I would recommend wearing some covering over the knees and gloves on the hands when diving around coral.

• MOLLUSCS, OR SHELL ANIMALS

Among the molluscs there are two types of animal of concern to the diver—the cone shells and the head-foots, or octopuses and squids. The cone shells are a problem to the shell-collecting diver in tropical waters. Some of the over 400 species of this attractive animal are extremely toxic. The diver may see a pretty shell on the bottom, dive down, pick it up, and get stung on the hand by the poison radula. All this happens rather slowly and the diver can handle the shell safely if he is aware of the problem. The activity of cone shells and their reaction to being handled varies greatly from one species to another. Most are

129

timid and will hide in their shell when handled. A few of the Indo-Pacific species may try to stick the diver with their poisonous dart. They must be handled by the large end to avoid being injured. All contact with the soft parts of the animal should be avoided.

The octopus and squid have been given great play by Jules Verne and others. Fortunately, their stories are just that—stories. The great kraken of mythology was a 1,000-armed octopus a mile in diameter that used to chase fishermen off the banks in the North Atlantic. These stories are fun to read and exciting to imagine. Unfortunately, they have come down through history and been with us for so long that they almost seem to have credence.

The diver is always hearing the question from his nondiving friends: "How about the dreaded octopus?" The octopuses the diver encounters are generally less than three feet in diameter. In areas where they get bigger, such as the Pacific Northwest around Puget Sound, they may be 15 or 20 feet in diameter. The divers who dive these waters say they are no problem at all. In fact, they have an octopus wrestling championship in some areas where the divers bring up specimens over 15 feet in diameter. They cannot use spears, but must bring them up using just their bare hands. The octopus is like most other animals; if he is handled properly by a knowledgeable person, he is not dangerous. If you are not familiar with octopuses, stay away until you are. Then enjoy them as part of your new world.

Of all the octopus stories I have heard, there is one that I would particularly like to share with you. It does not concern a diver, but it is the only one I know that I am sure is true. In my younger days, I worked on Catalina Island off the coast of California. There was an old fisherman who had lost his arm in an accident years before but, undaunted, he went to sea every morning to fish his long lines in the deep water off the island. Each afternoon he would come into the fish house and sell his catch, which was comprised of various bottom fish. One day he came in and told this story. I shall repeat it as closely as I can remember.

He had had his line out over the stern of his boat and was pulling it in. (The long line had hooks about every three feet, and as it was pulled in, the fish were taken off and the hook rebaited. You can imagine a one-armed man doing this job.) He was intent on his work when an arm came over the side of the boat. He said he jumped up and ran to look. By this time several more arms were aboard. He didn't know what to do for a moment, and just stood there.

Then a head came up over the transom and a gigantic octopus was aboard. Its tentacles were waving in the air and reaching over both sides of the 40-foot boat. Our hero raced into the cabin and grabbed an ax. He came back to the cockpit to do mortal battle with the creature from the deep. After much hacking, he killed it. I can just picture this sixty-year-old man, one-armed, all by himself at sea in combat with this giant.

The octopuses the diver usually encounters are less than three feet in diameter.

Even the larger octopuses are generally timid and inoffensive creatures.

After killing the octopus, he found it had been hooked on his line and he had pulled it right up to the transom of the boat. He cut the head up for bait and brought the arms in to sell at the fish market. I was there when he brought them in and each arm was ten feet long and four inches in diameter. With the head, the animal must have been 23 feet in diameter.

Who says a fisherman's life is dull?

The old fisherman had caught the octopus in 500 feet of water. Another good reason not to dive deep.

The diver often finds small octopuses while he is diving and pulls them out of their holes and plays with them. This is called an octopus break. It is fun and a good way to pass a few minutes of time. However, be careful of two things: first, don't let the octopus bite you, as they possess a powerful beak and a toxin and, second, don't injure him. He is a quiet, shy creature that should be enjoyed and not harmed.

While the octopus is a bottom dweller, the squid is a swimmer. The big squid are deep-water animals, so the only ones divers see are the one- to two-foot squid which are found swimming at times near the surface. They avoid divers but nonetheless are exciting to watch as they glide along on their single jet engine. I feel extremely clumsy as I watch their sleek bodies shoot through the water like torpedoes. Squid as long as 60 feet have been recorded. I hope I never see one that large!

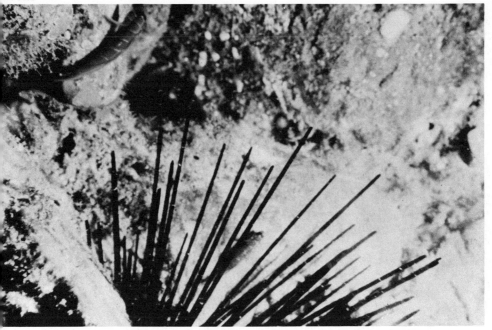

The long spines of the sea urchin must be avoided by the diver.

• THE SEA URCHIN

One of the most dangerous of all marine animals is the sea urchin. It is not dangerous in a way that will kill you, but it can cause pain and wreck a day's diving.

The urchins cause a problem because of long, thin, sharp spines that, like porcupine quills, will stick into the diver. Urchins are bottom dwellers and the diver must bump into them to get stuck. The spines are very brittle and break off after they enter the skin.

The spines should be removed as soon as possible. This is not an easy chore. They break when touched with a needle and some of them cannot be withdrawn. Most spines will be absorbed in several days, or will fester and pop out of their own accord. Some of the long-spined tropical forms can cause severe pain and paralysis, and should be treated by a doctor.

The best way to avoid getting stuck by the sea urchin is to avoid the animal. This means staying off the bottom as much as possible. I stepped on an urchin one time and drove a spine up into my heel. I went to the hospital, where they dug a hole in my foot about one-half inch deep trying to remove it. They never did get it. Four days later the one-inch spine festered and came out of its own accord. The hole in my foot took eight weeks to heal. I figure I learned a lesson—it's just that I'm not quite sure what it was!

133

The danger of the dreaded stonefish lies in its powerful venom and the ease with which it can be mistaken for a piece of coral or a stone on the bottom.

• FISH SPINES

Most fish have sharp, bony spines to support their fins, which protrude and also act as a protective device. The diver must always be alert to these sharp spines as a wound from one of them could lead to a bad infection. Some fish have evolved their spines as defense weapons and rely on them for protection. These fish range from the trigger fish which sports a long, single dorsal spine that he can raise and lock in place at will, to the stone fish which has a poison gland in a hollow dorsal spine with venom so powerful that a man undergoes severe pain and often dies if injected with it. There are a great many fish which have poison spines of one kind or another; only the more famous ones will be described here.

Most poisonous of all is the stone fish, so named, I've been told, because it looks like a stone. These fish have large poison glands beneath the spines on their body. Their extremely efficient protective coloration makes them hard to spot as they hang out along the ocean floor. The diver must take care not to brush against or step on one. Stone fish live in warm, tropical waters and pose a problem particularly to the vacationing diver who will not be looking for them, because they do not appear in his usual diving areas.

The zebra fish is also poisonous but, due to the much smaller poison glands present in the spines, is not nearly as dangerous as the stone fish. The diver has

134

This scorpion fish is a camouflaged, poison-spined fish of temperate waters.

another advantage with the zebra fish. It is colored strikingly and therefore is easier to see. Zebra fish are beautiful to observe in the water.

Scorpion fish are found in temperate waters as well as tropical; therefore more divers are confronted with them. Their poison gland is small and, although the wound from their spines is painful, it is not generally debilitating after a few hours. This species can change color rapidly and is difficult to see because it blends right in with its environment.

The toad fishes have a painful but nonfatal sting. They hide and use protective coloration to go unobserved by the diver. Like the stingrays, they are frequently found on the ocean bottom and the same method of avoiding them should be used. Shuffle your feet as you wade and push them out in front of you.

The weever fish are more pugnacious. They will attack anything which threatens them. Their poison spine on the side of the head is highly toxic and in some cases has caused death. These are found in the Mediterranean and around the British Isles. Again, the main hazard is to the wader. Get the "shuffle your feet" habit. It is a good protective device for you in any waters.

Obviously, the information about marine life given in this chapter is in no way complete and covers only a few localities. A diver should be well read about the dangerous marine animals of his particular diving area, and he should *always* seek the advice of knowledgeable local people in unfamiliar diving areas *before* he dives there.

135

10

THE DIVER GOES A-HUNTING

For today's society of concerned conservationists a chapter dealing with the best way to kill fish would seem almost out of place. This is, in fact, the main reason I felt I had to write one. Not because I want to wipe out the fish population or because I don't think it can be wiped out; divers can, and have, made serious inroads in certain fish populations. But rather, because I believe the diver can be a spearfisherman and still wear a white hat at the local ecology club.

As a marine biologist and chairman of the National Committee on Conservation for the National Association of Underwater Instructors, I am aware of and extremely concerned about our marine environment. I have been active in antipollution activities and support to my fullest underwater parks in almost any area. I have also been an active spearfisherman for many years. I have dived in two national spearfishing championships and made numerous expeditions to the Gulf of California and other places just to spearfish. I have found what I believe to be a blend of two worlds: conservation and sportsmanship.

The majority of fish in the sea offers no challenge to the hunter.

• THE EVOLUTION OF THE SPORTSMAN

In earlier days of spearfishing the diver would go into the water and kill any fish he came across that was big enough for him to hit. In fact, there was a certain amount of prestige in shooting a three-inch sardine because it was so hard to hit that the diver had to be a great shot to hit one. There are some divers, of course, who still do this. The diving community is working to educate these persons. They have not yet realized that most of the fish they kill are harmless little creatures that in their innocence give no challenge at all and therefore no glory in their taking. The majority of fish are friendly, curious, and about as difficult to spear as your pet dog would be to shoot with a .22 rifle. Nearly all new divers go through the "trigger happy" stage and generally get over it in one or two dives. The best cure for those who have not yet learned these simple facts seems to be a negative peer group response to their actions.

To me, the most important step toward sportsmanship is psychological. The diver has to realize that each fish is an individual and has its own personality and habits, just as people do. Some are cunning, others are shy, and still others are just plain tough. When the diver feels these qualities in his prey, he begins to become a true sportsman. Hemingway's Old Man said it very well, as he prayed, "Blessed Virgin, pray for the death of this fish, wonderful though he is." The old man's compassion for the fish is unmistakable. He loves this fish he is trying to kill and, because you know he loves it, you do not question his right to kill it. We humans

137

are strange at times, but I guess that is why we are special. The divers who dive because they love this new world they have discovered soon learn to have sympathy and respect for their new environment, which makes them happy and safe divers. They do not become game hogs. The few who persist in killing thoughtlessly must do so because it makes them feel somehow superior. I am sure that a psychologist would say that if they were sure they were superior to these aquatic residents, they would not need to keep proving it to themselves. As Steinbeck so aptly wrote, "We are not better than animals, in fact in a lot of ways we aren't as good."*

Hunting with Slurp Guns and "Goody Bags"

The concept of underwater hunting is far broader than spearfishing alone. Another type of underwater hunting becoming common today is hunting with a slurp gun. This is a device for catching small animals alive. Used *carefully,* it sucks them up into a chamber, unhurt, and a diver then can put them in his aquarium to be enjoyed by others. If a club were formed to go slurping, they should name themselves the "suck-em-ups"!

The general design of the slurp gun is a simple piston arrangement. By pulling back on the piston the diver creates a suction at the opposite end. To increase the amount of suction, the tube leading into the piston is smaller in diameter than the piston section. The object is to place the end of the small tube next to a little critter, pull back on the piston, and create a suction through the tube at the other end which is so powerful the wee beastie is sucked up. Slurping is indeed a lot of fun. Depending on the size of the slurp gun, you can catch various size animals. The largest slurp gun I have ever seen was five feet long. The piston cylinder was eight inches in diameter and the catching tube was three inches in diameter. It could catch fish up to one foot long, and it took two men to work this inverted cannon effectively.

The most humorous thing I ever saw involving a slurp gun was when some friends of mine tried to catch a moray eel. The eel was of medium size, about three feet long. They worked their way to Mr. Moray with a piece of fish tied to the front of the small tube, in order to entice the eel close and into the right position. The unsuspecting eel smelled the bait and came out of his lair to investigate. When his head got close to the opening, our divers let loose and the piston slammed back. There was a gigantic suction which devoured a great chunk of ocean. The eel, who was about to have a peaceful snack, found himself in a raging torrent of water.

When it all quieted down, everyone concerned was surprised. The eel was surprised to find himself halfway engulfed in a long plastic tube. The divers were surprised to find the eel halfway encased. The divers were also surprised to find the

* *Log from the Sea of Cortez,* Bantam Books, New York, 1971.

Increasing in popularity is a bring-em-back-alive device for small animals called the slurp gun.

eel backing out of the tube looking a bit disturbed at the divers through the Plexiglas. They tried to hold the eel back so he couldn't get his head out but he finally tied a knot with the end of his tail, slipped it down his body, and used it for leverage to pull his head out of the tube.

About now the shock had worn off and the eel was quite unhappy. The divers, being devout cowards, dropped the gun and backed off a considerable distance. The eel freed himself, swam a circle around the gun as though he were looking for the divers, and took off for his hole, where he disappeared in the rocks. The story grew into a pretty good one by the time the divers got home—about how, when freed, the eel looked around for them. The poor eel was probably just trying to get his bearings after the shock of practically having his eyes sucked out of his head. The divers decided to stick to smaller victims the next time!

I know of no marine aquarium club consisting of divers, that is, divers who have a club specifically to catch and share aquarium species. Keeping a marine aquarium is an exciting thing, and catching your own critters makes it cheap. Just be sure that you know how to take care of whatever you keep. Consider becoming a sucker—it's fun!

Others hunt with what is called a "goody bag," a bag with net sides or bottom that a diver carries with him to store his "goodies"—lobsters, abalone, scallops, pismo clams. Divers also use their goody bags to collect shells, rocks, and even seaweed. A diver and his wife sent me a Christmas card last year which they had

Lobsters are a prime type of game for the diver to stalk. The landing of a really big lobster is a day to remember.

COURTESY ALICE HOLLENBEC

The abalone is prized for its flesh as well as its decorative shell.

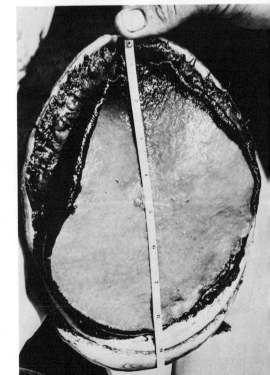

140

JIM G

made themselves. It had a small piece of seaweed pressed on one side and a cheery, handwritten greeting on the other. It was unique, personal, and meant more to me than all the "store bought" cards I received.

One woman made unusual candles from shells she collected. She used abalone and scallop shells as forms and poured colored wax into them. To decorate them she used smaller shells, driftwood, and seaweed. Other people make jewelry from sea life. Some items such as sea-urchin teeth are so light when they are dried that they make excellent earrings. The operculums of many of the sea snails (gastropods) make unusual pendants. Only the imagination and creativity of the individual limits what can be done.

A great number of divers are taking to hunting with a camera. I am glad to see this seems to be the main trend. The aquatic cameraman does not harm the environment as much and, because of his slow movement through the water and the necessity of close inspection of the area looking for a subject to photograph, he enjoys seeing the small inconspicuous things that most divers hurry past and never spot.

Spearfishing

I have devoted the rest of this chapter to the underwater hunting that is normally done with a spear gun. There are three basic components of spearfishing: (1) mental attitude, (2) physical ability, and (3) equipment. Each one is equally important and all must be in coordination if the underwater hunter is to be successful.

(1) MENTAL ATTITUDE • Let's discuss the phenomenon of mental attitude first. The underwater hunter should hunt for one of two main reasons: one, to put food on the table or, two, to accept a challenge. The food hunter or, as he is commonly called, the "meat hunter," generally will take practically any fish he comes across which is edible. As a rule, he will spear the smaller, more common varieties. This is perfectly acceptable as long as he quits when he has enough to make a meal for his family. Fresh fish is so much more pleasing to the palate than the frozen substance they call fish in the supermarket! Families that are fortunate enough to have someone bring them fresh fish enjoy a luxury that others can never know. There seem to be an endless variety of ways fresh fish can be prepared and all of them are very tasty and provide excellent protein.

Fish markets took a drop in business when the facts on the mercury content of fish meat became known. The public became upset because pollution was rendering fish unfit for human food. After research was conducted it was found that fish caught in the 1800s and preserved in museums had as much mercury in their flesh as do their modern cousins. It seems there is a natural level of mercury in the ocean. In the case of mercury, Mother Nature and not man is the culprit for a change. There are, of course, some specific local problems that raise the mercury

141

content in fish, but the mercury in tuna and sword fish is not entirely a man-made problem. The mercury level is highest in the bigger fish that the diver never gets a chance to spear anyway. Thus, the diver should not have to worry unduly about the mercury problem in the fish he spears.

Meat hunting is honorable if the game taken is used as it should be. The diver who hunts for sport must also be careful that he does not waste the fish he takes, lest he become a hyprocrite of the worst kind. If he does not eat his catch, he should give it to someone who will. There is a secret to giving game away, whether it be fish or venison. The secret is simple: All game must be cleaned and prepared for cooking *before* it is given away. Too many "sportsmen" kill their prey and then dump it on someone else to clean and prepare. Generally the recipient thanks the giver profusely and, as soon as he leaves, throws the "gift" out. It is easy to see why. Picture a quiet household after dinner some evening with the wife puttering about in the kitchen and the man of the house doing some menial male chore in the garage, when up drives Joe Diver. He jumps out of his cigar-smoke-filled car with a string of cold, slimy fish and lays them on the lawn. With great pride he announces, "Look what I have for you!" He carries the fish, which by now have grass sticking to them, into the kitchen where he places them in the clean sink. As the little housewife looks on with horror, the fish lie there and stare back at her. What she is thinking she doesn't say. Our diver, his good deed done, heads for home to clean up and relax in front of his TV. By the time Joe Diver leaves the house, the fish have already begun to make their presence known in the house via the air. What happens to them is obvious.

On the other hand, had the fish been cleaned at the beach when they were caught and the fillets brought to the same family, they would have been wrapped, put in the refrigerator, and later enjoyed. The cleaning of fish, which is a small job at the beach where the scales can fly and do no harm, becomes a monstrous task at home in a clean kitchen. We must educate Joe Diver in the proper protocol as regards dead fish.

To be a true sportsman and a spearfisherman at the same time, you must feel a challenge in the stalking and a sense of accomplishment in the landing of your prey. In order to do this, you must pick your fish. That's right—pick your fish. In your area there is a type of fish which will present such a challenge. I can't tell you what it is, but I can give you some guidelines on how to select it. Choose a fish that, when you seriously go after it, you succeed in catching one about one-third of the time. The size is of no importance. It might be a one-pound gar or a hundred-pound black sea bass. Don't pick one that you rarely see or you will become discouraged. It is equally important not to pick a type of fish which you can spear easily or you will become bored. As you concentrate your thoughts and efforts on one fish, you will find your knowledge of its life-style and habits increasing, and, with this knowledge, your degree of success will increase. When you become 75 percent effective, change fish. You will find your enjoyment

Gamefish like these "Jacks" are what the sportsman spends his time looking for.

Your physical diving limits and endurance will be one of the main factors in choosing the fish you will hunt.

UL TZIMOULIS/*Skin Diver* MAGAZINE

THE DIVER GOES A-HUNTING

increasing in direct proportion to your expanding understanding of the environment and consequently your increased relaxation during your dives.

(2) PHYSICAL ABILITY . The next area of importance to the diver in deciding what he can or cannot do is his physical ability. We all have a tendency to remember the last time we did something and assume that conditions are still the same as they were then. This can be disastrous. The diver who spent his summer diving last year and was in good physical condition but has not been in the water all winter just cannot do the things he was able to when last summer ended. You must *realistically* evaluate your own capabilities in the here and now. Analyze what you personally can do and work within these limits. It is good to push your limits so they will expand, but you must be certain to remain within your present physical range. Your physical diving limits will be one of the main factors in choosing the fish you will hunt. As your skill and endurance increase you will naturally and safely progress to more difficult types of fish and enjoy yourself more. With increased competence in the water you gain inner satisfaction and pride in yourself.

How does a diver get himself back into shape and/or improve the shape he's in? Undoubtedly the best way to train for a specific activity is to participate in that activity. Specificity of exercise is an important concept in any training. That is to say, the diver does more good for himself by putting on his fins and swimming a mile than he does by running a mile. Only by practicing free, or breath-holding, diving, can the diver become good at it. There is no exercise that he can do at home in the front room that will do the trick. The best way is to set aside a time, perhaps two or three times a week, when you can use a pool. If you can give yourself an hour, then establish a base line for your activities. Perhaps you are going to spend the first 30 minutes working to increase your underwater time. You should time yourself while actually underwater, so at the end of a 30-minute period you can say you were underwater for, say, 12 minutes. Then try for 12 minutes 15 seconds the next day. Each day you should strive to do better within the same time limit. This overloading principle is the secret to improving your physical ability. (As I mentioned, this can be dangerous so don't push too hard.)

The last 30 minutes of your workout might be a fin swim to build the legs so you won't tire on a dive. Each day try to swim one-fourth of a lap farther in the same time as the day before. This is a type of training which allows you to increase your ability without needing more time than you have available.

(3) EQUIPMENT . The time has come to talk about equipment. I have put this off as long as possible because no one agrees on what is best. No matter what I say, someone will violently disagree. I will try to stay on general ground and discuss basic philosophy rather than to be specific, through the first part of the discussion anyway.

144

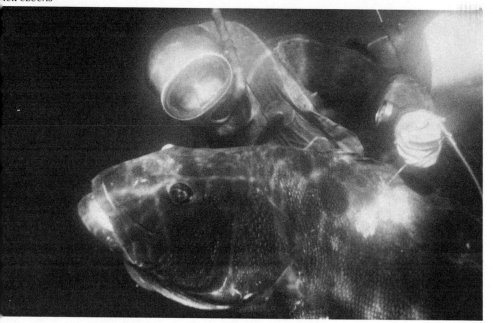

Equipment must be matched to the hunter and the hunter's prey. This diver has bagged a fine grouper in the Sea of Cortez.

The most important factor to be considered when thinking about equipment is that it must be matched to the hunter and to the hunter's prey. An archer matches the strength of his bow to his physical ability, then matches his arrows to the bow very carefully. He then selects the type of point he wishes on his arrows, depending on the type of prey he is going after. A rifleman matches the weight of his bullet to his game. The spearfisherman must be just as concerned with his weapon. The spear, whether it be a gun seven feet long or a pole two feet long, serves only one purpose—to connect you to the fish in such a manner that you can maintain control.

The critical thing in choosing the correct spear is the range or distance at which you will spot most of your game. If your fish is a catfish in the Mississippi River, where the visibility is practically zero, a two-foot wooden pole with a barbed head of some kind is the "right" equipment. You cannot expect, however, to take a white sea bass off Catalina Island where the visibility is 80 feet with the same pole spear, because the range at which you normally encounter sea bass is too great. A general rule of thumb is the clearer the water, the greater the range. This will vary, of course. There are some fish that live in holes so the range will be close, even though the water is clear. The long gun increases the range in clear water and is not necessarily for bigger fish.

Certain modifications will increase the range on all guns. One such modification is to keep the shaft highly polished. This is not really a modification, but rather a maintenance consideration. The shaft on most of the guns I see is so badly tarnished that a clean shaft would almost seem a modification. Any rust or corrosion on a shaft will cause increased drag and will slow it down considerably. The shaft should be polished with steel wool before every dive.

Another major factor in slowing down the shaft and therefore decreasing the range is the line tied to it. The large diameter which comes on most stock spearguns from the store is ridiculous. The best line for the general small gun is a 125-pound test nylon or linen fishing line. This gives all the strength that is needed and has far less drag to hold the shaft back. It will chafe more easily and must be changed every few trips, but the increased effectiveness of the gun more than compensates for the small amount of effort it takes to replace the line.

Most guns have lines about four times the length of the gun as standard gear. If you change the line to a lighter fishline, use six gun-lengths of line so the shaft can carry out farther. It will still have the power to penetrate. If you leave the line short, the shaft will break it when it hits the end due to the increased velocity. If the area in which you do most of your hunting is shallow, such as a coral lagoon, a lake, or shale area where the fish really can't get away from you easily, then perhaps you can dispense with the line. A "free shaft" can be effective at ranges up to 40 feet even from a short gun. The total absence of drag on the shaft makes such a dramatic difference in performance that it is hard to believe. Try it and see what I mean.

Now that you have selected a weapon which will give you the right range, let's talk about the different sizes of shafts that are available. When a diver considers the diameter of the shaft to use he is concerned with penetration and speed. A light shaft traveling fast will penetrate as well as a heavier shaft traveling slowly. The most commonly used shaft in the smaller guns is $5/16''$ in diameter. This size is used

Most spearguns are powered by rubber slings much in the same way as a slingshot is.

so that notches can be cut into it and still leave enough strength to get by without breaking the shaft. There are many circumstances where the lighter ¼″ shaft would do the job better. The diver generally has to make these himself. A hint that may help is not to cut notches in the shaft at all, but instead drill ¹/₁₆″ holes and put small pins of stainless steel or piano wire in these upon which to notch the rubbers (most guns are powered by rubber slings in much the same way as a slingshot is). This does not weaken the shaft as much as notching would, although it does create more drag.

Light shafts are particularly good if the diver is using a "free shaft." The lighter ⁵/₁₆″ and ¼″ shafts work well on the smaller fish, but if the diver's fish is in the 15-pound or larger class, a ⅜″ shaft is better. It will bend less easily and is heavier for the fish to carry around while he fights. Because of the weight of this shaft, more power is needed to get it underway at a reasonable speed. Generally, two rubbers are sufficient if the shaft is under three feet long. I have seen guns with many rubbers on the shaft, but too much power gives the shaft a "speed wobble" that is inconsistent with accuracy. I saw one seven-foot gun that had a half-inch shaft with six rubbers being carried by a diver at Cabo San Lucas once. I looked at it and asked him what he intended to shoot. He said, "Whatever I see; they get big down here." I ran into the same diver a month later and found he had landed nothing. In the same month, and in the same general area, I had landed dozens of fish, the largest of which was 605 pounds and the sexiest of which was a beautiful 20-pound Mahi Mahi. The differences were that my equipment (seven different guns) was matched to my prey and I knew what I was looking for. My diver friend had wandered without a specific objective and with a piece of equipment he could not handle in the water. I think if he had fired it, the recoil would have pushed him right out of the water.

The spear points available are as varied as the fish in the sea. Keep the point as simple as you can. The point has one job—holding the shaft to the fish. If your fish is small, say under five pounds, you are probably better off with a three- or five-prong head. If you find that you cannot hold the fish with this head, change to a different one. If the fish you are looking for is known to have soft flesh, such as the white sea bass or the yellowtail, a detachable head is probably your best bet. This head has the added advantage of allowing your shaft to pull out of the fish so that it will not be bent while the fish is fighting. Fish of 15 pounds or so have the ability to bend a shaft and render it useless. The detachable head helps prevent this.

These are things that each diver must work out for himself. I make my own shafts, so the expense is not great. Because of this, I seldom use a detachable head. I prefer what I call my "cactus patch." This is a shaft which is ground to a sharp point with large barbs placed right on the shaft. I use two or three barbs about three inches apart on the shaft and placed so they face out in different directions. I rarely lose a fish. A complete shaft and head can be made with not too much effort for less than $5 for the biggest gun. It is possible to spend over $25 to buy a commercial shaft and head for one of the larger guns.

It is worth mentioning where you should aim when you shoot at a fish. I have listened for years to divers talk about how they aim "right behind the head on the lateral line," or some other favorite spot. I'm rarely lucky enough to have such a shot. I always aim "dead center." When you shoot this way there is less chance of a fish getting away because of a poor shot.

LINE MODIFICATIONS • The way you are attached to the fish after you spear it is important. If your fish is under 30 pounds, then you probably have just the line from the gun to the shaft and no modifications at all, but as the fish run into the larger categories over 30 pounds, then some type of modification is necessary. I think the most common modifications made on the gun concerning the line fall into three basic types: reels, drag lines, and break-away gear.

Most divers use break-away gear with fish over 50 pounds. This gear consists of a line attached to the shaft or to a detachable head on one end and to a float of some kind on the other end. When the diver shoots the fish, the fish pulls the line out of a pack of some sort on the gun and takes off. The line unfolds and the fish pulls the float around. When he tires, the diver catches the float and lands him. He may go down and shoot the fish again to kill him before he brings him up.

I don't like this type of fishing. The bigger fish are not all that frightened of the diver and generally are not a problem to get close enough to shoot. If the diver uses break-away gear he has shown zero sportsmanship in my eyes. Anyone can shoot a harpoon into a cow with an anchor on it and wait for it to die. This method of hunting doesn't take skill or talent. I would place it just one step above dropping a stick of dynamite into the water and then picking up the dead fish. Needless to say, I don't consider it a proper method of sport fishing but rather a commercial fishing technique which brings no laurels to the sport diver.

The other two methods are similar in principle, but the diver hangs on to his fish by keeping the line in his hands. There is no way to explain the excitement of being towed by a big fish. Your mask will be pushed down around your neck or ripped off altogether by the water as you are pulled through it. The rush of water past your ears sounds like the roar of a crowd cheering you on. Hemingway came close to expressing what goes through your mind at times like these when he had his "Old Man" say: "I'm being towed by a fish and I'm the towing bit. I could make the line fast. But then he could break it. I must hold him all I can and give him line when he must have it. Thank God he is traveling and not going down."

There are two dangers in this type of fishing. One is losing your gear, gun and all; the other is becoming tangled in the line and losing your life. Because of the danger of becoming tangled in the line, I use a reel on my gun and at no time let the line slack in the water. Any time there is line drifting around in the water you have a potential hazard. The reel allows the diver to keep a hundred feet of extra line on hand to play the big ones. I personally prefer the reel to any other rig.

The second of the two methods I mentioned earlier is a drag line. This works well but has the inherent danger of entangling the diver in loose line. Drag lines are

148

JOHN RESECK, JR.

A large fish like this bass can pull a diver through the water so fast that his mask is pulled off his face from the water pressure. There is no way to explain such a feeling.

Any line loose in the water means tangles—and troubles.

ON MERKER

generally 50 to 100 feet long and are tied to the gun so that if the fish pulls the gun out of the diver's hand, the diver has a hundred feet of line to play the fish with. There is a float on the other end of the line so it can't be lost. The drag line is the cheapest and easiest way to rig your gear for the big ones. It is a compromise between the break-away and the reel. If you use one, make sure you know where the line is at all times so you won't become entangled in it.

Special Techniques

There are special ways to fish special areas that are too numerous to list. One example of what I mean by "special ways" would be the fishing that is done around the oil rigs in the Gulf of Mexico. It is difficult to hang onto a fish in the oil rigs because the fish will careen in and out of the maze of pipes. The divers who try it wear football helmets and use a short line so the fish can't wrap the line up. That's one way to get a thrill!

Other enterprising divers in the same situation decided that lines of any kind were dangerous under an oil rig, so they devised a lineless way to fish the big ones. They take a CO_2 gas gun, which shoots a shaft by issuing a blast of high-pressure CO_2, and make a special shaft for it. This shaft has a large brass ball on the end of it. The next modification is to take the barrel of the gun and sharpen it to a point. Then they drift in and out of the pipes below the rigs until they can sneak up on a big one. They shoot the brass ball shaft and conk the fish right between the eyes. The fish is stunned for an instant. In that instant, the diver swims up, sticks the sharpened barrel of his gun into the fish, and pulls the trigger. A blast of CO_2 gas—and we have a fish that floats to the surface, where the diver then picks him up.

In areas where you must take fish such as trout on a hook and line, there is a fun thing that you should try. Put on all your diving gear and then take a light fly rod or spinning rod with you into the water. You can bait fish or troll, but do it while you are swimming. It is fun to troll in clear water where you can watch the fish come out and hit your lure.

There are a thousand ways to enjoy underwater hunting. The rules are simple: Check the fish and game laws for any area you intend to fish (especially for any provisions that pertain specifically to divers). Never take more than you can use at one time. You are not a commercial fisherman; don't try to fill your freezer. Give yourself an excuse to go more often! Remember that you *can* harm the environment by over-fishing. Never have slack line around you in the water; this is hazardous. Always share your dives with a buddy—it gives him a good excuse to go, and you need him. Be considerate of others at all times. Match your equipment to your prey. Be objective about your own physical ability. Have a good time!

11

"SAY CHEESE"

Sooner or later almost every diver tries his hand at taking pictures underwater. It is a natural thing to do. Whenever we travel, we take pictures to show where we have been and what we did there. Every dive to the diver is like a trip abroad. The things we see change hourly and the scenery is as exotic, if not more so, as it is anywhere else we could go in the world.

In the first chapter I mentioned how difficult it is for a diver to communicate with a nondiver. Photographs help this situation a great deal. Underwater pictures inspire great interest in an audience simply because they are totally different from the pictures they are used to viewing. This novelty, however, is short-lived and to hold the interest of an audience the pictures must be of at least moderate quality. A poor movie of random underwater shots is just about as interesting as a poor movie of someone else's children. Slides must be clear and in focus and should show something. When the commentary runs something like this, you know you've got a problem: "This is John getting a lobster. The lobster is in that hole to your left. You can't see him because it was too dark in the hole to take a picture. John's head is out of the picture because I wanted to get close enough to get the lobster in. You can see how he has his hands back in the hole. He's wearing gloves but you just can't see them because his hands are back in the hole where it is too dark and it's a little bit blurred because I had to use a slow shutter speed to try to get the picture of the lobster in the hole and I guess I didn't hold the camera quite still enough." This photographer will find it difficult to arrange for a second gathering of his friends to view his subsequent attempts at underwater photography!

Just as boring to an audience as a bad picture is the slide show that never ends. A general rule might be to never show more than 45 slides at one sitting, or to limit the showing time to approximately 30 minutes. If, when you do end the show, your audience asks for more, this is great! But, don't show any more at this time. Tell them you will get together some more slides and will present them at another showing. They will then look forward to coming back.

If your first show was really good, you may be able to "con" them into inviting you over for dinner some evening so they can see the rest of your slides. It works for me—in fact, that's how I pay for my film! Another trick is to suggest that they might have some friends who would enjoy the pictures and, if they do invite additional people, this is all to your advantage. Firstly, it could mean the difference between hamburgers and fondue, as, the more people invited, usually the more effort goes into the meal! And, secondly, it gives you an opportunity to reshow some of the same slides. For, if you have more than 30 or 40 really excellent slides in your collection, you are either an outstanding photographer or you've been at it a long time. As you generally show your best pictures the first time around, it helps to be able to pull a few of them back in for your second show. (It also helps to be a bit of a psychologist, as well as a photographer!)

Movie rules would be about the same—they should be no longer than 15 minutes and, if the footage isn't perfectly smooth, cut it. Make the movie tell a story. It doesn't necessarily have to be a true story; instead of showing what you actually did on your trip, show what you want your friends to think you did. This is a great way to build a wild reputation for yourself without actually getting into trouble! I have found that small innuendoes are best. When someone asks who that gorgeous girl is I was talking to in the movie, I just blush and hem-haw around like I'm at a loss for words and then say, "Oh, yeah, that girl—I was just asking her for a cigarette." As they all know I don't smoke they can draw their own conclusions! Have a little fun in everything you do.

There are several questions that must be answered before you can start taking underwater pictures. What type of camera? What type of case to put it in? And—*how* do I do it?

Let's talk about the camera first. I never like to see anyone spend a lot of money

The sea has an endless—often colorful and active—range of subject matter for the photography-minded.

they don't have to and it's very easy to spend money on underwater photography equipment. Go slowly; think before you buy is always a good practice, but in underwater photography it really applies. The first step is to be objective and ask yourself the question: how good (or motivated) a photographer am I? Are you a snapshot photographer who likes to bring back snapshots of all your trips and catch your friends (and yourself) in fun moments? If so, you probably own an Instamatic-type camera or a Polaroid. You can stay in this class without spending much money and still go underwater. The divers who use this type of equipment have as much fun, if not more, than the serious photographer.

If you are one of the more serious amateurs you probably have one or two cameras in the $150 to $500 range. You will be much more choosey about the quality of your pictures because you are the one who will project them for shows. When a picture is enlarged to about 50″ × 50″ it has to be good to be tolerated. You recognize a good picture and will be very demanding of yourself. You are the one who will find great frustration and challenge working in this new media.

Once you have determined which of these two categories you belong to then you can make some realistic judgments as to what equipment you wish to purchase. The first two questions, What camera and What case, are not hard to answer for the snapshooter. The Instamatic-type cameras are so common and widespread that several manufacturers have created underwater cases for them on a mass production basis. This is good for the diver because the greater the quantity made, the cheaper they become. There are several cases manufactured for approximately $40. If you are interested in this type of case, just check the ads in one of the diving magazines. Some cases have a place for a flash cube also. This is not as big an advantage as you might think at first. The common assumption is that a flash will give you a good picture if the visibility is low. In actual practice, the opposite often is true. The more floating material in the water, such as plankton, the less good a flash located on the camera will do. The flash cube, of course, is located directly on top of the camera above the lens. The little objects floating in the water between your camera lens and your subject will act like mirrors and reflect back small particles of light. As a result, your picture will have spots all over it. A flash is a great help if it can be held away from the camera at an angle such that the reflected light from the particles is eliminated or greatly minimized. Therefore, a flash which is detachable from the camera with a four- or five-foot cord is a much better choice than one which is attached to the camera.

The flash cube is then actually useable only in clear water, where it's used for additional light. There is one good additional reason, however, to use a flash cube, for in some Instamatic cameras there is an automatic slowing down of the shutter when the cube is in place. For example, a standard camera might take a normal picture with no flash cube in place at about one-ninetieth of a second. This would stop most average action and yet pass a fair amount of light through the lens to the

154

Before becoming deeply committed in the (expensive) matter of photographic equipment, you must ask yourself: How serious a photographer am I?

This photo was taken in 1955 with a $1.50 camera. The camera was placed in a rubber glove and round glass from a face plate was placed in the hole where the wrist should be. Total cost of camera and case, $1.75.

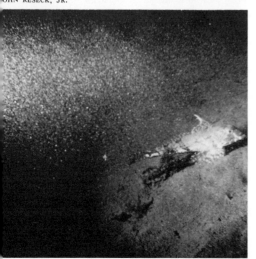

A flash located on the camera will cause particles suspended in the water to reflect back tiny spots of light.

film. When a flash cube is placed in the camera the shutter is automatically slowed down to about one-sixtieth of a second. This slowing of the shutter speed allows more light to pass through to the film, which is a great help at night when taking flash pictures. It is also easier to synchronize the shutter with the flash at a slower shutter speed. A good idea, then, is to put a *used flash cube* in place on the camera. There will be no flash of light to reflect back into your camera lens but the shutter will be automatically slowed down to let in more light and, underwater, you need all the light you can get. When using this technique, the diver must be very careful to hold the camera as still as he can. One-sixtieth of a second is not fast enough to stop the blurring of the picture if the camera is not held steady. I would recommend placing your elbow against a rock for stability if at all possible.

Acceptable pictures can be taken by practically anyone with one of these small, inexpensive outfits. Their total cost, including camera and case, would be around $70. There are limitations, of course. You must stay in shallow, well-lit waters. You can not get too close, perhaps four feet, without blurring the image, and you must hold the camera very still while taking the picture. Of all the things that can go wrong, an unsteady camera hand seems to move more pictures from the acceptable pile to the not acceptable pile than any other single mistake the photographer may make. Inhale, hold your breath, press slowly and gently. A professional cameraman once told me that "you press the shutter release on a camera just like you pull the trigger on a gun. Gently but firmly."

These same two questions regarding camera and case are more difficult to answer for the serious amateur. There are two ways he can go. He can take a camera he has now (for underwater work 35 mm and 2¼ × 2¼ cameras are most commonly used, with the latter being preferred for clarity) and make a case for it, or he can purchase a new camera that is made to work underwater without a special case. The decision can be a hard one, for both alternatives have advantages. Let's look at the advantages and disadvantages of both.

First—the self-contained camera. The most common of these in the United States is the Nikonos. This little camera is a real boon to the serious amateur. Its lens is sharp enough to give clear slides; it has several interchangeable lenses which the photographer can use to whatever advantage he can find for them; it is not too expensive, about $300; and, it can be used in or out of the water with equal ease. Because of these features, a great number of the Nikonos cameras are being sold. As they are becoming more and more popular, the list of accessories is growing. Right now, if you bought all the accessories that are made to fit the Nikonos, you would spend approximately $4,000. The list includes electric flash slave units, close-up lenses, extension tubes, and just about everything else you can imagine—even fish-eye lenses. This is undoubtedly a good way to go. As I said before, it is not a simple decision. As good as the Nikonos is, the lens system is not as good as the better lenses on the better cameras. You might have guessed

The Nikonos is such a popular camera that almost everyone makes some kind of accessory or attachment for it. This picture shows a few of the items available.

Underwater photo cases can be constructed for any camera. Generally when a special case has to be made, plastic is used. Plastic makes a good case and is easier to work with than metal.

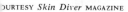

Cast metal underwater housings for cameras are expensive but highly durable and their greater weight is easier to handle in the water.

that the lens on a camera that sells for $300 cannot be as good and as sharp as a lens that alone sells for $300.

The best way to get professional quality pictures suitable for commercial reproduction in magazines is to use a camera with one of these better lenses. To do this, you must take the camera that you already have, put a good wide-angle lens on it, and build a case or have the case built for it. This can be expensive. Cases alone, for instance, cost as much as $400. Most of these cases are fairly bulky; much more so than the Nikonos. The two things which are gained by this seemingly more complicated alternative are things that are needed by the professional photographer more than by the amateur: first, the highest quality rendition on the film from the sharpest possible lenses and, second, great versatility in the ability to modify the system.

These "custom-rigged" cameras can have any number of lens changes, automatic electric eyes to make sure the exposure is correct, and other such accommodations that for the professional are worth the money—anywhere from $600 to $700 to around $1,500 for a complete system. The average person would do no better with one of these rigs than with a Nikonos. The advantage of the more sophisticated unit is that it makes all of the infinite techniques known to the professional on land available to the underwater professional. If you don't know any of these techniques, then you don't need a sophisticated rig.

As to *how* to take pictures underwater, there are a few basic rules which should always be observed. Several have already been mentioned: hold the camera perfectly still when firing it and keep the flash away from the lens whenever possible. Another general rule is to use scuba gear when possible. Scuba allows you to move slowly and deliberately and set up your picture with no fast movements involved which might stir up the bottom. Take time to look for good pictures and add to them what is needed before you snap the shutter. One picture well thought out is worth a hundred poor or random ones. Try to have people in most of your pictures, or at least use photos showing people when presenting a slide show, to give your audience something with which to relate. People lend interest to the scene, as their presence implies that action is taking place.

Think in terms of shooting sequences, not just random single pictures. There is nothing wrong with a good single shot, but it is not as interesting as a series of shots that tell a story. If you get a good single shot, have a print made and mount it. A few good underwater pictures hanging on the wall help to show your friends what your world looks like. They also make excellent gifts at Christmas, or other gift-giving occasions. Try making Christmas cards with an underwater scene. People love them. Be creative and think of ways to use your pictures to best advantage.

Shooting a picture story is fun and showing the story is equally fun. People love a story. Make up one and shoot slides which depict it. Write a short script. Plan the pictures you need to get your point across and then set them up. This can be a great club or family project.

Be sure your exposure is correct. Use a light meter when possible. Light meters are a must underwater for the serious photographer, just as they are on land. To capture that "perfect" picture we are all in search of, the exposure must be right. The proper exposure underwater is very difficult to judge, due to the light absorption and the scattering effect of all the particles floating in the water. A light meter will give the best setting to obtain whatever effect the photographer has in mind. Special effects can be had by over or underexposing.

Meters run from $20 to several hundred dollars. Just like cameras, they have a wide range. The best way to find the right meter for you is to get one that you feel comfortable using, and which matches the ability of your camera. The meter should read directly, if possible, in f/stops. The diver can then simply glance at it and set his camera. Simplicity of design is advantageous in a meter, as it is in all underwater equipment.

Underwater photographers have a habit of diving alone. They make all kinds of rationalizations for doing it, such as "I don't go anywhere; I just sit on the bottom so I don't want to bore someone else." Or, "Anybody else with me will stir up the bottom and make my picture-taking more difficult." Or, "I don't want to worry about anyone else." All of these are just excuses.

The photographer has no more business diving alone than anyone else. It is true he moves rather slowly and doesn't go far, but there are buddies who would enjoy these easy, relaxed dives. If I may make a suggestion, I would recommend taking your wife on such expeditions. Most women cannot physically keep up with their diving husbands; underwater photography presents an ideal situation for a wife to help her husband, as well as being able to share an interest. A buddy is invaluable in setting up good pictures. He or she can also act as your model, or take your picture for you. Most photographers never have photos of themselves.

Most of the things said in this chapter also apply to using a movie camera underwater. The most interesting possibilities for the amateur are offered by the new types of Super 8 cameras. Most of these have electric wind and electric eye exposure so about all the diver has to do is focus the camera, point it, and push the button. If your camera has a zoom lens, put the lens in the widest possible wide-angle position and the depth of field or the area which is in focus will be so extensive you won't have to worry about focusing it. You can set the camera at about five feet and just go out and shoot away. Do not pan. Pans are even more objectionable underwater than on top. Movies are fun; plan your scenes carefully and edit them ruthlessly. If a scene is jumpy or unclear or out of focus or too dark, cut it out. Better to have a good five-minute movie than a poor 15-minute one. Very few amateurs cut out all their bad scenes; they apparently are afraid of wasting the film. Be different! Be an individual! Cut out the bad stuff—give your

The professional movie unit is beautiful to behold. Unfortunately it is far too expensive for the average underwater photographer.

friends a good show! When you have the film cut the way you want it, put music to it with a small cassette tape recorder. The music will make a fantastic difference in how well your movie goes over with your friends.

One way to make sure that your pictures are in sharp focus is to make a wand. This wand is held out in front of the camera to measure the distance to the subject. Some divers use a short spear of three feet or so. The principle behind this is simple: water makes everything look closer due to refraction, so if your camera is set for two feet the subject underwater must be farther away than the two feet in order to appear to be two feet away from the camera. For the underwater cameraman a foot is not 12 inches—an underwater focus foot is equal to 16 inches. If you carry a small stick that is 32 inches long and use it to measure the distance from the subject to your camera, you will get good pictures with your camera set at two feet. It is well worthwhile to take great care to ensure the sharpest focus available with your equipment.

Keep the flash away from the lens if possible. This was mentioned earlier but is important enough to repeat. Try to keep the flash at at least a 45-degree angle from the lens, and especially in dirty water.

If possible, choose white sand bottoms to work over. They reflect a lot of light and will let you use a smaller iris diaphragm opening. The smaller opening will increase your depth of field and aid you in attaining a sharp image.

Try not to take pictures more than one-fifth of the distance you can see clearly at

Say Cheese!

any given time. If the visibility is 100 feet you will be able to get clear photos up to a distance of 20 feet. If visibility is five feet, then plan all your picture-taking at one foot or less. This procedure will insure that your pictures are not ruined by dirty water. You can take good photos with a Nikonos and a close-up tube when visibility is only one foot. Whatever the conditions where you dive, with a little forethought and much perseverance you can be a successful underwater photographer.

There are numerous books and classes dealing with underwater photography. Many of the books are available through the NAUI Diving Association (NDA). You can obtain a book list by writing to NDA, P.O. Box 630, Colton, CA 92324.

12

SPECIAL PLACES AND NEAT THINGS

This chapter discusses some of the areas in diving that are of special interest, but which also create special problems. It is not my intent to solve these problems, but rather to bring to the attention of the new diver the fact that there are topics which are not adequately covered in a basic class, for which additional instruction as well as special safety precautions are necessary.

Each of these areas warrants its own book of information. In fact, books have already been written about some of them. The diver should be sure to read all he can about each of these specialties before he attempts them, and then should attempt them only with an experienced diver who has not only knowledge, but actual practical experience in that specialty. Caution and good common sense are very important. Keep cool, and don't attempt something you know you shouldn't do just because a friend with less sense than you wants to.

. DEEP DIVING

Deep diving, as I have made clear many times in this book, is something the average sports diver should avoid. I would consider any dive over 100 feet to be a deep dive. However, there are times and circumstances when the recreational diver has a need to dive deeper than 100 feet, and it is important that he understand the special physiological problems associated with deep diving. These include excessive diuresis, loss of thinking ability due to cold water, excessive inert gas narcosis, absorption rates under high partial pressures of various tissues of the body, and many others, all of which, if the diver is not knowledgeable about them, could have a most serious effect.

I think it becomes obvious why we call this a "specialty area." If the opportunity comes to make a deep dive and you feel you have to do it, be sure you know how to work the decompression tables before the dive. Also, a shot line (a line weighted so it will hang down straight, even in current) should be hung from the boat to a depth of 30 or 40 feet. The shot line should be marked as to depth so the diver has an exact reference point. The diver can use this line when he comes to the surface to tell how deep he is. When it comes to make a decompression stop, let's say ten feet, the diver wants to make sure he is at exactly ten feet. Guessing at depth by looking at the surface or reading a depth gauge just won't cut it. The gauge could be as much as five or six feet off. Another must is an extra tank and regulator for each diver at the planned decompression depth. They should be tied onto the line so that, if for some reason the diver should run out of air during his decompression, he has a spare supply handy with which to finish his time decompressing.

Any dive below 100 feet without specific purpose in mind or a specific job that

The author photographing "black coral" with a light. This species is found only in deep water and requires a well-planned dive.

164

RON MERKER

must be done, I feel, is just an ego trip and should be avoided. I also would recommend not diving with individuals who like to brag about their deep dives, for they have some type of ego problem and you don't particularly want to be around when they solve it.

. CAVE DIVING

There are many fabulous underwater caves throughout the world which lure divers. Florida is one area that has a great many. The diver must realize, however, that cave diving is probably one of the more dangerous types of diving he can do. If you think about it for a moment, you can see why. The diver enters a small hole, goes down a shaft, bends around a couple of curves, and finds himself totally immersed in darkness and with many passages to follow, only one of which leads to the outside. Caves are exciting to explore and they can be dived in safety, but cave diving takes special equipment and very precise pre-dive planning.

You should never attempt a cave dive without someone there who is very much experienced and whose judgment you feel you can trust. It is always a good idea, for instance, not to get so far from the opening that you could not, if necessary, make an emergency breath-hold ascent to the opening. This, of course, is not always possible. I heave heard divers say that if you should have to make an emergency ascent in a cave, many times you can find air pockets which are trapped against the ceiling. But such pockets may not be all that they are cracked up to be. Admiral Momsen believes that some of them could be filled with gases other than air and would not support the diver if he breathed them. It is only speculation, but divers have been found drowned in caves for no apparent cause, with air in the tank and all gear functional. Possibly, these divers came up to an air pocket, took a deep breath of this air, and blacked out, which would have caused them to sink and drown.

Avoid breathing the gas in a cave unless you have someone right there with you to watch and make sure that you are all right. Never take your tank off so that you can fit through a small hole in a cave. You are only asking for trouble if you have to take your tank off to get through a passage into a larger chamber. What would happen if you had any type of trouble after you had passed through the small opening? The percentages just aren't with you at that point. So, why ever put yourself in that position? If you feel you must explore such a place, use a Hooka-surface supply air rig. It is safer. A small scuba bottle should be carried as a back-up air supply.

The cave diver always carries *two* underwater lights. Light to find your way is so important that a back-up light is a must. A large one for the primary light, and a smaller one as a spare is the usual procedure.

165

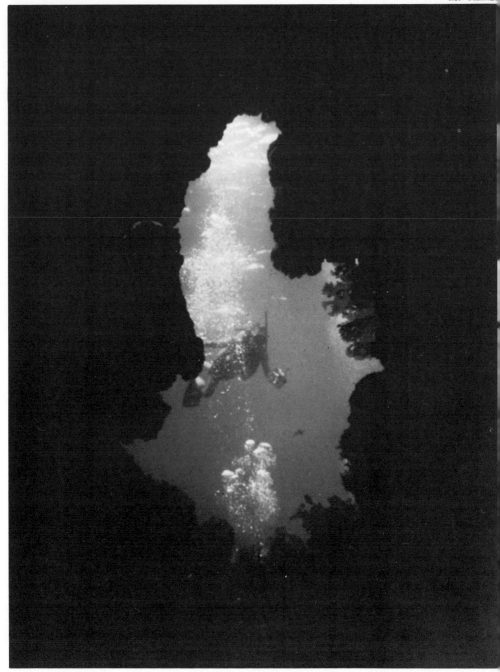

The mouth of this underwater cave draws the attention of the passing diver.

Most people who have diving accidents in caves are people who didn't follow the rules and did not have the proper lifelines, light, and safety equipment to make the dive safely to begin with. Don't you be one of these!

One last item about cave diving: A cave is one place where you *do not* wear a flotation vest. How would you like to be pulled away from your buddy and lost because your vest accidentally inflated? In a cave the vest becomes a hazard. Leave it home.

An excellent book on cave diving, *The Complete Guide to Cave Diving*, can be purchased from NDA Headquarters, P.O. Box 630, Colton, CA 92324.

. WRECK DIVING

The waters of the world have wrecks of many kinds in them. A wreck is always a fascinating place to dive but, like anything else, it could become dangerous if the diver is not careful. For instance, you should not approach a wreck from the current side, for many wrecks have spikes and extrusions sticking out from them which the current could push you against, causing severe injury. So, always approach a wreck from the down-current side.

Make sure you understand a wreck from the outside before you go in. Looking at the outside of a wreck is an adventure in itself and not all that dangerous. Once you go inside, however, you get into an area that can rapidly become dangerous. If the wreck is a large one, you must realize that you are entering a giant maze, in which you cannot always see well enough to get out of.

Much the same as in cave diving, in wreck diving you need a lifeline and lights. At times you can enter a wreck and see quite well, but as you swim along, the fine sediments that have settled inside are stirred up behind you in the water by your fins so that when you turn around to come out you can't see anything. A lifeline is an absolute must! Even if you have all the necessary things like lifelines, and a tender to watch the line, plus bright lights, you should still not penetrate too far into this maze of wood and steel. You should never be in the wreck so far that you cannot hold your breath and swim to the outside to make an emergency ascent. Again, the flotation vest is a consideration. If you are deep in a wreck you should not wear it.

Plan all wreck dives carefully and *follow* your dive plan. It is mandatory that everyone know what to expect so there will be as little confusion as possible.

Collecting in wrecks is a no-no. A wreck should be enjoyed and not desecrated so the next diver can enjoy it, too.

There is a wreck off the coast of California's Catalina Island that was absolutely breathtaking the first time I dove on it in 1955. It is about 180 feet long and sits in

Make sure you understand a wreck from the outside before you go in.

A diver has a look at what is believed to be the wreck of a Revolutionary War longboat, deep in Lake George.

Playing captain to an old sunken boat makes for pleasant memories.

168

100 feet of water. It was in perfect shape and the fish and general sea life on it were triple the population found in one spot anywhere else on the island. All was well for a few years until one of the local California dive shop owners found out about the wreck. First he chartered boats and took 75 people a weekend to dive on it. This wouldn't have been too bad, except that they took spearguns and in two weeks all the fish were dead or had split. Next they took wrenches and stripped the wreck of all they could. Then the big blow. The dive shop owner tried to *blast* the prop off with dynamite. Now this once majestic wreck is an open hull and a pile of scrap iron on the bottom. It doesn't make any difference to the fellow who did all the damage because he has found other wrecks in Florida to destroy, but to the divers of Southern California it is a great loss.

Protect your area and your environment. Don't let people destroy it, and even more important, don't *you* destroy it.

• ICE DIVING

As mentioned previously, diving in cold water can seriously hamper the ability of the diver to think and to act rationally. Therefore, if you are going to make an ice dive, which can be an incredible experience in a world of dim light and general eeriness, it should be done on a very simple basis with experienced personnel on hand to monitor you. Do not expect to go under the ice and do anything complicated. The cold water just won't let you do it.

You should always try to keep the hole in the ice you came through in sight. Sometimes this is difficult, but it is a good idea anyway. Heavy lifelines are again the order of the day. These lifelines should be tied to the diver's waist with a bowline knot. The "wet suit system," which is excellent for ice diving, has been discussed in Chapter 3. You should not dive as long as you can or, in other words, until you get severely cold. The chill factor occurs so rapidly in this cold water that it is best to come out before you get really chilled. In case any problem arises, you will then not be so cold that you lack the thinking ability and manual dexterity with which to handle it. For further information, you can obtain a list of books on ice diving by writing to NDA Headquarters at the address given under "Cave Diving."

• NIGHT DIVING

One of the most beautiful times to dive is at night, when the water is cut only by the beam of your light and your entire world seems to exist within that beam. If you are in shark "infested" waters, however, I would advise against night diving. It could be dangerous.

Along the Southern California coast, a great many divers go night diving for a very specific reason—to catch lobsters. Lobsters crawl out of their holes at night to feed and the diver who is present while they are feeding usually has little trouble picking them up off the bottom. A diver can go into the same area at night where he had spent all day and perhaps had seen two or three lobsters, and he might see two or three dozen and get his limit.

Night diving is very similar to day diving except that buddies must stay very close together so as not to lose each other. However, I do not believe in buddy lines—that is, a line tied between the two buddies. There are many problems which can arise from being tied together.

If you are in the ocean at night and turn off your light and let your eyes become accustomed to the darkness, you will see all kinds of little things moving in the water due to the phosphorescence which is often present. The barnacles on the rocks will appear to be little flashing stars in the sky. Such sights can add up to some of the most memorable experiences you have ever had. Night diving is also interesting because of the various extracurricular activities which can go along with the dive. I shall not elaborate on these.

A practical rule for all night diving is to always dive in the area first in the daytime so that you are totally familiar with it and, only then, venture out to investigate it at night.

• SEARCH AND RECOVERY

Everybody seems to drop something overboard from time to time when they get on a boat, so anyone with diving gear sooner or later finds himself in the salvage business. There are many patterns which can be run by a diver to locate a lost object. Probably the simplest is to drop a line with a weight on it directly to the bottom where the object was supposedly dropped, and then attach another line to the weight and swim in increasingly wider circles around the center weight. This allows you to cover a fairly large area quite thoroughly.

If you are looking for a large item such as an automobile, then you can take your line and swim a very wide circle because the object you are looking for is big enough to snag the line. When the line snags, you then come back along it and check to see what it is snagged on—hopefully, the car. Once while diving in Mexico I used this method to find a downed airplane which had just crashed hours before in a large bay.

When you have located your object, it has to be lifted from the bottom. There are special books that will advise you on ways to rig lifting devices. One of the simplest devices might be your flotation vest, though if this is used care must be taken not to place yourself in a dangerous position. If you need more than that, you

Learning to use lift bags may help you to recover an old anchor for your backyard, like the author.

These divers are using a hand-held sonar which can give dial readings and audio indications through earphones as to the direction of an object underwater. This is especially useful in search and salvage in dirty water.

171

might try using an old duffel bag or an inner tube which has been designed to hold a harness and can be filled from a scuba tank. One of the favorite lift devices of the commercial diver is the old 55-gallon drum. When full of air, this drum will lift in the neighborhood of 400 pounds, but watch out if it breaks loose!

Check your library for books on salvaging procedures and equipment. You will find them interesting, and perhaps some may be useful. Unfortunately, when the actual need arises to do a salvage job, you can rarely be picking up books and reading them, so the time to absorb the general information is when you don't have any particular project in mind—then when a job crops up at the spur of the moment you can hop right to work as if you knew exactly what you were doing.

If the item being searched for is something that involves great emotional appeal, don't let yourself get so caught up in the emotion that you endanger your life looking for it. Remember, if someone reports that a swimmer has drowned in a lake some 25 minutes ago, there is no hurry in looking for him and, if you do hurry and forget your safety procedures, they may be looking for you an hour later. Always take an objective view of the situation and act reasonably, not emotionally.

• SPECIALTY AND ADVANCED DIVING PROGRAMS

The special interest activities discussed in this chapter involve enough curiosity and special equipment and skills for an international program to have been devised to teach each specialty separately from the others in what is called a Specialty Diving Program. This program offers courses to the general public through the National Association of Underwater Instructors. You can thus take a course that will make you an adequate cave diver or an adequate salvage diver or the like and feel confident that you have had the proper training to handle these various situations, remembering of course that any class can only give you the basic details of safety and procedures. It takes years of experience to be really good.

The Specialty programs available as of 1976 include: Cave diving, Deep diving, Diving Leadership, Ice diving, Professional diving, Search & Recovery, Underwater Environment, Underwater hunting & Collecting, Underwater Photography, and Wreck diving. These Specialty courses are being taught as club activities in many clubs. What better activity could a club have than an educational program that involves no pressure, is fun, and teaches a new skill. Get your local instructor to spark up your club's life.

172

Instruction in these specialties is also included in some advanced diving programs. The term ADP (Advanced Diving Program) is commonly used by instructors for courses taken after a basic course is completed. What is an advanced diver? I can find no one who can define him, but there are two ADP programs I can recommend: Los Angeles County's ADP program, which takes many weekends over a four-month period, and NAUI's ADP program. To give the reader an idea of what a good ADP involves, I am presenting here the *minimum* requirements for the NAUI program. An instructor or group of instructors can exceed these minimal requirements as they have the expertise and equipment to do so.

	Minimum Hours	
Curriculum	*Classroom*	*Practical Application*
Subject Area	*Presentations*	*and Water Time*
1. Applied Sciences	1	0
2. Diving Equipment	1	0
3. Diving First Aid	1	1
4. Diving Lifesaving	1	1
5. Underwater Navigation	1	1
6. Limited Visibility Diving	1	1
7. Search and Recovery	1	1
8. Light Salvage	1	1
9. Diving Environment	1	1
10. Deep, Decompression, Repetitive, and Altitude Diving	1	1
11. Evaluation, Review, and Enhancement of Skills	0	8
Subtotal	10	16
12. Electives	6	8

Increased coverage of the foregoing subjects, special or local interest subjects, such as:

Underwater photography	Aquariums
Cave diving	Collecting
Lake or river diving	Spearfishing
Boat operation and diving	Wreck diving
Underwater archaeology	Military diving
Commercial diving	Diving organizations
Ice diving	Diving for gold

Minimum total hours	16	24

13

WHERE DO WE GO FROM HERE?

The growth of diving in the United States, as well as in other parts of the world, has been rather phenomenal over the last 20 years. In 1950 when the two-hose regulator designed by Cousteau was first used by the sports diver in the United States, we had no idea where we were going. The growth of the sport has been so rapid and so extensive that even Cousteau's dreams must have fallen short of reality. The National Association of Underwater Instructors alone is certifying divers at the rate of 10,000 a month. If we were to combine certifications issued by all other organizations, we would arrive at a total number in the area of 16,000 to 18,000 per month. More people are coming to the realization that scuba diving is a great way to escape the pressure of this "topsy, turvy world."

One of the most significant advancements took place when diving equipment became sophisticated enough for women and young people to use it safely. We

The testing of new gear, though not always pleasant, is a vital step toward the extension of man's underwater abilities.

now have in our ranks a high percentage of young people and women of all ages and occupations who thoroughly enjoy the sport. With all this growth, the firms in the business of manufacturing the equipment used in diving have found it difficult to meet the demand. They often do not have the time or manpower for extensive research and development. Our equipment today is not so very different from the original regulators manufactured in the late '40s and early '50s. It has fewer moving parts and is more fail-safe, but it operates on basically the same principle as earlier equipment.

During the middle and late 1960s there was a move toward the cryogenic scuba gear, which worked on liquid gas. Gas was cooled until it condensed into a liquid, which was then stored in a sort of oversized thermos bottle. The problems were many. The unit had to be filled just before use as the gas would leak as it became warm. The only advantage seemed to be that the diver could store more gas in a smaller tank than by just compressing it. There were several different units being developed and a great deal of research was done in order to make them practical and inexpensive enough for the sports diver. By 1974, these cryogenic units were no longer being manufactured as they apparently did not prove satisfactory.

Recently a new concept has been cropping up—the closed-system oxygen rebreather. Those of you who have done some reading on this subject will say that this is not new at all. It is what the Navy used long before Cousteau invented his demand regulator. But, like the cryogenic systems, those old oxygen rebreathers fell by the wayside because of their many problems. In the last 20 years, probably due to the aerospace race, our electronic technology has doubled, tripled, and quadrupled to the point where we may now have, in the 1970s, the know-how needed to produce simple, reliable, and safe closed-circuit scuba gear within the price range of the average sports diver. I have had the experience of diving with

175

two different units of this design; unfortunately, their cost at this writing is prohibitive and they still have many limitations to be overcome. One problem is that the design uses an excess number of "O" rings to seal the water from the vital inner works. Those of you who are familiar with O-rings know that in a camera case we are concerned about the case leaking with only three or four O-rings. With any scuba unit using in excess of ten O-rings, I would be skeptical as to its watertightness when handled roughly or mistreated, as all diving gear is. However, the principle is there. The units are working. The expense, as pointed out, is prohibitive—between $5,000 and $10,000 per unit, and more. But, the possibility is there. With the closed-circuit unit a diver rebreathes the same air so he never loses the air he takes down with him. He exhales into a bag and this air is then put through a device called a "scrubber," which removes the CO_2. A second device places oxygen back into the "cleaned" air mixture, thus maintaining a balanced supply of breathing gas. This process enables the diver to stay underwater with a very small amount of gas—as long as four to six hours—with a unit weighing 30 pounds or less. He only needs to emerge when he has metabolized all of the oxygen he brought with him. With further development, this excellent concept could easily become the "new way."

There have been many attempts to develop a device enabling divers to converse while underwater. The ones presently available are not workable enough to be practical, but I am sure that during the late '70s such a unit will be produced. The ability to carry on a normal conversation underwater would be the same kind of breakthrough as the rubber suit. Now, when a diver is down with his buddy, he still feels alone because if his buddy is not looking directly at him, he has no real way of communicating. Many divers with a problem have watched their companions swim off and disappear. The ability to converse will give added confidence to the diver and be a great safety factor. But, with all its good points, this communication may spoil one of the most enjoyable facets of diving, the "alone" time a diver has with his thoughts. Now when we are diving we are forced to think to ourselves and spend some time in self-communication. This process of self-communication is difficult to accomplish in our modern world, where we are surrounded by others, all making noise, a major portion of the time. But then, although I hate to lose my peace and quiet, I will be happy to be able to share what I see with my buddies.

Another item I can see being developed in the future is a control-panel board for the diver. Perhaps it will be worn on his wrist, perhaps on the upper part of his thigh, possibly even on a flip-down board over his face so whenever he wants to see it he can just flip it down and look at it. This board would include a depth gauge, a temperature gauge, a decompression meter, an underwater tank pressure gauge, a compass, a watch, and perhaps some other items not yet manufactured. All of these would be in one place, so that with a single glance the diver could totally coordinate his dive. I can also see the possibility that these items might lead into a small micro-circuit computer which would fit on the diver's chest or back, and which would monitor all information and thus keep the diver well-informed at all times.

A piece of gear which is becoming more common lately is the electric-powered underwater scooter, a small torpedo-like gadget which you can hang onto and which will pull you through the water at a higher speed than you can swim. This has been around for a long time but has always been rather expensive—in the $1,000 range. Now our modern electronic technology seems to be putting it within the reach of the sports diver's pocketbook. I am looking forward to owning my personal torpedo. In my torpedo I will have enough power to travel at least ten miles at three knots. Lights will be built into it in such a way that they can be unsnapped and used for photography away from the scooter itself. It will also contain a power source so that a few, simple underwater tools can be used to enable me to work more efficiently. Hopefully by 1980 such a scooter will be made within my price range—around $200. (Perhaps by then the scooter will also have a TV camera built into it, so Big Brother can watch, too.)

Presently, several companies are working on new materials for wet suits, and advances can be expected in this area, too. One of the problems with the present rubber suit is that as we go deeper the pressure compresses the suit and the buoyancy of the diver changes. This is one reason the flotation vest is such a distinct advantage, as it allows for compensation of the change in buoyancy. A material is presently under development which will not compress; thus, a diver, having once adjusted his buoyancy, would retain that buoyancy throughout his entire dive. It would also mean that the suit would not compress at depth and lose part of its insulating qualities, but remain the same thickness at all depths. Another advantage would be that it would not tend to constrict the diver, which can be most uncomfortable. When this material is fully developed it will present a major breakthrough in diving equipment; just think, a diving suit which is as comfortable to wear as a business suit!

I am sure that if I could look into the secret files of the major manufacturers in the country, I would find things that the diver of today has never even wildly imagined. Manufacturers, in the past few years in particular, have become alerted to the fact that the field needs improvement. Up to this point they have simply modified the same old gear over and over again. Divers are more sophisticated now and are demanding new and better equipment, and companies are being forced to comply with this demand in order to stay in the competition. I have a sincere belief that they are on the verge of moving out into research and development programs far beyond anything they have done in the past. These programs will benefit divers enormously. We aren't quite to the stage yet of the three-pill diving that I mentioned earlier—one pill to breathe underwater, one to keep warm, and one to keep safe—but I think that ten years from today we will be much closer to this point. Every time I read an article about new research on things such as a semipermeable membrane that allows oxygen through, but not water, or about the

A design such as this thermal protective suit may someday replace the wet suit. This model has been inflated with air to show that it is watertight. The diver stays dry while wearing it.

possibility of filling a man's lungs with water and having him subsist from the oxygen in the water, my mind wanders into all types of fantastic possibilities. The frontiers are wide open and the future is truly an exciting thing to which one can look forward.

If the membrane I mentioned were efficient enough we could go down to the beach, take out our little plastic bag, put it over our head, seal it around the neck and go diving to any depth for as long as we like. When we came out of the water we would rinse out our bag and put it back into our pocket or purse and be on our way. Sounds great, doesn't it? We have such a plastic bag now. It doesn't work quite like I described as yet, but who's to say it won't in ten years?

Along with all of the good things we can foresee in the future there are two very serious problems that could stop us all from diving forever. They can be summed up in a few words—pollution and conservation. These are very real problems already which must be dealt with if there is to be a future in diving. In the last several years prime areas of the California coast have been closed to swimming and diving due to pollution. Monterey, Newport Beach, and Laguna Beach have all been closed for periods of time because of raw sewage leaks. Santa Barbara was closed due to oil in the water and the residue of "gunk" on the beach. Cases of hepatitis have been reported from eating shellfish, and the amounts of *E. coli,* a bacteria from the sewer pipes emptying into the ocean is higher than ever. The diver's environment is being destroyed by the general population because of plain numbers. The sewage treatment plants are overloaded and therefore the treatment of waste has been reduced in order to handle the necessary volume. We can improve our sewage treatment but it will raise the tax bill. No one likes high taxes; on the other hand, no one likes hepatitis. It becomes a trade-off. Which is more important to us—health or our bank account?

DDT and other chemicals like it cause one of the most devastating types of pollution to the ocean. These chemicals are sprayed on crops, and then are washed via streams and rain run-off to the ocean, where they kill the marine life. The bad thing about this group of insecticides is that they don't break down for a very long period of time. They last for years, and thus their total amount in the ocean grows annually as more accumulate. The diver must join with other conservation groups to halt the use of these long-lasting insecticides.

This becomes necessary so that we can protect both our health and security. Be a concerned, informed citizen. Become concerned enough to read all the information possible about your local area and its pollution problems. Read about the national pollution problems and keep informed regarding pending legislation which will affect the environment. Work to influence the voting public in your area to vote on the side of anti-pollution and conservation whenever possible. Write to your state and national legislature. Let them know that you are for or against what is going on. What most people don't realize is that a postcard saying "I favor" or "I oppose" the issue is all that is needed. A long letter isn't necessary; just cast

179

Divers have hopped on the ecology bandwagon. Organized trash dives have helped to clean up many unsightly areas. The diver must be careful not to overdo it and wipe out *good* trash that is making a home for some marine animals.

your vote with your representative so he is truly able to represent you in his decisions. The pollution problem is a massive one and extends far beyond the diver's environment into our air, food, medicines, cosmetics, and even the games our children play. Be a concerned citizen and take action NOW.

The conservation problem is equally serious, although its immediate effect is not as drastic. (The end effect of both pollution and the failure of conservation could be, and is predicted to be, death for mankind.) The conservation problem is one of not wasting consumable resources such as wood, coal, and oil, as well as not destroying the various populations of wild animals and plants with which we cohabit the earth. It is not much fun to dive into a sterile pond. If we could stop pollution so as not to poison or starve the animals of the diver's world, we still would have to worry about proper game laws so we, the divers, would not destroy the population directly. The diver must be aware of game laws and help to enforce and improve them where necessary. He must start by adhering to them himself and "putting down" anyone who doesn't adhere to them. If you personally know of someone who is a "game hog" talk to him—try to convince him he is wrong and harming the sport for everyone. Make fun of him in front of his friends—cut a hole in the bottom of his goody bag—anything goes. Stop him from destroying our sport. Take an active part in helping to form underwater parks—places where we will be able to go for years to come and take pleasure in their beauty.

14

WHERE CAN I LEARN?

The aspiring student, when he decides to attend diving instruction classes, is at the mercy of the person to whom he talks. He assumes that the individual behind the counter of a shop or the instructor he runs into at a club or elsewhere is an expert. He really has no other choice because he has no background or knowledge upon which to base a judgment. The individual tells him that he is an instructor. The average person accepts this as fact.

Unfortunately, in the diving field there are a great number of self-acclaimed instructors. There are, in fact, entire organizations which qualify certain of their membership to teach diving with no real instruction in how to teach it at all. The fact that there is a Certified Scuba Card issued at the end of the course has little to do with the quality of instruction. It is possible, by telling a few little white lies on a piece of paper, to receive a nationally recognized Instructor's Certification through the mail from one organization.

In short, there really are no tight, stringent controls on who is teaching you and your spouse and children to be scuba divers. So the burden is on you to pick a competent instructor.

In the United States, there are two national organizations which qualify their scuba instructors only through stringent and exhaustive procedures to ascertain and guarantee that their skill and knowledge level, as well as their teaching ability, meets a certain standard for scuba instruction. These two organizations are The National Association of Underwater Instructors (commonly referred to as NAUI) and the YMCA. To become a NAUI instructor you *must* attend an eight-day program or a multi-weekend session with other candidates for instructor at a special course site and participate in both testing and learning. The entire time is spent on drilling in safe diving and good teaching techniques. High standards, such as a student to instructor (not assistant) ratio of 4 to 1 in open water, are the sign of a good instructor and a well-organized course.

The YMCA instructors have maintained a good reputation for being safety conscious and teaching a good program. The particular stronghold of the YMCA seems to be the Northeast Atlantic region. In that area the YMCA is training some of their instructors by running them through a NAUI course. You might say that the YMCA is using NAUI as one of their training arms for instructors.

A number of other national organizations boast about their programs. Upon close inspection, however, it is obvious that some of these groups spend more time on how to sell equipment than on how to teach safe diving. Having your own equipment is good. It is cheaper than renting all the time and the gear fits you better. Equipment sales is the backbone of the diving industry, but in an instructor training course the emphasis should be on how to teach diving. Teaching is in many ways a learned skill and the best of us need training.

If I were looking for someone from whom to take scuba lessons I would seek out either a NAUI or YMCA instructor. I would not take an individual's word that he is qualified. I would ask to see his current credentials. If an instructor is indeed representing an organization of which he is proud, he will be happy to show you his credentials.

There are also some *local* organizations that train scuba diving instructors. As an example, I have mentioned the Los Angeles County program. This program, although local, is excellent. The instructors go through rigorous training over a long period of time and must pass stringent tests. The program is run on weekends and consists of approximately 15 days of training and testing. It is worth noting that the Los Angeles County program was one of the first official programs for diving instructors in the world. It was an idea derived from this program which gave Mr. Neil Hess the vision he called the National Diving Patrol.

This was in 1958. In 1960 Mr. Hess was the spark that started a one-week training course and the name was changed from National Diving Patrol to National Association of Underwater Instructors. The first NAUI course was run

Sound *practical* instruction is of prime importance for safe diving. The National Association of Underwater Instructors is the largest organization of quality instructors in the world.

in Houston and the information and general standards used were based on the Los Angeles County program.

Because the Los Angeles County program is as good as it is, and due to the fact that NAUI started out using nearly the same standards in 1960, the two programs run quite parallel. In 1970 a merger, if you wish, was made whereby all Los Angeles County courses added a day of NAUI orientation to their normal time and the candidates receive both Los Angeles County and NAUI certifications.

A similar thing is happening between NAUI and YMCA, and NAUI and SCIP (Southern Council Instructor Program). NAUI ran a special testing program for SCIP instructors which took into account their formal training. The YMCA in some areas is issuing its instructor cards to candidates who successfully complete a NAUI program. The YMCA in such cases maintains members on the staff at the course and has an orientation similar to the NAUI orientation in our Los Angeles County course. What all this really means is that the organizations with high standards are joining forces.

Though there are other local programs throughout the country, I do not have firsthand knowledge of them. Some of these local programs are probably excellent; some are poor. Each one, of course, claims it's the best. I would discuss with the instructor the type of training he had and the number of hours involved in his training before I considered him qualified to teach my children how to dive. If his training consisted of one weekend, or even two, I would say that it was inadequate. If, on the other hand, he has attended five or six weekend sessions, totaling seven or eight days, then he has probably gone through an adequate instructor preparation program—*if the time was spent learning to teach diving.* I would emphasize, however, the advantages of a nationally recognized certification card.

With people traveling as they do nowadays, it is not uncommon to find yourself in some foreign port with time on your hands. Perhaps they have good diving there and you'd like to get in the water and take a look. Many of the local certification cards are not recognized in foreign ports, whereas NAUI and YMCA are recognized worldwide. This is certainly worth considering.

There are certain ethics in diving instruction that the student should also be aware of, for he can use them to judge his instructor a little more accurately. The teaching of diving is a separate activity from the sale of diving gear. By this I do not mean that an instructor cannot work in a dive store or that he cannot, if asked, recommend certain gear. But the instructor who spends *time in class* promoting the sale of gear is in conflict of interest. The normal course is 27 to 32 hours and there just is not time to spend on anything but diving instruction.

I am always leery of an instructor who starts recommending various gear by brand name. I would much rather see him tell you the good points and bad points of the different types of equipment and then show you all the different brands and let you pick the one you feel is most comfortable and most satisfactory in your particular situation. In all too many dive shops, the instructional program is

185

nothing more than a come-on to sell gear. Many times a store will get a real buy on a line of gear. The "real buys" are generally on items that are not desired by the public; that's why the company can't move them. The shop will make a high profit on them so they are "pushed" onto the unsuspecting student.

Be aware of and cognizant of your instructor's ethics as you go through the course. It is true that the diver who owns his own gear will generally dive more often and have more fun than the diver who does not. I am in favor of purchasing your own gear. I am not in favor of your being "hustled" by your instructor to buy gear *while you are taking* a diving class. The person who will hustle gear to his students will generally be tied to one or two manufacturers. Unfortunately, no one manufacturer makes all the best gear. If they want to hustle you over the counter when you walk into their store, that's great; we expect that. But the student looks at his instructor as a god for some unknown reason, and this situation should not be taken advantage of.

A good instructor who is interested in teaching will spend his time working with the student to develop and perfect diving skills.

What about the diving course itself? The National Association of Underwater Instructors has a standard instruction course that must run no less than 27 hours of pool and classroom work and must include, in addition, at least three open water dives. The YMCA standards are very nearly the same. When the two largest diving certification organizations say that this is the minimum time necessary for safe diving instruction and they arrive at this opinion independently, I think it bears consideration. I don't see how the world's best instructor can teach anyone to be safe in the water in less than this time. It has been tried and it didn't work.

I can take practically anyone off the street and teach him how to blow bubbles underwater in a period of 10 or 12 hours, but there is no way I can truly feel that he is safe. To be safe, he must have experienced enough time with the equipment to have lost most of his anxiety, and to have been guided slowly and deliberately through the list of skills in this book.

None of the University of California's campuses will allow a student to dive on any school project unless he has undertaken a minimal 100-hour course. The diving officers of the various branches of the university, even though their students are sharp mentally, young, and in good physical condition, feel this time is necessary. Even then the students are restricted to diving in less than 50 feet of water.

There are a great many substandard scuba courses being run across the country. There are also divers who drown each year. I think we would find a very interesting correlation between quality of instruction and these divers. In 1971, the majority of the divers who drowned had had no formal training of any kind. A description of minimum basic scuba diving course standards is included in Appendix B.

If NAUI or YMCA certification is available, use it, and if it is not available then check out your local organizations carefully. You may find one that is excellent. Like anything else, the *individual* who is doing the teaching is more important than the organization for which he teaches. There are good and poor diving instructors in every organization, so choose your man carefully. He is playing with your life.

APPENDICES

APPENDIX A
Basic Swimming Skills

The new student must possess basic water skills to become a diver. While some people and even organizations claim that "you don't have to be a swimmer to dive," this is idiotic. It is true that you don't have to be a "good swimmer," but you must be "water safe." If a student knows he is very poor in the water and would be in trouble without the fins, he will never relax to the point where he will be a safe or competent diver. He must have complete peace of mind in the area of his safety before the learning process can take place. To insure that he possesses the necessary competence and confidence, the following general swim levels should be accomplished *before* diving training takes place, and *without* the help of swim fins.

Swim Levels

1. Swim 50 yards on the back and be relaxed when finished.
2. Swim 50 yards using either breast stroke or side stroke and be relaxed when finished.
3. Swim 200 yards nonstop using any stroke without undue stress.
4. Complete a 20 minute float-tread water combination without stress.
5. Hold the breath while sitting on the bottom in shallow water for 25 seconds.
6. Swim under water for 15 yards.

These swim levels are not difficult and are *extremely* important for the mental attitude of the student. When they are achieved learning will take place and not be pushed out of the student's mind by survival thoughts. If a student cannot pass all of these items, he should take the time to get coaching in swimming skills before starting to train to be a diver. In most cases, two or three hours with a good swimming teacher or eight to ten times in the pool, building endurance, will do it.

APPENDIX B
Minimum Basic Scuba Diving
Course Standards

The terms Basic Scuba Diver and Qualified Scuba Diver are used interchangeably in the NAUI Standards and on NAUI materials. They refer to the same certification course.

1. Minimum age for Basic Scuba Certification is 15.
2. Minimum course duration is 27 hours. Of this time, 16 hours or more are to be in-water activities, and the remainder is to be spent in classroom/lecture activities. Of the time spent in water activities, at least two (2) hours are to be in open water; the balance of the water time may be in open water or pool.
3. The Basic Scuba Course is a combined Skin and Scuba Diving Course. Therefore, skin diving is to be taught where it will best enhance the total learning outcome of the course.
4. A minimum of three (3) open water dives are required. One of these is to be a skin dive and two (2) are to be scuba dives. No more than two (2) dives per day can be counted toward this requirement. At least one (1) of these open water training experiences is to take place to a depth of 20 feet. Exposures in excess of 40 feet are not recommended.
5. The required curriculum subject areas which are to be covered in a Basic Scuba Course are:
   a. Applied Sciences
   This area is to provide the student with a basic knowledge of physics, physiology, and medical aspects as they relate to a diver's performance in the water. Emphasis is to be placed on the diver's physical fitness, diving hazards, personal limitations, and the behavioral changes needed to function safely as a diver. Material is to be presented in a manner which is of practical application to the sport and is to specifically include: gases, pressure, volume, temperature, density, buoyancy, vision, and acoustics; the definition, cause, symptoms, signs, first aid, treatment, and prevention of decompression sickness, nitrogen narcosis, respiratory accidents, squeezes, overexertion and overexposure, air embolism, and related injuries. Decompression tables are to be covered to the extent required for the students to be able to safely calculate repetitive no decompression dives.
   b. Diving Equipment
   This area is to provide the student with a basic knowledge of the purpose, features, types, and use of sport skin and scuba diving equipment. The student is to be prepared to intelligently select, use, and care for the following: mask,

192

snorkel, fins, surface float with flag, personal flotation vest, knife, weight belt, protective suit, depth gauge, watch, pressure gauge, compass, regulator, and cylinder, including valve and harness or backpack, plus any other useful accessories.
  c. Diving Safety
  This area is to provide the student with a basic knowledge of lifesaving and first aid as applied to diving. Underwater communications, underwater orientation, dive planning, and safety rules are also to be covered. Shock, wounds, and drowning are to be covered under first aid. Lifesaving is to include rescues, tows, and artificial respiration as they apply to open water.
  d. Diving Environment
  This area is to provide the student with a basic knowledge of the physical and biological aspects of the environment in the area where the course is conducted. The fundamentals of conservation, regulations, dangers, water movement, and water characteristics, including the environment's effect on the diver, are to be covered.
  e. Diving Activities
  This area is to provide the student with a basic knowledge of the who, when, where, what, and why of diving. Specific references to dive clubs, dive boats, dive stores, diving locations, diving books and magazines, plus related courses are to be included. A limited introduction to specific diving activities should be given.
6. The required water skills which are to be covered *during* a Basic Scuba Course are:
  a. Swimming Skills (no equipment)
    (1) Distance swim of 220 yards, nonstop any stroke.
    (2) Survival swim for 10 minutes, treading, bobbing, floating, downproofing, etc.
    (3) Underwater swim of 20 yards.
  b. Skin Diving Skills (mask, snorkel, and fins)
    (1) Distance swim of 440 yards, nonstop, using no hands.
    (2) Complete rescue of another diver in deep water.
    (3) Practice and perform without stress proper techniques including: water entries/exits, surface dives, swimming with fins, clearing the snorkel, ditching the weight belt, buoyancy control with the personal flotation vest, underwater swimming, and surfacing.
  c. Scuba Diving Skills (skin and scuba equipment)
    (1) Repeat all listed skin diving skills while using scuba.
    (2) Tow another fully equipped scuba diver 100 yards.
    (3) Practice and perform without stress proper techniques including: mask and mouthpiece clearing, buddy breathing, emergency swimming ascents, alternating between snorkel and scuba.
  d. Open Water Skin and Scuba Diving
    (1) Perform without stress water entries/exits, surface dives, buoyancy control and surfacing techniques that are required to do surface, underwater, and survival swimming with both skin and scuba equipment.
    (2) Make a complete rescue of a buddy diver.
    (3) With scuba equipment clear mask and mouthpiece, buddy breathe, alternate between snorkel and scuba, and make a controlled emergency swimming ascent.

7. Sample Minimum Schedule:

Session Number	Session Type	Typical Days	Hours	Topic
1	Dry	T	1½	Skin Diving Equipment
	Wet		1½	Swimming Skills and Evaluation
2	Dry	TH	1½	Applied Sciences
	Wet		1½	Skin Diving Skills
3	Dry	T	1½	Applied Sciences
	Wet		1½	Skin Diving Skills
4	Dry	TH	1½	Scuba Diving Equipment
	Wet		1½	Scuba Diving Skills
5	Dry	Sat.	1	Diving Safety
	Wet		2	Skin Dive (Open Water)
6	Dry	T	1	Diving Safety
	Wet		2	Scuba Diving Skills
7	Dry	TH	1	Diving Activities
	Wet		2	Scuba Diving Skills
8	Dry	Sat.	1	Diving Environment
	Wet		2	Scuba Dive (Open Water)
9	Dry	Sun.	1	CPR Introduction
	Wet		2	Scuba Dive (Open Water)

TOTAL 27

APPENDIX C
Questions and Answers About Breath-Hold Diving

When I talk to people about breath-hold diving I am asked many questions. I have included a few of the more common ones here.

1. Q. Isn't it true that it is best to exhale about half your lung capacity *before* you dive to make it easier to go down?

   A. Very definitely *NO*. You want to carry with you all the air you are able to. A reduced amount of air will also mean a reduced amount of oxygen. The less oxygen, the easier it is to get shallow water blackout and the shorter time you can stay down. If you are a little buoyant with a full breath, then wear two or three pounds of weight.

2. Q. Is there an exercise I can do to increase my lung capacity?

   A. I have talked to a lot of weight lifters and they tell me that you can increase the size of the thoracic cavity by just placing a broomstick behind the head, across the shoulders and placing your hands on either side holding the broomstick in place with the palms out while breathing as deeply as possible, lifting the rib cage. I think this is a good exercise but I don't believe it will increase the lung capacity. Any extreme deep breathing exercise is good. I like one where I stand feet together, toes pointed *straight ahead*. The arms are held straight out in front of the body *palms together*, back straight. I inhale slowly and deeply bringing the arms *straight* back to the sides with the palms still pointed straight ahead. When I have taken in all the air I possibly can, I *continue* to inhale hard and turn the palms up towards the sky and lift my arms. At the same time I lift my arms I rise on my toes. If you are doing it right, you will turn red and start to shake. Then relax and exhale as you go back to the starting position. About five times is all you can take at one session. Do this exercise in the morning and in the evening.

Such exercises may not increase your lung capacity, but they do make the chest muscles more elastic, and open all sections of the lungs for good ventilation. Most of us have never really taken an *extremely* deep breath. These exercises let us know what a really good *deep* breath feels like. I think the exercises are well worthwhile.

By the way, done properly, they will also reduce the waistline because they strengthen the abdominal muscles.

3. Q. I can only hold my breath a few seconds. Is there any hope for me?
   A. Yes. Read the section on relaxation.
4. Q. Does smoking hurt my breath-hold diving?
   A. Good grief, *yes*. When you smoke, your system is in a perpetual state of low level carbon monoxide (CO) poisoning. The CO utilizes a portion of the hemoglobin that carries oxygen and CO_2. The effects are low-level anemia, which means inefficient oxygen transport. Quit smoking. You will dive better, feel better, not get as tired during the day, and live longer.
5. Q. Is my diet important for diving?
   A. Of course it is. Your diet is important for good health. The better your health, the better your diving will be. Diet is a very complicated thing, but extremely worthwhile to be concerned about. I would recommend that you read a paperback book by Adelle Davis called *Let's Eat Right to Keep Fit*, published by Signet. It is an easy and fun book to read and covers general nutrition. If you are like practically everyone else, you will be shocked to discover what good nutrition really is.
6. Q. Should I take lessons to learn breath-hold diving?
   A. You always learn faster and better from a competent instructor in a semiformal situation. Good instruction will keep you from learning bad habits and get you diving deeper and longer, sooner. Remember, "Only perfect practice makes perfect." The National Association of Underwater Instructors (NAUI) has a special category within its ranks called "Skin Diving Leader." These instructors are specialists in teaching breath-hold diving, basic and advanced.
7. Q. Why should I breath-hold dive when I have a scuba tank?
   A. Scuba is a relaxing and fun way to dive but there are times when it is too much of a hassle or too limiting. If you have to carry your gear a long way, scuba is difficult. If you are going to be out all day at the beach, scuba limits the time you are in the water. A breath-hold diver can move farther, faster, and stay longer. The only thing he can't do is go deep for long stays. Good free divers can spend 30 seconds at 60 feet without undue stress. If you want to work at it, you can, too. It is a matter of technique and physical conditioning.
8. Q. Should I drop my snorkel out of my mouth when I dive?
   A. *No*. In fact, the snorkel can be used to help you dive deeper and also help clear the ears. When the diver turns head down in a dive some air is trapped in the snorkel. If he has taken a maximum breath then he can (and should) continue to inhale as he descends. As he descends, the increasing pressure will compress the air in his body as well as in the snorkel and the extra air in the snorkel will be pushed into the body. The compression factor is small,

but if the diver allows the air to be compressed by the water to the point where the mouth is full of water, it is a significant factor. It is a difficult technique to learn, but once learned it gives the diver compressed air to breathe, makes ears easier to clear, and provides more oxygen to reduce chance of shallow water blackout. It does, however, create the theoretical *danger of air embolism.* Exhale as you approach the surface, preferably during the last three feet of ascent to clear the snorkel.

APPENDIX D
U.S. Navy Standard Air Decompression and Repetitive Dive Tables

Taken from
U.S. Navy Diving Manual of March 1970
Prepared by
National Association of Underwater Instructors

TABLE 1-9.—*Decompression procedures*

GENERAL INSTRUCTIONS FOR AIR DIVING

Need for Decompression

A quantity of nitrogen is taken up by the body during every dive. The amount absorbed depends upon the depth of the dive and the exposure (bottom) time. If the quantity of nitrogen dissolved in the body tissues exceeds a certain critical amount, the ascent must be delayed to allow the body tissue to remove the excess nitrogen. Decompression sickness results from failure to delay the ascent and to allow this process of gradual desaturation. A specified time at a specific depth for purposes of desaturation is called a decompression stop.

No-Decompression Schedules

Dives that are not long or deep enough to require decompression stops are no-decompression dives. Dives to 33 feet or less do not require decompression stops. As the depth increases, the allowable bottom time for no-decompression dives decreases. Five minutes at 190 feet is the deepest no-decompression schedule. These dives are all listed in the *No-Decompression Limits and Repetitive Group Designation Table for No-Decompression Dives* (No-Decompression Table (table 1–11)), and only require compliance with the 60-feet-per-minute rate of ascent.

Schedules That Require Decompression Stops

All dives beyond the limits of the *No-Decompression Table* require decompression stops. These dives are listed in the *Navy Standard Air Decompression Table* (table 1–10). Comply exactly with instructions except as modified by surface decompression procedures.

Variations in Rate of Ascent

Ascend from all dives at the rate of 60 feet per minute.
In the event you are unable to maintain the 60-feet-per-minute rate of ascent:
   (a) If the delay was at a depth greater than 50 feet: increase the bottom time by the difference between the time used in ascent and the time that should have been used at a rate of 60 feet per minute. Decompress according to the requirements of the new total bottom time.
   (b) If the delay was at a depth less than 50 feet: increase the first stop by the difference between the time used in ascent and the time that should have been used at the rate of 60 feet per minute.

Repetitive Dive Procedure

A dive performed within 12 hours of surfacing from a previous dive is a repetitive dive. The period between dives is the surface interval. Excess nitrogen requires 12 hours to be effectively lost from the body. These tables are designed to protect the diver from the effects of this residual nitrogen. Allow a minimum surface interval of 10 minutes between all dives. For any interval under 10 minutes, add the bottom time of the previous dives to that of the repetitive dive and choose the decompression schedule for the total bottom time and the deepest dive. Specific instructions are given for the use of each table in the following order:
   (1) The *No-Decompression Table* or the *Navy Standard Air Decompression Table* gives the repetitive group designation for all schedules which may precede a repetitive dive.
   (2) The *Surface Interval Credit Table* gives credit for the desaturation occurring during the surface interval.
   (3) The *Repetitive Dive Timetable* gives the number of minutes of residual nitrogen time to add to the actual bottom time of the repetitive dive to obtain decompression for the residual nitrogen.
   (4) The *No-Decompression Table* or the *Navy Standard Air Decompression Table* gives the decompression required for the repetitive dive.

U.S. NAVY STANDARD AIR DECOMPRESSION TABLE

Instructions for Use

Time of decompression stops in the table is in minutes.
Enter the table at the exact or the next greater depth than the maximum depth attained during the dive. Select the listed bottom time that is exactly equal to or is next greater than the bottom time of the dive. Maintain the diver's chest as close as possible to each decompression depth for the number of minutes listed. The rate of ascent *between* stops is not critical for stops of 50 feet or less. Commence timing each stop on arrival at the decompression depth and resume ascent when the specified time has lapsed.
For example—a dive to 82 feet for 36 minutes. To determine the proper decompression procedure : The next greater depth listed in this table is 90 feet. The next greater bottom time listed opposite 90 feet is 40. Stop 7 minutes at 10 feet in accordance with the 90/40 schedule.
For example—a dive to 110 feet for 30 minutes. It is known that the depth did not exceed 110 feet. To determine the proper decompression schedule : The exact depth of 110 feet is listed. The exact bottom time of 30 minutes is listed opposite 110 feet. Decompress according to the 110/30 schedule unless the dive was particularly cold or arduous. In that case, go to the schedule for the next deeper and longer dive, i.e., 120/40.

NOTES ON DECOMPRESSION AND REPETITIVE DIVING PREPARED BY NAUI

DECOMPRESSION SICKNESS

1. All scuba divers should know the cause, symptoms, treatment, and prevention of decompression sickness, plus have available the telephone number, location and method of transportation to the nearest chamber. Call ahead to the chamber to be sure it is operational.

2. Factors which increase the likelihood of decompression sickness are: Extreme water temperatures, dehydration, age, obesity, poor physical condition, fatigue, alcoholic indulgence, old injuries which cause poor circulation, and heavy work during the dive.

3. The most frequent errors related to the treatment of decompression sickness are the failure: To report symptoms or signs early, to treat doubtful cases, to treat promptly, to treat adequately, to recognize serious symptoms, and to keep the patient near the chamber after treatment.

DECOMPRESSION TABLES

4. There is no safety factor built into the U.S. Navy Standard Air Decompression Table.

5. A "no decompression dive" is a dive which requires no decompression stops; it still causes nitrogen to go into solution within the body. This nitrogen must be taken into account as residual nitrogen in repetitive diving. The ascent rate of 60 feet per minute is a form of decompression.

6. Bottom time starts when the diver leaves the surface and ends only when the diver starts a direct ascent back to the surface.

7. If a dive was particularly cold or arduous, or the depth/time determination may be inaccurate, or some factor increases the likelihood of decompression sickness, decompress for the next deeper AND longer dive.

8. After diving, do not fly for 12 hours or, if you must fly, use the tables for altitude diving (see Skin Diver Magazine, November 1970).

9. An exception to the tables occurs when a repetitive dive is to the same or greater depth than the previous dive AND the surface interval is short enough that the residual nitrogen time from Table 11-13 is greater than the actual bottom time of the previous dive. In this case, add the actual bottom time of the previous dive to the actual bottom time of the repetitive dive and decompress for the total bottom time and deepest dive.

10. Plan repetitive dives so that each successive dive is to a lesser depth. This will aid in the elimination of nitrogen and decrease the need for decompression stops. Always keep surface intervals as long as possible.

11. Plan your dive and dive your plan; always having an alternate plan if the actual depth and/or time of the dive is greater than planned.

REASONS FOR REPETITIVE DIVE PLANNING

12. To avoid decompression stops.
    a. Be able to use tables to compute maximum time of a repetitive dive without decompression stops.
    b. Be able to use tables to compute minimum surface interval needed to avoid decompression stops.

13. To stay within a particular decompression schedule or repetitive group.

14. To dive maximum depth or time on limited air.

15. To make minimum decompression stops.

16. To make the dive and take whatever decompression stops are required.

EMERGENCY INFORMATION AND NUMBERS

USCG: Telephone _____ Radio _____

POLICE: State _____ County _____ City _____

FIRE DEPARTMENT _____ AMBULANCE _____ HARBOR PATROL _____

CHAMBERS:
1. Location _____ Day _____ Night _____
2. Location _____ Day _____ Night _____

M.D. QUALIFIED IN UNDERWATER MEDICINE:
Name _____ Day _____ Night _____

TABLE 1-10.—*U.S. Navy Standard Air Decompression Table*

Depth (feet)	Bottom time (min)	Time to first stop (min:sec)	50	40	30	20	10	Total ascent (min:sec)	Repetitive group
40	200						0	0:40	(*)
	210	0:30					2	2:40	N
	230	0:30					7	7:40	N
	250	0:30					11	11:40	O
	270	0:30					15	15:40	O
	300	0:30					19	19:40	Z
50	100						0	0:50	(*)
	110	0:40					3	3:50	L
	120	0:40					5	5:50	M
	140	0:40					10	10:50	M
	160	0:40					21	21:50	N
	180	0:40					29	29:50	O
	200	0:40					35	35:50	O
	220	0:40					40	40:50	Z
	240	0:40					47	47:50	Z
60	60						0	1:00	(*)
	70	0:50					2	3:00	K
	80	0:50					7	8:00	L
	100	0:50					14	15:00	M
	120	0:50					26	27:00	N
	140	0:50					39	40:00	O
	160	0:50					48	49:00	Z
	180	0:50					56	57:00	Z
	200	0:40				1	69	71:00	Z
70	50						0	1:10	(*)
	60	1:00					8	9:10	K
	70	1:00					14	15:10	L
	80	1:00					18	19:10	M
	90	1:00					23	24:10	N
	100	1:00					33	34:10	N
	110	0:50				2	41	44:10	O
	120	0:50				4	47	52:10	O
	130	0:50				6	52	59:10	O
	140	0:50				8	56	65:10	Z
	150	0:50				9	61	71:10	Z
	160	0:50				13	72	86:10	Z
	170	0:50				19	79	99:10	Z
80	40						0	1:20	(*)
	50	1:10					10	11:20	K
	60	1:10					17	18:20	L
	70	1:10					23	24:20	M
	80	1:00				2	31	34:20	N
	90	1:00				7	39	47:20	N
	100	1:00				11	46	58:20	O
	110	1:00				13	53	67:20	O
	120	1:00				17	56	74:20	Z
	130	1:00				19	63	83:20	Z
	140	1:00				26	69	96:20	Z
	150	1:00				32	77	110:20	Z
90	30						0	1:30	(*)
	40	1:20					7	8:30	J
	50	1:20					18	19:30	L
	60	1:20					25	26:30	M
	70	1:10				7	30	38:30	N
	80	1:10				13	40	54:30	N
	90	1:10				18	48	67:30	O
	100	1:10				21	54	76:30	Z
	110	1:10				24	61	86:30	Z
	120	1:10				32	68	101:30	Z
	130	1:00			5	36	74	116:30	Z
100	25						0	1:40	(*)
	30	1:30					3	4:40	I
	40	1:30					15	16:40	K
	50	1:20				2	24	27:40	L
	60	1:20				9	28	38:40	N
	70	1:20				17	39	57:40	O
	80	1:20				23	48	72:40	O
	90	1:10			3	23	57	84:40	Z
	100	1:10			7	23	66	97:40	Z
	110	1:10			10	34	72	117:40	Z
	120	1:10			12	41	78	132:40	Z
110	20						0	1:50	(*)
	25	1:40					3	4:50	H
	30	1:40					7	8:50	J
	40	1:30				2	21	24:50	L
	50	1:30				8	26	35:50	M
	60	1:30				18	36	55:50	N
	70	1:20			1	23	48	73:50	O
	80	1:20			7	23	57	88:50	Z
	90	1:20			12	30	64	107:50	Z
	100	1:20			15	37	72	125:50	Z

TABLE 1-10.—*U.S. Navy Standard Air Decompression Table*—Continued

Depth (feet)	Bottom time (min)	Time to first stop (min:sec)	50	40	30	20	10	Total ascent (min:sec)	Repetitive group
120	15							0	2:00	(*)
	20	1:50						2	4:00	H
	25	1:50						6	8:00	I
	30	1:50						14	16:00	J
	40	1:40					5	25	32:00	L
	50	1:40					15	31	48:00	N
	60	1:30				2	22	45	71:00	O
	70	1:30				9	23	55	89:00	O
	80	1:30				15	27	63	107:00	Z
	90	1:30				19	37	74	132:00	Z
	100	1:30				23	45	80	150:00	Z
130	10							0	2:10	(*)
	15	2:00						1	3:10	F
	20	2:00						4	6:10	H
	25	2:00						10	12:10	J
	30	1:50					3	18	23:10	M
	40	1:50					10	25	37:10	N
	50	1:40				3	21	37	63:10	O
	60	1:40				9	23	52	86:10	Z
	70	1:40				16	24	61	103:10	Z
	80	1:30			3	19	35	72	131:10	Z
	90	1:30			8	19	45	80	154:10	Z
140	10							0	2:20	(*)
	15	2:10						2	4:20	G
	20	2:10						6	8:20	I
	25	2:00					2	14	18:20	J
	30	2:00					5	21	28:20	K
	40	1:50				2	16	26	46:20	N
	50	1:50				6	24	44	76:20	O
	60	1:50				16	23	56	97:20	Z
	70	1:40			4	19	32	68	125:20	Z
	80	1:40			10	23	41	79	155:20	Z
150	5							0	2:30	C
	10	2:20						1	3:30	E
	15	2:20						3	5:30	G
	20	2:10					2	7	11:30	H
	25	2:10					4	17	23:30	K
	30	2:10					8	24	34:30	L
	40	2:00				5	19	33	59:30	N
	50	2:00				12	23	51	88:30	O
	60	1:50			3	19	26	62	112:30	Z
	70	1:50			11	19	39	75	146:30	Z
	80	1:40		1	17	19	50	84	173:30	Z
160	5							0	2:40	D
	10	2:30						1	3:40	F
	15	2:20					1	4	7:40	H
	20	2:20					3	11	16:40	J
	25	2:20					7	20	29:40	K
	30	2:10				2	11	25	40:40	M
	40	2:10				7	23	39	71:40	N
	50	2:00			2	16	23	55	98:40	Z
	60	2:00			9	19	33	69	132:40	Z
	70	1:50		1	17	22	44	80	166:40	Z
170	5							0	2:50	D
	10	2:40						2	4:50	F
	15	2:30						5	9:50	H
	20	2:30					2	15	21:50	J
	25	2:20				2	7	23	34:50	L
	30	2:20				4	13	26	45:50	M
	40	2:10			1	10	23	45	81:50	O
	50	2:10			5	18	23	61	109:50	Z
	60	2:00	2		15	22	37	74	152:50	Z
	70	2:00	8		17	19	51	86	183:50	Z
180	5							0	3:00	D
	10	2:50						3	6:00	F
	15	2:40						6	12:00	I
	20	2:30				1	5	17	26:00	K
	25	2:30				3	10	24	40:00	L
	30	2:30				6	17	27	53:00	N
	40	2:20			3	14	23	50	93:00	O
	50	2:10		2	9	19	30	65	128:00	Z
	60	2:10		5	16	19	44	81	168:00	Z
190	5							0	3:10	D
	10	2:50					1	3	7:10	G
	15	2:50					4	7	14:10	I
	20	2:40				2	6	20	31:10	K
	25	2:40				5	11	25	44:10	M
	30	2:30			1	8	19	32	63:10	N
	40	2:30			8	14	23	55	103:10	O
	50	2:20		4	13	22	33	72	147:10	Z
	60	2:20		10	17	19	50	84	183:10	Z

*See table 1-11 for repetitive groups in no-decompression dives.

Table 1–11.—*No-decompression limits and repetitive group designation table for no-decompression air dives*

Depth (feet)	No-decom-pression limits (min)	Repetitive groups (air dives)														
		A	B	C	D	E	F	G	H	I	J	K	L	M	N	O
10	....	60	120	210	300											
15	....	35	70	110	160	225	350									
20	....	25	50	75	100	135	180	240	325							
25	....	20	35	55	75	100	125	160	195	245	315					
30	....	15	30	45	60	75	95	120	145	170	205	250	310			
35	310	5	15	25	40	50	60	80	100	120	140	160	190	220	270	310
40	200	5	15	25	30	40	50	70	80	100	110	130	150	170	200	....
50	100		10	15	25	30	40	50	60	70	80	90	100			
60	60		10	15	20	25	30	40	50	55	60					
70	50		5	10	15	20	30	35	40	45	50					
80	40		5	10	15	20	25	30	35	40						
90	30		5	10	12	15	20	25	30							
100	25		5	7	10	15	20	22	25							
110	20			5	10	13	15	20								
120	15			5	10	12	15									
130	10			5	8	10										
140	10			5	7	10										
150	5			5												
160	5				5											
170	5				5											
180	5				5											
190	5				5											

Instructions for Use

I. No-decompression limits:

This column shows at various depths greater than 30 feet the allowable diving times (in minutes) which permit surfacing directly at 60 feet a minute with no decompression stops. Longer exposure times require the use of the Standard Air Decompression Table (table 1–10).

II. Repetitive group designation table:

The tabulated exposure times (or bottom times) are in minutes. The times at the various depths in each vertical column are the maximum exposures during which a diver will remain within the group listed at the head of the column.

To find the repetitive group designation at surfacing for dives involving exposures up to and including the no-decompression limits: Enter the table on the *exact or next greater depth* than that to which exposed and select the listed exposure time *exact or next greater* than the actual exposure time. The repetitive group designation is indicated by the letter at the head of the vertical column where the selected exposure time is listed.

For example: A dive was to 32 feet for 45 minutes. Enter the table along the 35-foot-depth line since it is next greater than 32 feet. The table shows that since group D is left after 40 minutes' exposure and group E after 50 minutes, group E (at the head of the column where the 50-minute exposure is listed) is the proper selection.

Exposure times for depths less than 40 feet are listed only up to approximately 5 hours since this is considered to be beyond field requirements for this table.

TABLE 1–12.—*Surface Interval Credit Table for air decompression dives*

[Repetitive group at the end of the surface interval (air dive)]

Z	O	N	M	L	K	J	I	H	G	F	E	D	C	B	A
0:10 0:22	0:23 0:34	0:35 0:48	0:49 1:02	1:03 1:18	1:19 1:36	1:37 1:55	1:56 2:17	2:18 2:42	2:43 3:10	3:11 3:45	3:46 4:29	4:30 5:27	5:28 6:56	6:57 10:05	10:00 12:00*
O	0:10 0:23	0:24 0:36	0:37 0:51	0:52 1:07	1:08 1:24	1:25 1:43	1:44 2:04	2:05 2:29	2:30 2:59	3:00 3:33	3:34 4:17	4:18 5:16	5:17 6:44	6:45 9:54	9:55 12:00*
	N	0:10 0:24	0:25 0:39	0:40 0:54	0:55 1:11	1:12 1:30	1:31 1:53	1:54 2:18	2:19 2:47	2:48 3:22	3:23 4:04	4:05 5:03	5:04 6:32	6:33 9:43	9:44 12:00*
		M	0:10 0:25	0:26 0:42	0:43 0:59	1:00 1:18	1:19 1:39	1:40 2:05	2:06 2:34	2:35 3:08	3:09 3:52	3:53 4:49	4:50 6:18	6:19 9:28	9:29 12:00*
			L	0:10 0:26	0:27 0:45	0:46 1:04	1:05 1:25	1:26 1:49	1:50 2:19	2:20 2:53	2:54 3:36	3:37 4:35	4:36 6:02	6:03 9:12	9:13 12:00*
				K	0:10 0:28	0:29 0:49	0:50 1:11	1:12 1:35	1:36 2:03	2:04 2:38	2:39 3:21	3:22 4:19	4:20 5:48	5:49 8:58	8:59 12:00*
					J	0:10 0:31	0:32 0:54	0:55 1:19	1:20 1:47	1:48 2:20	2:21 3:04	3:05 4:02	4:03 5:40	5:41 8:40	8:41 12:00*
						I	0:10 0:33	0:34 0:59	1:00 1:29	1:30 2:02	2:03 2:44	2:45 3:43	3:44 5:12	5:13 8:21	8:22 12:00*
							H	0:10 0:36	0:37 1:06	1:07 1:41	1:42 2:23	2:24 3:20	3:21 4:49	4:50 7:59	8:00 12:00*
								G	0:10 0:40	0:41 1:15	1:16 1:59	2:00 2:58	2:59 4:25	4:26 7:35	7:36 12:00*
									F	0:10 0:45	0:46 1:29	1:30 2:28	2:29 3:57	3:58 7:05	7:06 12:00*
										E	0:10 0:54	0:55 1:57	1:58 3:22	3:23 6:32	6:33 12:00*
											D	0:10 1:09	1:10 2:38	2:39 5:48	5:49 12:00*
												C	0:10 1:39	1:40 2:49	2:50 12:00*
													B	0:10 2:10	2:11 12:00*
														A	0:10 12:00*

Repetitive group at the beginning of the surface interval from previous dive

Instructions for Use

Surface interval time in the table is in *hours* and *minutes* (7:59 means 7 hours and 59 minutes). The surface interval must be at least 10 minutes.

Find the *repetitive group designation letter* (from the previous dive schedule) on the diagonal slope. Enter the table horizontally to select the surface interval time that is exactly between the actual surface interval times shown. The repetitive group designation for the *end* of the surface interval is at the head of the vertical column where the selected surface interval time is listed. For example, a previous dive was to 110 feet for 30 minutes. The diver remains on the surface 1 hour and 30 minutes and wishes to find the new repetitive

group designation: The repetitive group from the last column of the 110/30 schedule in the Standard Air Decompression Tables is "J." Enter the surface interval credit table along the horizontal line labeled "J." The 1-hour-and-30-minute surface interval lies between the times 1:20 and 1:47. Therefore, the diver has lost sufficient inert gas to place him in group "G" (at the head of the vertical column selected).

*NOTE.—Dives following surface intervals of *more* than 12 hours are not considered repetitive dives. *Actual* bottom times in the Standard Air Decompression Tables may be used in computing decompression for such dives.

TABLE 1–13.—*Repetitive dive timetable for air dives*

Repetitive groups	Repetitive dive depth (ft) (air dives)														
	40	50	60	70	80	90	100	110	120	130	140	150	160	170	180	190
A	7	6	5	4	4	3	3	3	3	3	2	2	2	2	2	2
B	17	13	11	9	8	7	7	6	6	6	5	5	4	4	4	4
C	25	21	17	15	13	11	10	10	9	8	7	7	6	6	6	6
D	37	29	24	20	18	16	14	13	12	11	10	9	9	8	8	8
E	49	38	30	26	23	20	18	16	15	13	12	12	11	10	10	10
F	61	47	36	31	28	24	22	20	18	16	15	14	13	13	12	11
G	73	56	44	37	32	29	26	24	21	19	18	17	16	15	14	13
H	87	66	52	43	38	33	30	27	25	22	20	19	18	17	16	15
I	101	76	61	50	43	38	34	31	28	25	23	22	20	19	18	17
J	116	87	70	57	48	43	38	34	32	28	26	24	23	22	20	19
K	138	99	79	64	54	47	43	38	35	31	29	27	26	24	22	21
L	161	111	88	72	61	53	48	42	39	35	32	30	28	26	25	24
M	187	124	97	80	68	58	52	47	43	38	35	32	31	29	27	26
N	213	142	107	87	73	64	57	51	46	40	38	35	33	31	29	28
O	241	160	117	96	80	70	62	55	50	44	40	38	36	34	31	30
Z	257	169	122	100	84	73	64	57	52	46	42	40	37	35	32	31

Instructions for Use

The bottom times listed in this table are called "residual nitrogen times" and are the times a diver is to consider he has *already* spent on bottom when he *starts* a repetitive dive to a specific depth. They are in minutes.

Enter the table horizontally with the repetitive group designation from the Surface Interval Credit Table. The time in each vertical column is the number of minutes that would be required (at the depth listed at the head of the column) to saturate to the particular group.

For example: The final group designation from the Surface Interval Credit Table, on the basis of a previous dive and surface interval, is "H." To plan a dive to 110 feet, determine the residual nitrogen time for this depth required by the repetitive group designation: Enter this table along the horizontal line labeled "H." The table shows that one must *start* a dive to 110 feet as though he had already been on the bottom for 27 minutes. This information can then be applied to the Standard Air Decompression Table or No-Decompression Table in a number of ways:

(1) Assuming a diver is going to finish a job and take whatever decompression is required, he must add 27 minutes to his actual bottom time and be prepared to take decompression according to the 110-foot schedules for the sum or equivalent single dive time.

(2) Assuming one wishes to make a quick inspection dive for the minimum decompression, he will decompress according to the 110/30 schedule for a dive of 3 minutes or less (27+3=30). For a dive of over 3 minutes but less than 13, he will decompress according to the 110/40 schedule (27+13=40).

(3) Assuming that one does not want to exceed the 110/50 schedule and the amount of decompression it requires, he will have to start ascent before 23 minutes of actual bottom time (50−27=23).

(4) Assuming that a diver has air for approximately 45 minutes bottom time and decompression stops, the possible dives can be computed: A dive of 13 minutes will require 23 minutes of decompression, for a total submerged time of 36 minutes. A dive of 13 to 23 minutes will require 34 minutes of decompression (110/50 schedule), for a total submerged time of 47 to 57 minutes. Therefore, to be safe, the diver will have to start ascent before 13 minutes or a standby air source will have to be provided.

APPENDIX E
Nu-Way Dive Tables

TABLE 1-13 REPETITIVE DIVE TIMETABLE FOR AIR DIVES

RESIDUAL NITROGEN TIMES ABOVE (MINUTES) FOR REPETITIVE DIVE DEPTH BELOW (FT)

Group	40'	50'	60'	70'	80'	90'	100'	110'	120'	130'	140'	150'	160'	170'	180'	190'
A	7	6	5	4	4	3	3	3	3	3	2	2	2	2	2	2
B	17	13	11	9	8	7	7	6	6	6	5	4	4	4	4	4
C	25	21	17	15	13	11	10	10	9	8	7	7	6	6	6	6
D	37	29	24	20	18	16	14	13	12	11	10	9	8	8	8	8
E	49	38	30	26	23	20	18	16	15	13	12	11	10	10	10	10
F	61	47	36	31	28	24	22	20	18	16	15	14	13	12	11	11
G	73	56	44	37	32	29	26	24	22	19	18	17	16	14	13	13
H	87	66	52	43	38	33	30	27	25	22	21	19	18	16	15	15
I	101	76	61	50	43	38	34	31	28	25	23	22	20	18	17	17
J	116	87	70	57	48	43	38	34	31	28	26	24	23	20	19	19
K	138	99	79	64	54	47	43	38	35	31	29	27	26	22	21	21
L	161	111	88	72	61	53	48	42	39	35	32	30	28	25	24	24
M	187	124	97	80	68	58	52	47	43	38	35	32	31	27	26	26
N	213	142	107	87	73	64	57	51	46	40	38	35	33	29	28	28
O	241	160	117	96	80	70	62	55	50	44	40	38	34	31	31	30
Z (NEW GROUP)	257	169	122	100	84	73	64	57	52	46	42	40	37	35	32	31

TABLE 1-12 SURFACE INTERVAL CREDIT TABLE (TIMES IN HR:MIN)

(Enter vertically under the repetitive group carried down from Table 1-11; read the surface interval time; the new repetitive group is at the right.)

Starting group	Surface interval ranges → new repetitive group
A	A: 0:10–12:00
B	B: 0:10–2:10 · A: 2:11–12:00
C	C: 0:10–2:10 · B: 2:11–2:49 · A: 2:50–12:00
D	D: 0:10–2:10 · C: 2:11–2:49 · B: 2:50–3:20 · A: 3:21–12:00
E	E: 0:10–2:38 · D: 2:39–2:58 · C: 2:59–3:22 · B: 3:23–3:57 · A: 3:58–12:00
F	F: 0:10–… · E: … · D: … · C: … · B: 3:58–4:25 · A: 4:26–12:00
G	… A: 4:50–12:00
H	… A: 5:13–12:00
I	… A: 5:41–12:00
J	… A: 6:03–12:00
K	… A: 6:19–12:00
L	… A: 6:33–12:00
M	… A: 6:45–12:00
N	… A: 6:57–12:00
O	… A: 7:06–12:00
Z	O: 0:10–0:22 · N: 0:23–0:34 · M: 0:35–0:48 · L: 0:49–1:02 · K: 1:03–1:18 · J: 1:19–1:36 · I: 1:37–1:55 · H: 1:56–2:17 · G: 2:18–2:42 · F: 2:43–3:10 · E: 3:11–3:45 · D: 3:46–4:29 · C: 4:30–5:27 · B: 5:28–6:56 · A: 6:57–12:00

TABLE 1-11 "NO DECOMPRESSION" LIMITS AND REPETITIVE GROUP DESIGNATION TABLE FOR "NO DECOMPRESSION" AIR DIVES

BOTTOM TIMES FOR AIR DIVES (MINUTES)

DEPTH (FEET)	NO DECOMPRESSION LIMITS	A	B	C	D	E	F	G	H	I	J	K	L	M	N	O
10	–	60	120	210	300											
15	–	35	70	110	160	225	350									
20	–	25	50	75	100	135	180	240	325							
25	–	20	35	55	75	100	125	160	195	245	315					
30	310	15	30	45	60	75	95	120	145	170	205	250	310			
35	310	5	15	25	40	50	60	80	100	120	160	190	220	270	310	
40	200	5	15	25	30	40	50	70	80	100	110	130	150	170	200	
50	100	–	10	15	25	30	40	50	60	70	80	90	100			
60	60	–	10	15	20	25	30	40	50	55	60					
70	50	–	5	10	15	20	30	35	40	45	50					
80	40	–	5	10	15	20	25	30	35	40						
90	30	–	5	10	12	15	20	25	30							
100	25	–	5	7	10	15	20	22	25							
110	20	–	5	10	13	15	20									
120	15	–	5	10	12	15										
130	10	–	5	8	10											
140	10	–	5	7	10											
150	5	–	5													
160	5	–	5													
170	5	–	5													
180	5	–	5													
190	5	–	5													

CAUTION:

THESE "RESIDUAL NITROGEN TIMES" ARE THE TIMES A DIVER MUST ASSUME HE HAS ALREADY SPENT ON THE BOTTOM BEFORE HE STARTS A REPETITIVE DIVE TO A SPECIFIC DEPTH.

—— INSTRUCTIONS ——

ALL TABULATED BOTTOM TIMES (MINUTES), AND ALL TABULATED DEPTHS (FEET) HAVE BEEN TAKEN FROM THE U. S. NAVY DIVING MANUAL OF MARCH 1970.

1. TO CALCULATE A REPETITIVE DIVE UPON SURFACING FOR DIVES INVOLVING EXPOSURES UP TO AND INCLUDING THE "NO DECOMPRESSION LIMITS": ENTER TABLE 1-11 ON THE EXACT OR NEXT GREATER DEPTH THAN THAT TO WHICH EXPOSED, AND SELECT THE LISTED EXPOSURE TIME EXACT OR NEXT GREATER THAN THE ACTUAL EXPOSURE TIME. THE REPETITIVE GROUP DESIGNATION IS INDICATED BY THE LETTER AT THE HEAD OF THE VERTICAL COLUMN WHERE THE SELECTED EXPOSURE TIME IS LISTED.

2. CONTINUE THE VERTICAL MOTION ALONG THE STRAIGHT LINES JOINING TABLE 1-11 TO TABLE 1-12. ENTER THE TABLE VERTICALLY TO SELECT THE ELAPSED SURFACE INTERVAL TIME. THE NEW REPETITIVE GROUP DESIGNATION FOR THE SURFACE INTERVAL IS TO THE RIGHT OF THE HORIZONTAL COLUMN WHERE THE ELAPSED SURFACE INTERVAL TIME IS LISTED.

3. CONTINUE THE RIGHTHANDED MOTION TO ENTER 1-13 ON THE HORIZONTAL COLUMN TO THE RIGHT OF THE NEW REPETITIVE GROUP DESIGNATION. THE TIME IN EACH VERTICAL COLUMN IS THE RESIDUAL NITROGEN TIME. IT IS A PENALTY TIME; ie, THE TIME A DIVER MUST ASSUME HE HAS ALREADY SPENT ON THE BOTTOM BEFORE HE STARTS A REPETITIVE DIVE TO THE DEPTH SPECIFIED AT THE BOTTOM OF THE COLUMN.

APPENDIX F
Sample Repetitive Dive Problems

The following method of drawing your dive and entering the data is an easy way to visualize what is happening while you make the calculations necessary for your dive. Ideally, your diagram would reflect the varying depths of the dives.

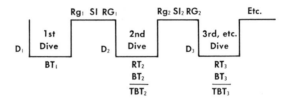

D   = Depth at deepest part of dive.
BT   = Bottom Time. The time elapsed from breaking the surface and starting down until leaving the bottom and starting up (start of descent to start of ascent).
Rg   = Repetitive group when getting out of the water after a dive (Table 1–11).
SI   = Surface Interval in hours and minutes.
RG   = Repetitive Group after surface interval (Table 1–12).
RT   = Residual Nitrogen Time in minutes for your next dive depth (Table 1–13).
TBT = Total Bottom Time. Residual time plus bottom time = TBT.
       TBT is what is figured in the table to find your Rg (Table 1–11).
D_1 = Depth first dive.
D_2 = Depth second dive, etc.

Problem 1

First Dive: $D_1 = 40'$, $BT_1 = 45$ min., $SI_1 = 1:45$ min.
Second Dive: $D_2 = 70'$, $BT_2 = 28$ min.
               Questions:
               1. What is the Rg on first dive (Rg_1)?
               2. What is the RG on first dive (RG_1)?
               3. What is the RT for second dive (RT_2)?
                  (*Note:* there is no RT or TBT on first dives, therefore, there is RT_1 or TBT_1. RT and TBT start on second dive so they a designated by RT_2 and TBT_2, etc.)
               4. What is the Rg for second dive (Rg_2)?

Problem 2

First Dive: $D_1=70'$, $BT_1=28$ min., $SI_1=1:45$ min.
Second Dive: $D_2=40'$, $BT_2=45$ min.
> *Questions:*
> Answer the same four questions given in Problem 1.

NOTE: After working Problem 1 and then Problem 2, you will realize that the numbers are the same. The only change is that in Problem 1, the shallower of the two dives was made first. You will have noticed that in Problem 1 you were right at the limit for No Decompression. Only a two-minute leeway was given. This is a situation in which it takes very little carelessness to cause a problem. On problem 2, however, although you spent exactly the same BT on both dives and with the same SI, at no time were you anywhere near the No Decompression limits. This was a safe dive.
Lesson to be learned: If you are going to make dives of unequal depth during a day's diving, be sure to make the *deepest one first*. This will increase your possible diving time enormously and help keep you out of trouble.

Problem 3

$D_1=60'$, $BT_1=30$ min., $SI_1=0:15$ min.
$D_2=50'$, $BT_2=30$ min., $SI_2=0:25$ min.
$D_3=40'$, $BT_3=45$ min.
> *Questions:*
> Give the values for the following:
> Rg_1, RG_1, RT_2, TBT_2
> Rg_2, RG_2, RT_3, TBT_3

Problem 4

$D_1=50'$, $BT_1=55$ min., $RG_1=F$
$RT_2=24$ min.
> *Questions:*
> 1. Within what range must the SI be (from what to what is tolerable)?
> 2. $D_2=?$

Answers

Problem 1
1. $Rg_1=F$
2. $RG_1=D$
3. $RT_2=20$ min.
4. $Rg_2=J$

Problem 2
1. $Rg_1=F$
2. $RG_1=D$
3. $RT_2=37$
4. $Rg_2=I$

Problem 3
$Rg_1=F$, $RG_1=F$
$RT_2=47$ min., $TBT_2=77$ min.
$Rg_2=J$, $RG_2=J$
$RT_3=116$ min., $TBT_3=161$ min.

Problem 4
$SI=1:07$ min. to 1:41 min.
$D_2=90'$

APPENDIX G
Some Diving Safety Rules

1. Make sure you are in good physical and mental condition; dive only when feeling well.
2. Maintain good swimming ability.
3. Take a certified diving class from a nationally recognized organization.
4. Get skin diving experience; this is a prerequisite to scuba diving.
5. Take first-aid training.
6. Be current in lifesaving techniques.
7. Have a first-aid kit.
8. Know your limitations (both personal and equipment).
9. Check and use correctly the proper equipment in good condition.
10. Use a flotation vest.
11. Attach your weight belt with a quick release so that it can be ditched with one hand.
12. Plan your dive.
13. Know your diving area.
14. Limit depth to less than 60 feet.
15. Dive with a buddy *and stay together*.
16. Develop and use methods of underwater communication.
17. Treat spear guns as dangerous weapons.
18. Equalize pressure *before* pain is felt.
19. Leave water when injured, tired, or cold.
20. Surface carefully and correctly.
21. Breathe regularly with scuba.
22. Avoid stage decompression or decompression repetitive dives.
23. Use only pure compressed air.
24. Maintain and handle compressed air cylinders properly.
25. In general: Know what you are doing; use good judgment and common sense; be prepared for emergencies; *avoid panic;* practice diving skills; read and study about diving and related activities, use moderation in depth and time in water; *build up experience gradually under safe conditions;* before diving do not indulge in alcohol, overeat, or eat gas-producing foods.

APPENDIX H
A Study Outline of Diving Diseases
and Accidents*

INTRODUCTION:

The following material, "A Study Outline of Diving Diseases and Accidents," is a comprehensive outline. It is designed to assist the instructor and his students in locating MINIMUM information about diving diseases and accidents.

For more detailed and technical information the U.S. Navy's "Submarine Medicine Practice," or "Diving Manual," along with other standard diving publications, should be consulted.

Category Key

1. ACCIDENTS OR DISEASES INVOLVING RESPIRATORY SYSTEM
2. EFFECTS OF PRESSURE DURING DESCENT
3. EFFECTS OF PRESSURE DURING ASCENT
4. INDIRECT EFFECTS OF PRESSURE
5. EFFECTS OF TEMPERATURE
6. EFFECTS OF GASES

   Note: A/R—Use when applicable: Artificial Respiration to be administered when necessary.

* From the *Los Angeles County Underwater Instructor's Manual*, courtesy of the Los Angeles County Underwater Instructors Program.

AEROTITIS, MEDIA (Middle ear squeeze)

Category: 2

Definition: Hemorrhage within the tympanic membrane and middle ear.

Cause: Failure or inability to clear ears either through neglect or blockage in the Eustachian tubes.

Symptoms: Extreme pain in the ear upon descent. Redness and swelling of eardrum. Bleeding into drum or middle ear space. Spitting up blood. Rupture of drum will result in bleeding outside drum.

Treatment: "Hands off!" Seek medical aid. Avoid pressure until damage heals. If rupture occurs do not dive until completely healed.

Prevention: Equalize ear pressure properly during descent. Do not dive with head colds or infections that block Eustachian tubes.

AERODONTALGIA

Category: 2

Definition: Acute pain in tooth caused by pressure increase on tooth with air pocket beneath filling or inlay, or sinus above tooth.

Cause: Pressure increase on air pocket beneath filling, inlay, dental cap, or unequalized sinus.

Symptoms: Excruciating pain experienced with change in pressure.

Treatment: Seek dental assistance. Do not continue diving until condition has been cleared up.

Prevention: Dental checkup and X rays. Replacement of filling or cap may be necessary.

AIR EMBOLISM (Traumatic air embolism—overexpansion of the lungs)

Category: 1, 3

Definition: Rupture of alveoli walls (air sacks in lungs) forcing air into bloodstream resulting in the plugging of blood vessels by air bubbles which enter the circulatory system directly from the lungs.

Cause: Holding breath during ascent.

Symptoms: Symptoms usually occur within seconds (up to 5 min.) after surfacing. May occur before diver reaches the surface. Prior to unconsciousness diver may experience: weakness, dizziness, paralysis or weakness of extremities, visual disturbance, pain in the chest, or convulsions. Often bloody froth at the mouth is visible.

Treatment: Immediate recompression. A/R when applicable. Treat for shock.

Prevention: Always breathe normally when using scuba. Never hold breath during ascent. Exhale continuously when making "emergency ascent."

ANOXIA (oxygen deficiency—hypoxia)

Category: 1, 6

Definition: Tissues fail to receive enough oxygen to maintain life and normal function resulting from the diver's not receiving enough oxygen to breathe.

Cause: Inadequacy or loss of air supply. Extended breath-holding.

Symptoms: None likely to give diver adequate warning. Pulse rate and blood pressure increase. Slowing of responses, confusion, clumsiness, foolish behavior resembling effects of alcohol. Blueness (cyanosis) of lips, nailbeds, and skin. May result in unconsciousness and stoppage of breathing.

Treatment: Get to surface and fresh air (oxygen if available). A/R when applicable.

Prevention: Careful equipment maintenance and proper use of apparatus. These precautions are especially important when closed circuit unit is being used.

ASPHYXIA

Category: 1, 6

Definition: Asphyxia involves both anoxia and carbon dioxide excess resulting in suffocation.

Cause: Inadequate air supply. Blockage of air passage (strangulation). Excessive carbon dioxide.

Symptoms: Breathing becomes difficult. Headache, weakness, and dizziness occur. Diver may experience symptoms of anoxia or carbon dioxide excess. Blueness of lips, etc. Motor skills impaired. Unconsciousness in severe cases.

Treatment: Rest and fresh air. A/R when applicable. Clear breathing passages if blocked.

Prevention: See anoxia.

BLEEDING

Category: 1, 2, 3

Definition: The appearance of fresh blood at the nose, ears, or mouth.

Cause: Bleeding from the mouth (*not frothy*) may be caused by a bitten tongue resulting from convulsions. *Frothy bleeding* may indicate lung rupture and air embolism. May also be caused from lung squeeze or breath-holding in skin diving. Bleeding from nose may indicate drainage from Eustachian tube, sinus, or from vigorous blowing to clear ears. Bleeding from ears may indicate rupture of eardrum or ear canal damage.

Symptoms: Coughing, blood in mask, etc.

Treatment: Depends on cause and condition of diver. Seek medical advice if bleeding does not stop.

Prevention: Prevention depends upon case in question.

BENDS (caisson disease—decompression sickness—compressed air sickness—diver's disease)

Category: 3, 6

Definition: Formation of gas bubbles (predominately nitrogen) as a result of releasing pressure too rapidly (inadequate decompression).

Cause: The respiratory system (lungs) takes up increased quantities of nitrogen from the inspired atmosphere and deposits it in the blood.

211

Now in a soluble state, the nitrogen in the blood is delivered to the tissues of the body and is held there by external pressure.

If the diver were to suddenly reduce pressure by surfacing, the increased nitrogen tension in the blood and tissues would be unable to remain in solution (Henry's law). At this point, the nitrogen rapidly returns to its natural state, which is a gas, and forms bubbles. Their location often refers to the type of effect produced, e.g., if in subcutaneous tissue "skin bends," in the pulmonary system "the chokes," in the extremities (arms, legs, etc.) the typical or classic "bends," in the central nervous system paralysis, convulsions, etc., and if in the orbital (eye) area, "eye bends," etc.

There are many characteristics that determine the rate, area, and degree of severity. One of the more common variables is the amount of fatty tissue in the body. Nitrogen being highly soluble in, and having an affinity for, fatty tissue, an obese person will be more grossly affected.

The depth, rate or degree of activity, and length of time exposed are the prime factors of determining the amount of excess nitrogen that is absorbed into the body.

Symptoms: In a majority of cases, localized pain in the joints (knee, ankle) of the lower limbs is the most common symptom. However, it is not uncommon to find the bends symptomatically as follows:
1. Localized pain—increasing in severity
2. Itching of skin
3. Nausea
4. Difficulty in breathing
5. Unconsciousness and/or paralysis
6. Convulsions
7. Death

Treatment: Little if anything can be done for a diver once symptoms have appeared. Immediate recompression in an adequately equipped chamber is mandatory. Returning a stricken person underwater could seriously compound his injuries and he could possibly drown. After notifying the Coast Guard, the victim should be treated for shock. Give oxygen if available and if respiration difficulty is encountered. A/R if necessary. Caution pilot about altitude if victim is to be transported by aircraft. Always send along his maximum depth, amount and frequency of dives and any information pertinent to the victim's activities and/or history.

Prevention: The only sure way of preventing decompression sickness is to carefully *plan* your dives. Taking into consideration, particularly, the depth, length of bottom time, and number of dives made is of absolute importance. Familiarize yourself with the U.S. Navy Repetitive Dive Tables and their proper use. Never rise faster than 60 feet per minute and avail yourself of additional study on this subject.

CARBON MONOXIDE POISONING (symbol for carbon monoxide is CO)

Category: 1, 6
Definition: Insufficient oxygen reaching the tissues (tissue anoxia) caused by carbon monoxide combining with hemoglobin in the blood and keeping it from carrying oxygen.

Cause:	Flashing of lubricating oil in compressor, or compressor intake too close to engine exhaust.
Symptoms:	Sometimes unconsciousness without warning. Headache, dizziness, nausea, and weakness. Abnormal cherry red lips, nailbeds, or skin. Motor symptoms resemble anoxia.
Treatment:	Fresh air, oxygen if available. A/R when applicable. 24 hours rest following treatment.
Prevention:	Keep compressor engine exhaust away from air intake. Analysis of air should be made periodically by air station or compressor operator.

EXTERNAL EAR INFECTION

Category:	None
Definition:	Infection in external ear canal.
Cause:	Infection in the external ear due to lack of proper drying or cleaning. May also be caused by infectious bacteria present in water.
Symptoms:	Pain in ear. Vertigo may be experienced. Swelling of external ear canal. Redness, tender to the touch.
Treatment:	"Hands off," seek medical advice. Do not dive until condition has been cleared up.
Prevention:	Dry and cleanse ears thoroughly after diving or swimming. Be particularly careful in areas where "ear fungus" is a prevalent disease.

CAROTID SINUS REFLEX

Category:	1, 2
Definition:	Fainting or blackout caused by inadequate supply of blood reaching the brain.
Cause:	Excessive pressure on the carotid sinus (located in the neck).
Symptoms:	Dizziness, headache, flush feeling, eyes may appear to "bug."
Treatment:	Loosen jacket collar or garment causing pressure.
Prevention:	Jacket or flotation vest should be snug and comfortable, never tight, as increased descent will increase pressure and possibility of accident.

EMPHYSEMA, SUBCUTANEOUS

Category:	1, 3
Definition:	Swelling or inflation due to abnormal presence of air in the tissues just under the skin. It usually appears in the neck or nearby areas.
Cause:	See Mediastinal Emphysema.
Symptoms:	Not extreme, perhaps only a feeling and look of fullness in the neck and a change in the voice. Difficulty in breathing and swallowing.
Treatment:	Seek medical advice. If air embolism has occurred, treat accordingly.
Prevention:	Never hold breath during ascent, breathe normally. Exhale during "emergency ascent."

213

EMPHYSEMA, MEDIASTINAL

Category: 1, 3
Definition: Presence of air in the tissues in the vicinity of the heart and lungs and large blood vessels in the middle of the chest.
Cause: Overexpansion of the lungs causing air to leak through the lungs and bronchial tubes into the surrounding tissues.
Symptoms: Pain under breast bone. Shortness of breath. Shock may occur. Blueness (cyanosis) of the skin, lips, or fingernails.
Treatment: Seek medical advice. If air embolism has occurred treat accordingly.
Prevention: Never hold breath during ascent. Breathe normally. Exhale during "emergency ascent."

CARBON DIOXIDE EXCESS (carbon dioxide toxicity—hypercapnia) (carbon dioxide symbol CO_2)

Category: 1, 6
Definition: An excess of carbon dioxide in the tissues (hypercapnia).
Cause: CO_2 builds up in mouthpiece. Loss of, or inadequate air supply. CO_2 absorption failure or inadequacy in rebreather scuba. Excessive skip (controlled) breathing.
Symptoms: Sometimes none. Diver may experience throbbing headache, weakness and fatigue, nausea, unusual sweating, inability to think clearly, other symptoms similar to anoxia. Unconsciousness may be followed by twitching in extreme cases.
Treatment: Rest and fresh air, oxygen if available. A/R when applicable.
Prevention: Avoid causes, always breathe normally. Rest when breathing becomes labored and if difficulty continues, discontinue dive. Avoid poor air supplies, poor ventilation, and faulty equipment.

DROWNING

Category: 1
Definition: Death caused by suffocation or strangulation in water or other liquid.
Cause: Any diving accident may result in drowning. Failure of air supply or the loss or flooding of mouthpiece. Surface exposure in rough water. Overexertion, exhaustion, unconsciousness. Any mishap followed by *panic!*
Symptoms: Similar to respiratory or cardiac arrest accidents.
Treatment: A/R immediately. Follow treatment procedures for other apparent accidents or problems.
Prevention: Never dive alone. Know and practice diving safety. Don't panic. Use proper equipment in good condition.

HEART STOPPAGE (cardiac arrest)

Category: 1
Definition: Heart stops beating.
Cause: Strain, age, related accident, etc.

Symptoms: Symptoms may resemble those of any respiratory failure. Lack of pulse or audible heartbeat is usually adequate evidence to presume need for action.

Treatment: Apply external heart massage at the rate of 15 heart compressions to three (3) mouth-to-mouth lung ventilations. With two rescuers, interpose a ventilation cycle between every five (5) heart compressions.

Prevention: Dive only with medical sanction—a YEARLY PHYSICAL IS A MUST FOR DIVERS!

PNEUMOTHORAX

Category: 1
Definition: Presence of air between the lungs and chest wall.
Cause: Excessive pressure in the lungs producing leakage of air into space between lungs and chest wall.
Symptoms: Blueness of skin, lips, or fingernails. Pain in the side of chest.
Treatment: With air embolism, treat for embolism. Without air embolism, do not recompress. However, in severe cases trapped air should be removed by doctor.
Prevention: Never hold your breath when diving. Do not dive with personal history of lung damage.

REVERSE BLOCK

Category: 3
Definition: Inability to clear ears or sinus during ASCENT.
Cause: Air or free body fluid trapped in middle ear or sinus during ASCENT, PREVENTING PROPER CLEARING.
Symptoms: Pain in ears or sinus during ascent.
Treatment: Slow rate of ascent, descend again if pain persists. Hold nose and "suck" while moving jaw to assist in relieving trapped pressure.
Prevention: Never dive when you have a cold. If difficulty is encountered when descending, stop, do not force dive.

SINUSITIS

Category: 2
Definition: Inflammation of the sinus.
Cause: Continuing descent even though sinus pain occurs.
Symptoms: Pain during descent, relieved upon ascent. Blood and mucus discharged upon surfacing. Sinus area tender to touch.
Treatment: Use nose drops, spray, etc., to permit discharge. Antibiotics for treatment of infection. Seek medical advice.
Prevention: Do not dive when you have a head cold. Clear up any sinusitis condition before diving.

SQUEEZE

Category: 1, 2, 4

Definition: Squeeze (barotrauma) refers to any injury that occurs because closed airspace in the body cannot be equalized to that of the outside water pressure.

Cause: Inability to equalize pressure between closed airspace and outside water pressure.

Symptoms: Symptoms of squeeze on any part of the body is evidenced when pressure on that part of the body is felt to be greater than on other parts. The following is a list of squeezes experienced by divers and their causes and preventions.

SINUS SQUEEZE

Cause: Blockage of openings leading from nose to sinuses. (See sinusitis.)
Symptoms: Pain in face, above, below, between, or behind eyes during descent.
Treatment: Avoid diving until cause of squeeze has been relieved.
Prevention: Do not dive with head colds. Discontinue descent when pain develops.

EXTERNAL EAR SQUEEZE

Cause: Use of ear plugs during dive (air trapped between plug and eardrum). Hood sealing over external ear, either "wet" or "dry" suit.
Symptoms: Pain in/on ear during descent even after clearing. Feels much the same as middle ear squeeze.
Treatment: See aerotitis.
Prevention: Never use ear plugs when diving. Allow air or water to enter hood to prevent squeeze depending on type of wet suit.

MIDDLE EAR SQUEEZE

Cause: Failure or inability to clear ears either through neglect or blockage in Eustachian tubes.
Symptoms: Pain in ear during descent. Relief will be sudden if eardrum ruptures (followed by bleeding and spitting up of blood).
Treatment: See aerotitis.
Prevention: Never dive when you have a head cold. Clear ears during descent (move jaws, blow gently against closed nostrils). See your doctor.

FACE MASK SQUEEZE

Cause: Rapid descent with failure to equalize when using eye and nose or full face mask. Failure of demand valve. (Danger *increases* with the use of goggles.)
Symptoms: Pain and suction sensation on face. Face swollen or bruised. Whites of eyes may turn bright red. Bleeding from nose, eyes, and lungs. Eyes may protrude with hemorrhage in eyeballs and in membrane lining lids.
Treatment: Best available treatment would be ice packs on affected area.
Prevention: Make all descents under control allowing for mask equalization. Do not adjust mask too tightly before entry into water. When wearing full face mask be sure equipment is functioning. *Never* wear goggles for diving.

LUNG (THORACIC) SQUEEZE

Cause: Too deep descent during skin dive. Holding breath on descent when using scuba. Air supply failure during descent.

Symptoms: Feeling of chest compression during descent, sometimes followed by pain. Difficulty in breathing after ascent. Bloody, frothy sputum.

Treatment: Surface—place diver in "drainage" position, head down. A/R when applicable. Use oxygen if breathing is labored.

Prevention: Breathe normally when using scuba. Know your limits for skin diving depths.

SUIT SQUEEZE

Cause: When using a dry suit air must be admitted to suit to equalize air spaces in folds, pressure on these spaces beyond a certain depth will cause squeeze.

Symptoms: Pinching sensation of skin—symptoms of external ear squeeze. Welts with skin bleeding in areas of squeeze.

Prevention: Provide means of admitting air into suit. Stop descent when pinching is felt, blow air into neck of suit. Blow into face plate allowing air to pass into hood.

GAS IN THE GUT

Category: 3

Definition: Swallowed or trapped air in the stomach expanding on ascent. If gas is not released, it cannot only become uncomfortable, but might cause actual harm.

Cause: Swallowing air during dive, or gas forming in the lower intestine during dive.

Symptoms: Sensation of abnormal fullness, in more serious cases pain and cramping followed by fainting.

Treatment: Stop ascent, redescend until pain subsides. Attempt belching (being careful not to swallow more air), and "break wind."

Prevention: Do not dive with stomach or bowel disorders. Avoid gaseous foods or swallowing air.

HEAT LOSS

Category: 5

Definition: Whenever the body is exposed to water colder than normal body temperature, heat loss will occur. The colder the water, the more energy must be expended to maintain normal body temperature.

Cause: Insufficient protective clothing.

Symptoms: Numbness of extremities, pains in head, shivering, increased breathing.

Treatment: Dry after dive. Hot soup or coffee. Warm up with heavy clothing.

Prevention: Adequate exposure clothing. Leave water as soon as chill is felt. Keep extremities especially well protected. Do not overextend yourself.

HYPERVENTILATION, DANGERS OF

Category: 1, 3, 6

Definition: After hyperventilation, a diver at depth is comfortable; however, upon ascent the partial pressure of oxygen will drop sharply. Diver fails to experience a desire to breathe and in some cases loses consciousness from anoxia. (See Anoxia.)

Cause: Deep breathing resulting in the lowering of carbon dioxide tension content (loss of triggering mechanism).

Symptoms: Weakness, dizziness, headache, blurring of vision, and fainting may be experienced during hyperventilated dive—or no symptoms—"blackout" resulting in death, usually due to drowning.

Treatment: If "blackout" occurs during dive, get diver out of water. Follow procedure for similar accidents.

Prevention: Avoid deep breathing to the point of lightheadedness. Avoid breath-holding and underwater distance contests.

NITROGEN NARCOSIS (rapture of the deep)

Category: 4, 6

Definition: A nervous and mental condition resembling that of alcoholic intoxication caused by the action of nitrogen and carbon dioxide under pressure.

Cause: Nitrogen in air along with carbon dioxide in the tissues begin to have intoxicating effects at about 100 feet.

Symptoms: Loss of judgment and skill. False feeling of well-being. Lack of concern for safety. Increasing dizziness. Difficulty in accomplishing even simple tasks. Foolish behavior, highly susceptible divers may be near unconsciousness.

Treatment: Get diver to shallower depths.

Prevention: Avoid exceptionally deep dives. Know your limitations and learn to recognize symptoms.

LIPOID PNEUMONIA

Category: 1

Definition: Pneumonia infection in the lungs caused by the present nonabsorbent fat in the lungs.

Cause: Nonabsorbent fat in lungs due to bad air.

Symptoms: Similar to any pneumonia ailment.

Treatment: Seek medical advice.

Prevention: Take special precautions in the filtration of compressed air.

OVEREXERTION AND EXHAUSTION

Category: 1, 4

Definition: Feeling of suffocation when diver is unable to breathe deeply enough for comfort.

Cause: Added breathing resistance underwater. Poor breathing apparatus. "Out of shape" diver trying to work beyond his capacity. Carbon dioxide buildup. Excessive controlled breathing. Bad air. Excessive cold.

Symptoms: Fatigue, weakness, and labored breathing. Anxiety and tendency towards panic.

Treatment: Rest. End dive if symptoms persist.

Prevention: Know your limitations (physical and equipment). Train in order to eliminate panic under such circumstances.

OXYGEN POISONING

Category: 6
Definition: Toxic effect of oxygen on the diver when breathing pure oxygen or oxygen mixtures under pressure.
Cause: Results from any exposure to increased oxygen partial pressure beyond acceptable limits (two atmospheres).
Symptoms: Muscular twitching, nausea, dizziness, difficulties in hearing and seeing (tunnel vision). Difficulty in breathing and performing motor skills. In very serious cases, convulsions.
Treatment: If victim is underwater, bring him up. Protect victim from himself during convulsions. Get medical assistance.
Prevention: Avoid the use of closed-circuit diving apparatus or the use of oxygen in open-circuit units. Never dive below 25 feet when using oxygen or 297 feet with compressed air.

SHALLOW WATER BLACKOUTS (see carbon dioxide poisoning and hyperventilation)

Category: 1, 2, 3, 6
Definition: Accidents in which divers lose consciousness presumably from *carbon dioxide* excess, without an adequate respiratory warning, are called "shallow water blackouts."
Cause: See carbon dioxide poisoning and hyperventilation for cause, symptoms, treatment, and prevention.

STRANGULATION

Category: 1
Definition: Obstruction of breathing process.
Cause: Inhalation of foreign material such as chewing gum, vomitus, false teeth, etc.
Symptoms: Extreme difficulty in breathing, choking. Breathing and consciousness will eventually stop.
Treatment: Relieve cause. Remove obstruction with fingers or forceps. Sharp blow to back may dislodge obstruction. Tracheotomy as last resort. A/R when applicable.
Prevention: Do not chew gum or wear dentures when diving.

VERTIGO (twirly bends)

Category: 2, 3, 5
Definition: Diver feels dizzy and as though he or his surroundings are whirling around.
Cause: Rupture of the eardrum allowing cold water to enter into the middle ear. Imbalance of pressure in the ears. Symptoms will cease when water warms in the ear.
Symptoms: Diver becomes disoriented to surroundings and may become violently nauseated.
Treatment: Hang on to something. Hug yourself until feeling passes. Do not attempt to surface during reaction. Breathe normally.
Prevention: Do not force descent if pain persists. Level off and if necessary terminate dive. Do not dive with a head cold. Stay with your buddy.

APPENDIX I
General Diving First Aid*

Proper first aid can make the difference between life and death. Every diver should have a good knowledge of first aid and Standard First Aid Training Course. This table is only a reminder of some vital points.

1. If nature of injury is not certain, check victim over quickly but carefully.
   a. Is he breathing?
   b. Is he bleeding?
   c. Any broken bones?
   d. Any sign of head injury?
2. Start artificial respiration if breathing has stopped.
3. Stop bleeding. (If bleeding is very heavy, do this before *anything* else.)
   a. Try direct pressure with snug bandage.
   b. Use "pressure points."
   c. Apply tourniquet only as last resort.
4. If victim is a diver, consider possible need for immediate recompression.
5. Combat shock.
   a. Know its signs:
      (1) Paleness
      (2) Skin cold and moist
      (3) Weak, rapid pulse
      (4) Fainting
   b. Remember that shock is a serious danger in almost any injury or severe illness. Take steps to prevent or treat it:
      (1) Keep victim flat (head slightly lower than rest of body—except with head injury or if this causes trouble breathing).
      (2) Keep warm by covering.
      (3) Try to calm him; do what you can to lessen pain.
      (4) If conscious, able to swallow, not vomiting, and with no abdominal injury, give as much *shock solution* as victim will take. (1 teaspoonful table salt and ½ teaspoonful baking soda per quart of water.)
6. Send for medical help, or get victim to hospital or dispensary, in anything but most minor conditions.
   a. If another person is present, send him at once for medical assistance.
   b. Do not move victim unless you can do it properly. (See 7.)

* From the *Los Angeles County Underwater Instructor's Manual*.

220

7. Handle any injured person with care.
   a. If victim must be moved, use stretcher (or improvise one). Transfer him to it with as little movement as possible. Use special precautions with possible back or neck injuries.
   b. Splint broken bones temporarily on the spot.
8. Cover wounds and burns.
   a. Avoid handling; do not try to clean or disinfect (let the doctor do this).
   b. Use sterile dressing (or cleanest cloth available) and apply bandage over it.
9. In head injuries:
   a. Keep patient lying down and quiet.
   b. Secure medical attention even if injury seems slight.
10. In convulsions:
    a. Put something soft between teeth.
    b. Try to prevent injury, but do not restrain movements.
11. In collapse in hot surroundings:
    a. Check for signs of heatstroke.
       (1) Skin hot, dry.
       (2) Pulse rapid but full.
       (3) High body temperature.
    b. If signs are present,
       (1) Get medical assistance.
       (2) Take immediate steps to lower body temperature.

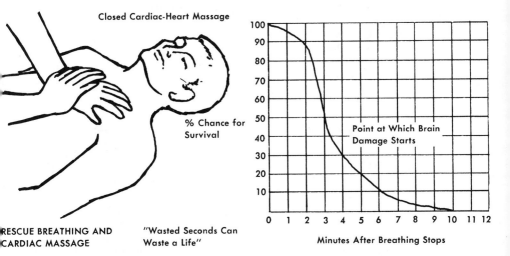

Closed Cardiac-Heart Massage

% Chance for Survival

Point at Which Brain Damage Starts

0 1 2 3 4 5 6 7 8 9 10 11 12

RESCUE BREATHING AND CARDIAC MASSAGE

"Wasted Seconds Can Waste a Life"

Minutes After Breathing Stops

1. If there is no response (breathing or return of normal color) after 9 full inflations of mouth-to-mouth, start cardiac massage by placing hand over lower third of sternum with second hand on top.
2. Apply very firm (75–95 lbs) pressure vertically downward toward the spine and release (once per second).

221

3. Continue for 15 compressions and then stop and inflate lungs 2 times by mouth-to-mouth.
4. With two rescuers compress heart 5 times, inflate lungs once then repeat 5-1, 5-1, etc. Interpose a ventilation cycle between *every five heart compressions*.
5. Continue alternating process until victim recovers or is turned over to doctor or hospital.
6. *Do not interrupt* the rhythm of *one compression per second*. Even minimal pauses will cause the oxygen supply to fall dangerously.

Seconds are Valuable

If the first inflations start within one minute after suspension of breathing you will have a good chance of saving 10 lives out of 10 rescue attempts.

Delay for 2 minutes—you lose 1 out of 10
Delay for 3 minutes—you lose 4 out of 10
Delay for 4 minutes—you lose 7 out of 10
Brain damage has started.

It takes approximately two minutes to read this far. Can you afford this time in an actual rescue? *Simplicity and speed must be stressed.*

% CHANCE FOR SURVIVAL
   100% = Immediate Action
    50% = 4 minutes
    10% = 6 minutes

MOUTH-TO-MOUTH METHOD

A.
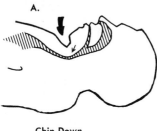
Chin Down
Air Passage Closed

B.
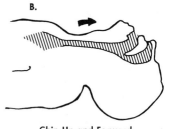
Chin Up and Forward
Air Passage OPEN

Immediate Action

Place victim on his back and begin rescue breathing! Any delay may be fatal. Don't waste time by: feeling victim's pulse . . . finding special equipment . . . moving victim . . . going for help . . . getting to shore. *ONLY* if foreign matter is visible at the mouth should the operator clean the mouth with his fingers or piece of cloth before the first inflations. *Those first inflations are the most crucial.*

APPENDIX J
"What Every Girl Should Know About Diving"*

by James Woodruff, M.D.

As the number of women interested and participating in diving increases, numerous questions are asked about their physiological adaptability to the rigors of diving. These questions are directed to doctors, physiologists, scuba and free diving instructors. When one turns to literature for a good factual base for responses to these questions, it is found that the research library is not replete with information on the subject. An attempt, therefore, is made to give some factual direction for responses, and hopefully dismiss some of the ancient mythology that remains to be overcome among a large segment of the lay population.

WOMAN'S ADAPTABILITY TO THE WATER ENVIRONMENT—For 1500 years, women have proved well suited for the strenuous occupation of free diving in the Orient. The "weaker sex" has also proved itself in the world of competitive swimming and in the more spectacular area of channel swimming.

Woman, through her more favorable distribution of body fat, generally has better buoyancy than her male counterpart. Although her system of muscle levers is not as good as man's, and she does not attain as fast a swimming record over a distance, she may expend less energy in remaining afloat, and so be ideally suited for longer distance work where speed is not necessary.

Her more favorable superficial adipose distribution also gives woman a 20% better insulation adaptability to withstand cold. Studies on the Korean diving women indicate they have also compensated for cold water work by increasing the basal metabolic rate, a higher shivering threshold, and peripheral vasoconstriction mechanism which acts as a heat sparing device. It would seem that her better buoyancy control would also help by requiring less energy output during resting.

IS DIVING HARMFUL TO THE MENSTRUATING WOMAN?—If menstruation is defined as the cyclic shedding of the endometrial lining of the uterus in response to hormonal control, then it is obviously a normal physiological phenomenon. During this period, averaging from three to five days, an amount of approximately 50 to 150 cubic centimeters of blood and cellular debris is lost. Most women have no adverse effects during this period and are able to continue full activity, remaining in excellent physical health.

Some women are adversely affected by menses. They may have excessive fluid retention at this time of the month, associated with severe headaches or peripheral edema. For a number of underlying causes, some women have severe uterine cramping, that is, dysmenorrhea. This results in pain and inability to function normally during the menstrual period. Abnormal menses, when it equates with illness, obviously means that diving should not be participated in during this derangement. People who are ill should not dive. For the

* Reprinted from an article in *Skin Diver* Magazine, March 1972.

223

woman who maintains good health through her menstrual flow, there is no contraindication to participation in aquatic sports, diving included. Conversations with numerous active women in water sports have indicated that immersion in cold water temporarily reduces the amount of menstrual flow and hot water may increase the amount of flow. This, however, readjusts itself to a normal amount after returning to a more normal temperature. It has been hypothesized that this may be due to sympathetic and parasympathetic reaction of the autonomic nervous system.

Some women are apprehensive about entering the ocean when menstruating, due to a real or imagined shark menace. It seems unlikely that such a small amount of blood would act to attract these dynamic predators. However, reassurance to the worried lady cannot be based on factual evidence. There is, however, a device on the market which may solve this problem. It is the Tassaway, an intravaginal disposable cup. This device can hold approximately thirty cubic centimeters of material. It fits well in the vagina, preventing any leakage or spill. In short, it seems a much more hygienic route for our aquatic sportswoman to go than the cotton tampon which has a tendency to become wet and, therefore, much less effective.

The answer to the question of diving when menstruating, then, is: As long as there are no ill effects associated with the menses, there would be no reason why women should not dive.

"THE PILL" AND LADY DIVER SAFETY—Considerable controversy wages across the globe about the safety of the birth control medication, primarily estrogen and progesterone combinations. Evaluation of research done in the United States and in England indicates there may be some increased blood clotting effect and a slowing or sludging effect in the micro circulation of some women. If this is true, and if disseminated intravascular coagulation is a contributing factor in decompression sickness symptomatology, then some increased risk may be run by a woman diver on oral contraception medication. This medication would be contraindicated in women participating in saturation diving projects such as TEKTITE II. However, for the sports diver who makes two or three dives in relatively shallow water and stays well within the no decompression limits, there should be little increased risk in mixing diving and oral contraceptive medication. The two recommendations to be made in this case are: 1) Do not push the decompression limits, 2) Remain well hydrated throughout the day. This, of course is good advice to any diver.

CAN A WOMAN DIVE WHILE PREGNANT? The working woman diver of Japan does not suspend her diving activities while pregnant. Numerous reports are found telling of these Ama delivering on the boat returning from a day's diving, or later in the evening after returning home. After 1500 years of successful history of diving, it must be assumed that no obvious adverse pathological effects have been noted in their offspring. If injury had been noted, the Ama surely would have stopped the diving during pregnancy hundreds of years ago. Although these women are free divers, that is, without scuba gear, forty feet is considered a good average working depth for the Ama. It is known that the partial pressure of nitrogen in the lungs is approximately doubled at forty feet. This depth, then, is sufficient to increase the nitrogen uptake in the tissues.

Very little formal research has been done on the effect of a hyperbaric environment on the fetus. That which has been done to date fails to show adverse effects on the unborn child.

If a pregnant woman should continue her diving activities, several changes will be noted by her. She will become more buoyant during pregnancy and will have to adjust her weight pattern accordingly. Her enlarging girth will require a wet suit design that can be adjustable to her increasing size, without binding. Many women report seemingly increased difficulty in deep breathing during pregnancy, but studies reveal relative absence of changes in forced vital capacity and forced expiratory volume.

Diving is out for those women who have adverse physical effects of pregnancy such as nausea, vomiting, increased motion sickness, or cardiovascular instability resulting in a tendency to become light-headed or faint. This is also a very poor time for the non-diver to enroll in a basic scuba course. Better for her to wait until the new family has arrived, when less of a physical adjustment needs to be made.

Doctor Eugenie Clark, founder of Florida Cape Haze Marine Laboratory, and noted shark researcher, reports having continued her underwater studies throughout pregnancy. She reports making repeated dives (30 minutes bottom time) at seventy feet, over an extended number of days. And recently there was a report by a woman diver eight months pregnant, who acted as photographer for her husband during a research project at a depth of 180 feet. No adverse effects were reported.

No contraindications to diving while pregnant have been reported. Some recommendations might be made. This activity should be restricted to less than 100 feet and the no decompression limits strictly observed. This, however, is only good advice for all sport diving. Boat entrances should be restricted to a gentle manner of entry; it is not necessary to leap into the ocean with full gear. Heavy surf should be avoided. As for all divers, there is no substitute for good common sense.

CONCLUSION—Women have successfully participated in diving for hundreds of years. During the past twenty years, the lady diver has developed into a scuba diving enthusiast. During the past ten years, an ever increasing number of women are involved in sport diving. When consulted, it would seem that an affirmative answer may be given when questioned about the safety of diving during menses, while taking oral contraceptive medication, and during pregnancy. The previous brief overview makes no pretense at final answers. . . . The answers definitely do not extend to the more critical subject of saturation diving experience. If the clinician who treats women divers has been stimulated by this article to pursue in depth research on this subject, then I shall consider this report a success.

APPENDIX K
High Altitude Procedures for
Repetitive, Decompression, and
Flying After Diving*

Introduction

The factors used as a base for the U.S. Navy Standard Air Decompression tables and the computation of altitude are primarily based on the studies of John S. Haldane, British physicist, in 1907. He brought to light the fact that a diver could ascend to a point where the highest saturated tissue in the body of inert gas was very near twice that of the outside ambient pressure before bubble formation becomes critical. "Haldane's theory" is more often referred to as the "2 to 1" law and was the basis for stage decompression.

Based on the above information, we know that a diver at sea level can enter the water and dive for as long as he wants at depths up to 33' and return to the surface without decompression regardless of whether it's a first dive or a repetitive dive. It's difficult for a diver to imagine why complications will occur when diving at a higher altitude than sea level. Why then is this a problem?

At sea level, we know the absolute atmospheric pressure is 14.7 PSIA. We also know that in sea water, the pressure increases at the rate of .445 PSIA per foot of water depth. It isn't difficult then to multiply .445 times 33 feet and find that every 33 feet we have added an additional atmosphere of pressure. This varies slightly in fresh water because fresh water, minus the salt deposits and other minerals, is less dense than salt water. In fact, for every foot of water depth in fresh water the rate of pressure increase is .434 instead of .445. If we divide .434 into our atmosphere of pressure at sea level (14.7 PSIA) we find that every 34 feet we have increased the pressure by another atmosphere. As long as our diver stays above 33 feet in salt water and 34 feet in fresh water at sea level he can return to the surface and not reduce the outside ambient pressure by more than one-half the partial pressure of the highest saturated body tissue. Example: 33' total pressure=29.4 PSIA; sea level total pressure=14.7 PSIA. One-half of the highest saturated body tissue or 29.4 would be 14.7 and our diver could ascend without violating the "2 to 1" law.

The problem occurs when our diver goes up into the mountains and dives in a lake where the absolute atmospheric pressure at lake surface is not 14.7, but something less.

Corrections of Error in Standard Diving Depth Gauges

Most depth gauges are calibrated to begin reading pressure at sea level or 14.7 PSIA. At 10,000 feet, that means you will be underwater almost eleven feet before your gauge even

---

* NOTE: These procedures are not scientifically tested. They were worked out by John Frederick, a NAUI instructor, and presented at the NAUI "Industrial Orientation Course." As there are no "tested" procedures, I am including these because they have been used by many divers without incident. I do not wish hereby to assume responsibility for their use.

lifts off the zero peg. The atmospheric pressure at 10,000 feet (10.11) is 4.63 PSI less than sea level. At the rate of .434 PSI increase per foot of depth, you are actually at 11 feet before you have again registered 14.7 PSIA. If you have a depth gauge with a peg at the zero foot mark and have had it much above 5,000 feet you have probably bent the needle and it won't be accurate. If you have a gauge that does not have a peg at zero, go dig it out and if you are at any altitude at all, the needle will be registering quite a bit behind zero. On some gauges, the cap can be removed and the needle can be reset. Care should be taken to insure that if you re-adjust the needle, that it be properly calibrated before relying on it for decompression purposes.

There is one depth gauge that corrects perfectly for the difference in altitude pressure. It's the one that has the little air tube in a circle with depth increments around the dial. These are usually flat and very inexpensive. To make sure you have the one I am talking about, check the 33-foot mark on the gauge. It should be one-half the distance around the tube. 66 feet should be two thirds the way around the tube, etc. This gauge is based on Boyle's law and as the pressure on a gas is doubled, the volume is one-half the original volume, right? Let's see how this gauge works at 10,000 feet. The little air tube is filled with atmospheric pressure, which is 10.11 PSIA. As the gauge is taken underwater, the pressure will be doubled when the diver gets to 20.22 PSIA or 23.29 feet of water depth. The gauge actually reads 33 feet at that point which is the depth you should be using for computation on the repetitive and decompression tables. At two atmospheres of water depth or three atmospheres absolute at 10,000 feet, this gauge will be indicating 66 feet. Your "true water depth" is actually only 46.58 feet.

Whatever the method you are using to determine your depth at altitudes, make sure it is accurate or at least that the error is in your favor.

Flying After Diving

Flying after diving can be safe. Most airlines pressurize the cabin at 5,000 feet. To be safe, make your dive according to the 5,000 foot altitude tables and hope that the cabin does not depressurize. If you are a military or airline flyer, to be on the safe side, you should compute tables that will cover you for the highest altitude you will attain, rather than just 5,000 feet. That may seem rather restrictive, but at least it's better than not diving at all 24 hours before flight time. Those of us that do a lot of lake diving should be aware also. Often times, you gain a great deal more altitude just getting to the lake you plan to dive. Figure for the highest altitude.

Below you will find the absolute atmospheric pressure at varying altitudes:

SEA LEVEL:	14.74	8,000:	10.91
1,000:	14.17	9,000:	10.50
2,000:	13.66	10,000:	10.11
3,000:	13.17	11,000:	9.72
4,000:	12.69	12,000:	9.35
5,000:	12.23	13,000:	8.98
6,000:	11.78	14,000:	8.63
7,000:	11.34	15,000:	8.29

NOTE: Some variance has been noted as to the exact atmospheric pressure at each altitude. The U.S. Weather Bureau has one set of figures and the United States Air Force Altitude chamber systems have another. The figures listed above are the Air Force ones and since very little difference is noted, no problems should be encountered in using the above figures for calculations.

Altitude Tables

Now, suppose a diver at 10,000 feet descends into a fresh water lake. If he goes to 34 feet and totally saturates himself with the increased partial pressure of the inert gas and comes back to the surface expecting to not require any decompression, what happens?

First, let's see if he violated the "2 to 1" law. The absolute pressure at 34 feet in a lake 10,000 feet above sea level is 24.85 PSIA. One-half of that pressure would be 12.43 PSIA or that point would be reached when the diver has ascended to five feet of water depth. If our diver ascended from five feet back to the surface without proper decompression, he would have violated the "2 to 1" law, right? and probably would end up with a case of the bends.

Let's find out what safe depth our diver can dive to at 10,000 feet to keep from violating this law and getting a case of the bends. First, we know that the atmospheric pressure at 10,000 feet is 10.11 PSIA. We also know that in fresh water, the pressure increases at the rate of .434 PSIA per foot of water depth. Let's divide .434 into 10.11 and see how many feet of water depth it takes to increase the atmospheric pressure by one additional atmosphere.

$$
\begin{array}{r}
23.29 \\
.434\overline{)10.11000} \\
\underline{868} \\
1430 \\
\underline{1302} \\
1280 \\
\underline{868} \\
4120 \\
3906
\end{array}
$$

Depth Required to Increase the Pressure By One Atmosphere

$$\frac{X}{.434} = Y = 23.29 \text{ feet}$$

The second part of our problem is to find the relationship between 23.29 feet at 10,000 feet, and 33 feet at sea level in 10 foot increments. We would write that mathematically as follows:

$$\frac{3.Y}{10} = 2$$

$$\frac{3.Y}{10} = Z \qquad \text{(Comparable depth to 10 feet at sea level on the tables for diving at 10,000 feet altitude)}$$

$$
\begin{array}{r}
23.29 \\
\times\ \ 3 \\
\hline
69.87
\end{array}
$$

$$Z = 6.98 \text{ feet}$$

Knowing this information, we can now formulate a set of tables that should render the standard Navy air tables useful to use at 10,000 feet.

If you are actually at "True" depth, use "Decompression" depth for repetitive decompression purposes to keep from getting the bends.

"True" depth 10,000 feet		U.S. Navy Standard Air Tables table depth "Decompression" depth at sea level	
6.98 =	10	76.78 =	110
13.96 =	20	83.76 =	120
20.94 =	30	90.74 =	130
27.92 =	40	97.72 =	140
34.90 =	50	104.70 =	150
41.88 =	60	111.68 =	160
48.86 =	70	118.66 =	170
55.84 =	80	125.64 =	180
62.82 =	90	139.60 =	190
69.80 =	100		

The next step is to change the fractions of feet into solid numbers, and make the tables more useful. This is what has been done on the following page.

1,000 ft.	2,000	3,000	4,000	5,000	6,000	7,000	8,000	9,000	10,000	11,000	12,000	13,000	14,000	15,000	TABLE DEPTH
5	5	5	5	5	5	5	5	5	5	5	5	5	5	5	10
10	10	10	10	10	10	10	10	10	10	10	10	10	10	10	20
20	20	20	20	20	20	20	20	20	20	20	15	15	15	15	30
30	30	30	30	30	30	30	30	25	25	25	20	20	20	20	40
40	40	40	40	40	40	35	35	30	30	30	30	30	25	25	50
50	50	50	50	50	45	40	40	40	40	40	35	35	30	30	60
60	60	60	60	55	50	50	50	50	45	45	40	40	40	40	70
70	70	70	70	60	60	60	60	55	50	50	50	45	45	45	80
80	80	80	75	70	70	70	65	60	60	60	55	50	50	50	90
90	90	90	80	80	80	75	70	70	65	65	60	60	55	55	100
100	100	100	90	90	85	80	80	75	70	70	70	65	60	60	110
110	110	105	100	100	90	90	90	80	80	80	75	70	70	65	120
120	120	110	110	105	100	100	95	90	90	85	80	80	75	70	130
130	130	120	120	110	110	105	100	100	95	90	90	85	80	80	140
140	140	130	130	120	120	110	110	105	100	100	95	90	85	85	150
150	150	140	140	130	130	120	120	110	110	105	100	95	90	90	160
160	160	150	145	140	135	130	125	120	115	110	105	100	100	95	170
170	165	160	150	150	140	140	130	130	120	120	110	110	105	100	180
180	170	170	160	160	150	145	140	135	125	125	120	115	110	105	190

If you are actually at the depth listed under each altitude, follow the table to the last number on the right, and that depth is the one you should use on the Standard U.S. Navy Air Tables for Repetitive and Decompression purposes.

APPENDIX L
How to Prepare Some
Good-Looking Specimens

"KEEPEN KREEPERS"
by Sam Miller, NAUI Instructor

There are as many ways to preserve critters from the deep as there are to spear a fish or bag a bug. There are complex, difficult, scientific methods employed by complex, difficult scientists and then there are my methods, simple and easy, void of scientific basis. Normal hand tools are adequate for most tasks, common household cleaning agents comprise most solutions, and measurements are approximate.

In order to assist you in your future efforts, I have prepared the following outline as a guide.

STARFISH (Use only fresh, live starfish):

KILL (anesthetize, for college kids) in a solution of Epsom salts and water. One tablespoon to a quart of water.
FORM to desired shape in Epsom salt solution.
FIX by boiling in fresh water for approximately ten minutes.
PRESERVE by coating legs and stomach area with household bleach.
DRY in a warm dry place.
COAT with clear spray (plastic, enamel, or other, available from your art supply or paint store).

SEA URCHINS:

REMOVE mouth and internal organs.
FORM by placing sea urchin top down in a container filled with sand super-saturated with glycerin, and leave in place for a week.
PRESERVE by removing from sand. Then coat the inside of the sea urchin with a 50/50 mixture of glycerin and formaldehyde.
FIX by hanging the sea urchin in an upside-down position until it is good and dry.
COAT with clear spray.

CORAL:

KILL in a solution of Hexol and plain water. Use one or two tablespoons to a quart of water.
BLEACH in a solution of diluted household bleach (approximately 1:20).

231

BIVALVE SHELLS (Pismo clams, scallops, etc.):

HINGE should be coated with glycerin. Repeat periodically to prevent the hinge from breaking.
COAT with baby oil to obtain natural luster.

SEASHELLS (All other shells not specifically mentioned):

CLEAN by placing in a solution of Hexol and water, one tablespoon per quart of water. You may also place them on a sponge in the solution. Remove the shell in a few days and wash the remaining meat from the shell.
COAT the shell with baby oil and repeat as necessary.

CONCHES (Large shells found in warmer water, Mexico, etc.):

CLEAN by hooking the meat or "foot" with a fishhook on a string. Hang the meat by the string away from your camp until the shell falls free of the meat. Place the shell in a large-weave net and suspend the net in the ocean beneath a float for one or two days, or soak in Hexol solution as described above.
REMOVE any outside growth from the shell.
COAT the shell with baby oil as needed.

FISH PRINTING:

CLEAN the fish with brush, cloth, etc., and rub with salt to remove oil if necessary.
COAT the fish thinly with a solution of Sumi Ink (available at art stores). The solution should be the consistency of ordinary fountain-pen ink.
APPLY rice paper to the fish and pat the rice paper flat against the fish skin. After you are sure the rice paper has come into contact with all of the skin, carefully peel off the paper.
COAT the rice paper with clear artist's fixative.

ABALONE SHELL CLEANING

One of the most enjoyable and rewarding activities associated with sports diving is the cleaning of abalone shells, to strip them down to pure luminescent mother-of-pearl on both sides. Although unknown to many, the procedure for cleaning shells is fast and simple and can be accomplished with a minimum of effort and tools.

The basic cleaning kit consists of the following items:

1. Hammer
2. Chisel
3. Wire brush
4. Box of paraffin
5. Small metal pan
6. Small paintbrush
7. One gallon of muriatic acid (pool acid)
8. Two large plastic containers
9. One pair rubber gloves

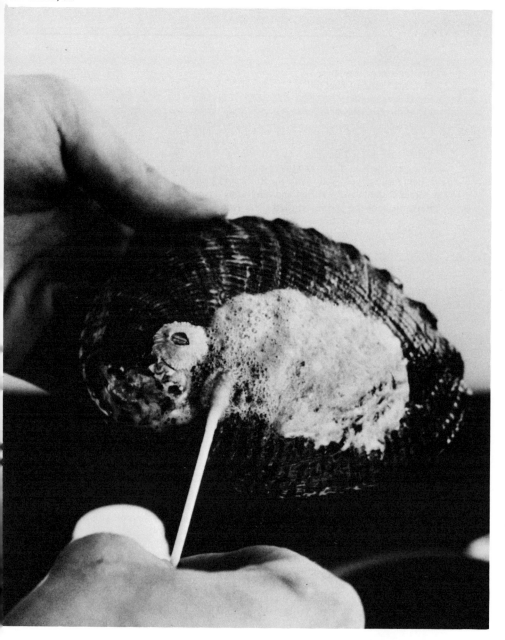

Cleaning off the back of an abalone shell with muriatic acid. Preparing and finishing your own shells can be a rewarding pastime.

233

10. One large stew pot
11. One bottle of baby oil
12. Power grinder
13. Polishing wheels
14. Jeweler's rouge

Experience gained through years of trial and error has revealed the best species for cleaning are the Red, Pink, and Sorenson abalones. These species have consistently given excellent results. If possible, avoid the Blacks or Greens; the Blacks have become pitted and the Greens' shells are stratified and tend to have soft spots and crumble.

Regardless of the species chosen, it is recommended that only those shells that are healthy and relatively free of marine growth be used. After the specimens have been selected, the following procedure should be followed for best results:

1. (a) Using the hammer or hammer and chisel (an abalone iron also makes a good chisel), remove all large marine growths such as barnacles, tube worms, and so on.
   (b) Wire brush the exterior, removing as much of the remaining growth as possible.
2. (a) Wash shells, removing all traces of meat and as much of the remaining external growth as possible.
   (b) Dry the shells completely.
3. Using the paintbrush, thoroughly coat the interior of the shell with paraffin. *Note:* The paraffin protects the surface of the shell from the acid; therefore, the shell must be completely dry; otherwise the paraffin will not adhere to the shell's surface.
4. (a) Put on rubber gloves and other protective clothing. Since acid will be used, it is *strongly recommended* that eye protection also be worn—a face plate with the purge valve removed makes an excellent eye protector.
   (b) Place two large plastic containers side by side; in one pour about three inches of muriatic acid, fill the other with fresh water.
5. (a) Place prepared shells in the acid, top down.
   (b) Check occasionally by removing shell and rinsing in fresh water.
   (c) When the exterior has attained the desired degree of cleanliness, remove from acid, rinse in fresh water, and wash under running water.
6. (a) Place completed shells in a large stew pot, and fill the pot with fresh water.
   (b) Place the pot on the stove and bring water to a boil.
   (c) Set aside, allow to cool. Skim solidified paraffin off the top of water and remove shells.
7. (a) Grind rough spots with power grinder.
   (b) Polish shell with polishing wheel and jeweler's rouge.
8. (a) Finish shell with a hand-rubbed coat of baby oil.
   (b) Periodically recoat with baby oil to renew the luster.

PRESERVING A LOBSTER OR CRAB AS A WALL MOUNT (Added by author):

Lobsters and crabs make pleasing wall mounts and are not difficult to preserve. Materials needed include:

1. Large pot
2. Sharp knife
3. Formaldehyde solution (10%)

4. Several pipe cleaners
5. *Clear* glue
6. *Clear* plastic spray paint

Procedure:

1. Boil the animal for ten minutes.
2. Disjoint it with the knife and clean out all of the meat you can.
3. Eat the meat. Don't worry about the meat that you can't get out of the legs.
4. Place the disjointed animal (parts) in the formaldehyde overnight.
5. Take it out of the formaldehyde, rinse in fresh water, and dry well in the sun.
6. Glue it back together using the pipe cleaners as supports *inside* the legs. Make sure the animal is in the position you want it to remain in.
7. Spray with clear plastic spray, eight or ten coats.
8. Glue it to some type of mount. FANTASTIC!

INDEX

237